Truth on the Run:

Christian Advaita

by
Bill Lindley
(Ahimsananda)

For

Tom, Bill's brother

And Bill's Facebook Friends

Contents

Preface Note

Bill wrote in his blog profile:

"I am a former Anglican Monk and Teacher of Non-Duality and Christian Mysticism. After a transformation as a result of reading The Cloud of Unknowing, my partner and I were asked by the Dean of Lincoln to form a Contemplative / Service Religious Community. I wrote the rule, and The Community of the Living Sacrifice was born. The Community worked with young Gay people, and we housed ex-prisoners, newly released psychiatric patients, and the homeless. As the Community was coming to a close, I discovered Ramakrishna, Sri Ramana Maharshi, and Nisargadatta Maharaj. This revitalized the spiritual search, and in 1990 a final understanding occurred, and all seeking stopped. After about ten years, I attempted to 're-write' The Rule for the Community of the Living Sacrifice in Advaitic terms. After another decade, and a series of dreams where Nisargadatta appeared to enter the dream and indicated to me that I should share my understanding with others, I decided to start 'teaching'."

The first edition of Bill's book Truth on the Run, published by In the Garden Publishing in 2014, is out of print. This second edition is expanded, insofar as more contributions (beginning with: Nothingness or Unlimited Potential?) and also poems by Bill have been added.

Reference should also be made to Bill's films on youtube.

I thank John Adams very much for the permission to compile this second edition.

Gabriele Ebert (ed.)

Introduction

Bill Lindley wrote his book during his last run around the sun from October 2010, to October 2011, in a series of blogs. Bill was a heart teacher. He held no degree and could not claim any special lineage. If someone wished to fence or argue he would simply decline and say that love was all he had to offer. But he would not soft about it. In the end, one of his friends remarked, "This guy really challenged me with his love."

This non-dual spiritual teaching was from his own, uniquely American point of view with his special gift for simplifying difficult concepts. One of his readers said, "The really great thing about Bill is that he didn't go in for the non-dual party-line. His notes and post were always truthful, but they had a really wonderful folksiness." He encouraged everyone to go ahead and look, see for themselves, re-invent the spiritual wheel, and then, integrate one's spiritual life into his or her everyday life.

Chapter one, *Fearlessness in Divergence: Beyond the Safety of the Masters*, is typical of his objective, independent point of view.

Toward the end of our religious work at Lincoln Cathedral in England, the Sub-Dean accused Bill of becoming too independent. Many who are interested in non-dual philosophy come from a religious tradition, which has let them down. This was Bill's experience as well, but he made use of it as a jumping off point, diving into the limitless pool of his expression of that "no thought" side.

When writing these essays, Bill demonstrated an urgency and single-mindedness which I had never seen in all the forty years we were together. A fierce earnestness became his compass on a daily basis, as exemplified by Nisargadatta.

Nisargadatta Maharaj was Bill's guru. Though he passed away before Bill was aware of him, Nisargadatta's books sufficed to provide direction and inspiration. In this book, Bill relates two dreams in which Nisargadatta appears, but there was also a third dream.

Bill was standing just inside Nisargadatta's mezzanine room when his guru walked in to present him with a golden model of a Hindu chariot. The second dream prior to this was about the unspoken question, "Do you want this love?" Bill's answer is in these pages, which I recommend reading again and again.

John Adams

Fearlessness in Divergence:
Beyond the Safety of the Masters

One of my earliest philosophical ideas came when I was no more than eight or nine years old. It occurred to me that just because I and my friend both called the same color crayon red, did not mean that we both saw the same color. His view of red might be what I see as green, just as his perception of green might be what I perceive as red. But we both use the same color names, so we assume we both see the same color. And more perplexing still, we will never know the answer, as we cannot see for each other. No outside person can tell us, as they too live in a world of their own color perception.

This is much like it is on the search. We all seek in a way that works for us. If we try to follow a path, it must be our own. We would be unwise to ignore the paths that have gone before, but we must not try to imitate or re-live lives past.

As a Christian seeking monastic formation, one follows rules. First, the rules of the Church, then the rules of an order, and immediately, the rules and instructions of your superior. These include instructions from what to clean to how to contemplate. Some are good and some are bad, but the institution requires they be followed.

The belief system also requires following dogma: how to pray, how to envision the Trinity, how to think of heaven and hell, and all the rest of it. This is where I broke down. I reached a point where I no longer believed in the part of the creed that calls Christ, "Our only mediator and advocate." I saw infinite possibilities. It was here I found Ramana Maharshi, Nisargadatta Maharaj and Advaita.

One of the things I have felt called to do is try to break the fear that causes seekers not to go on beyond the confines of what they know, or feel they should. Christians fear hell if they fail to see Jesus as "Lord". Fundamentalists feel they must find some approval in the words of the Bible. They will go to the extreme of doubting Darwin or trying to find Noah's Ark rather than simply look for themselves at what is in front of them.

I find fundamentalists in Advaita as well. Not just the Neo-Advaitins, but many who follow a stricter, more traditional path.

I recently used a word in a blog that is not the usual word used for describing the indescribable. I was told, "The *realized* use a different word as a reference." This is a way of appealing to authority. This reference to the realized is no different than referring to the Roman Catholic Church's Magisterium or referencing the Bible itself. It is fine to read and learn. The Masters from Buddha, Christ, Shankara to Ramana and Nisargadatta were different from society and different from each other. They all had a slightly different message, resulting in the same awareness.

Each master, each one of us, has an ongoing connection to the ultimate reality. Most of us have a hallway full of junk in our spiritual house that blocks the view, but it's there. Only we can clean our hallway. It's our junk. Sometimes someone comes along to help in the cleaning. Not in the cleaning itself, but in the organization of the effort. Some will find Christ is the one to sort out the situation. Others will not like his methods and turn to Buddha, or Ramana. The sheep know the shepherd, and the shepherd knows the sheep. The important point here is that each realized being interprets the message differently. Each has his references and his body/mind conditioning, so different words will be used, different concepts employed. So we must be very careful in quoting *the realized*, just as we should things from the Bible or any text.

But really, the important thing is openness. If we restrict our path to awareness only to those things, ideas, experiences, and practices recommended by others, we may miss our salvation.

There is a story I heard long ago, about a man who was sure he could trust God. He knew that God would create a miracle if only he needed one. One day, while crossing a high bridge over a bay, the man fell in. The water was swift and the man was immediately in trouble. The man went into deep prayer, "Only God can save me now," he thought. Just then, he was spotted by a ship passing by. But he was lost in prayer and deep meditation, and the ship could not reach him without his cooperation.

An airplane spotted him next and tried to contact him, but by this time he was lost in prayer and beseeching, and he heard nothing. Next, a helicopter flew over, and even let down a net, but even though he saw it this time he was going to leave it to *trust* in the lord to save him. He drowned.

Upon arriving in Heaven, and being introduced to God, the man asked God why he had not saved him. God scratched his head and said, "I don't know what happened. Didn't you see the ship, plane and helicopter I sent?"

We don't want to miss something because someone, no matter who disagrees. We all arrive at awareness in a unique way. Christ in his and Ramana in his, and yours, too, will be unique.

This is where trust, and what Nisargadatta calls absolute fearlessness, come into play. Being bound by the restraints of a Church doctrine, a Bible or the writings of the masters will not let us find awareness in our self. While the writings and words of the masters are our guides, we may be given a different path, and their words may be stumbling blocks in its way.

To step beyond the teaching, beyond the gate of fear and the comfortable, allows you to *be* the teaching.

Education: Help or Stumbling Block?

When I was a Christian monk, it took me some time to find the simplicity of Christ's teachings. There were so many concepts to learn, so much stuff to fill the mind. It took what appeared to be a very long time to get it all down and organized. Then, realizing that the Church was not really following Christ's message or teaching, I began to read and study Hinduism and some Buddhist literature and teaching: more mind-stuff.

Learning is fun. Education is an asset in many endeavors. But it can be a stumbling block to realizing. Many here, as well as many gurus, are vastly educated, Masters in Religion, Doctorates in Philosophy, Doctorates in Eastern Studies, and all the rest of it. But are they aware?

Many here, and on other spiritual websites post long, scholarly blogs using all the words and concepts they have learned through long, hard study. This is commendable, and done for many reasons, commendable or otherwise. It is not for me to judge. However, learning can be like any other attainment or acquisition: a source of pride. Nisargadatta comments that we learn our identity from others. Our parents, friends, and everyone we have contact with add to our image of ourselves. Our minds believe the projections these others tell us we are. So it is with education. As children, as well as in adulthood, we discover many things for ourselves. But if you look closely, you find that in order to fit in, many of us trade our own discoveries, our own intuition, for the commonly accepted view. I, and others, are constantly being told that our ideas or methods do not fit with the realized as if we should care. Ramana Maharshi had his realization, Nisargadatta had his, and you and I have our own. They do not need to fit.

Realization will not fit your concept of it. If you can fit your realization into your concept, your realization is in the mind only. We all seem to agree that awareness, enlightenment, the Absolute, are not available to the mind. Yet we study to fill the mind with concepts. Many, like me, spend time learning concepts of one religion or belief and later spend more time learning about another

18

philosophy, religion, or belief system. Then we compare, combine and organize the whole into new concepts. This, of course, is all done in the mind, which cannot possibly use it for enlightenment.

Many on these spiritual websites love to play one-ups-man-ship. A "my mind's full of more concepts than yours" kind of thing. Or we call out someone's ego or criticize their concepts as not as good as ours. This is done because the mind does not want enlightenment. Enlightenment means silence to the mind. Enlightenment ends the control of the mind. If we have filled our minds with a large education, this is an investment we have made. This is something to protect. So even if we know that enlightenment is not available to the mind, we still pursue it with the mind and judge others, even gurus, with the mind. This is why so many are skeptical of every guru, every teacher that they can outsmart or challenge with their superior education.

The wisest teachers in spirituality are the ones who are mostly silent. Ramana was one such. He talked only out of compassion. And this is the key. Gurus are often questioned as to why they teach. And, of course, the answer is compassion. Just as those who search for awareness or enlightenment are driven by an unexplainable compulsion, the guru is compelled to teach. I am not talking here of those who see enlightenment as an achievement to add to their education or the guru who seeks an ego boost, a following, or riches. I am talking about those who realize that enlightenment brings nothing (and teaching is often thankless work), but who are compelled to search and to help.

I find it terribly funny that those who many see as enlightened like Ramana, Nisargadatta, and Jesus Christ were only educated in a very cursory manner. Yet many think that they need to have a large education to understand these simple men. Education can be a source of pride beyond almost anything else. Western gurus and teachers are almost all very well-educated. Many, like Ken Wilber, Andrew Cohen, and many others are very full of themselves. This does not a guru make. Many of the seekers who attend Satsangs are very educated people who are hoping to top off their education with enlightenment. They seek confirmation from their guru that they "have made it". Enlightenment is simple. Christ tells us to "become as little children".

I am not saying that education is bad. As I said, learning is fun and can be used to help others, but it makes neither seeker nor guru. The thing that defines a real guru or teacher is his compassion and the living of his teaching, not his educational level. If you seek awareness, enlightenment or whatever, then be as the guru: live a compassionate life. Earnestness, love, and selflessly helping others will lead you to what you seek without the seeking and without caring whether you find enlightenment or not. Living compassion is enlightenment. Be that.

Nebulous Clarity

The oxymoron that titles this blog needs some explanation.

The only way one can express the Absolute is by silence. This makes it a challenge to those who try to teach. When the call comes to teach with concern for the ultimate understanding, a kind of confusion comes that makes teaching at first seem impossible. This is often why those who are awakened either do not teach or wait a very long time to do so.

After waiting for twenty years, and finding a sense of establishment, I have been trying to encourage others to step into the unknown in this search.

I explain my understanding as love being your true nature. Of course, this is not accurate as the seeker will interpret love in their own way. The masters use words like Absolute or Self to explain the unexplainable or they will talk of nothingness or no-self. None of these things are at all accurate. This is why the early masters referred to this as neti-neti: not this, not this. Only by describing what something is not, can one come close, as the Absolute is beyond explanation.

I use the word love, as most of us have a vague idea of love, or at least sadly, the lack of love. This love of which I speak cannot be explained as the opposite of hate or a feeling or an emotion, but as the creative force that not only holds all together but creates the objects and the *flow* between them. This is not a true explanation, but how my mind explained it to "me".

For some years, I struggled with the second verse from Chapter One of the *Avadhuta Gita:*

"How shall I salute the formless Being, indivisible, auspicious, and immutable, who fills all this with His Self and also fills the self with His Self?"

I knew myself to be one with all. After years of practice, I was established in the I Am. Still, I felt love for God, even as I recognized that God and I were not separate. Silent awareness would bring a response of tearful bliss. "How can that be?" I asked. How can love exist between two objects in this awareness? The answer came as "myself" and "God" vanished. Only love was left. This was, of course, an answer in my mind. The mind called it love. It was an explanation I could pass on to others, but not the truth. The truth is here. I am the truth, but I can't explain it. I can only be it. This is the meaning of nebulous clarity.

When this *happens,* all is clear. There are no questions left. No more seeking. But you cannot explain it to others. Moreover, you cannot explain it to yourself! It is an understanding without knowledge. It requires the suspension of knowledge and the suspension of a conclusion. There is no judgment. There is no labeling, only silent awareness, without even an awareness of being aware. Nebulous clarity.

Some years ago, I saw a play about Oscar Wilde starring Vincent Price. It was presented as a lecture and talk, as given by Oscar Wilde at the end of his career. At the conclusion, he said, "I've lied to you, you know! But you don't know where." This is the problem with the teacher of spirituality. They all lie. Not in an attempt to fool you or mislead you, but in an attempt to explain the nebulous clarity they live but can't explain, even to themselves. For any explanation is false. As soon as it is put into concepts, or words, it is false. It can only be and yet is beyond being.

A teacher can only give pointers. You must look closely for yourself. Find who seeks, who wants clarity. But don't accept the explanations of others or those of yourself. If you can explain it to yourself, it is false. You must find and accept nebulous clarity.

Emotion in the Search Beyond "I Am"

Ramana Maharshi recommended exploring *Who am I?* Nisargadatta advised the earnest examination of the I Am.

But this only leads to the "I". This is a comfortable place. It is a place, where anyone, with proper diligence (earnestness!), can find rest. It gives one an intellectual sense of who one is, but it is only the first step to oneness. The mind can only go as far as the I Am. All else is speculation based on memory or imagination. How then to go beyond?

The mind, in Advaita circles, has often become the devil. It lies in wait to catch hold of spiritual experiences, and insights, to confuse and falsely entertain itself. This, almost bestowing intent on the mind, paints an erroneous picture. The mind is often portrayed as protecting itself from extinction. This too is giving motive to the mind which simply does not exist. The body, the mind, and the emotions are all part of the functioning of the whole. All have their purpose and require acceptance. But the mind is the tool of choice for the student of Advaita, even though it is held in suspicion and contempt.

Most students of Advaita, as well as most people, see emotions as part of the mind. Some see them as bodily sensations caused by particular thoughts in the mind. Others think the thoughts arise out of certain bodily sensations. Clearly, the mind and body are intimately linked, but ultimately it is all linked, so this is no answer. The emotions are only reflections, like everything in my world. But they are not in the mind.

The emotions all stem from love. Now, here I am not speaking of love, the emotion, but the impersonal love. Here again, we have the semantics problem. We all have our attachments to the word love. Here I am talking about agape, in its fullness. David Jenkins, former Bishop of Durham before his election as Bishop, gave a lecture in which he gave a wonderful description of agape. He described God as having so much compassion, so identifying with man, that he became one (Jesus) in order to manifest love (Christ). In the Christian sense, this is the humbling of God to bring compassion to the cosmos. But it also demonstrates the creative power of love as *essence* (the Absolute).

Emotions are often looked at as distractions to spirituality, both in the East and in the West. But they are there, and trying to eradicate them only makes them stronger. Also ignoring or suppressing them is useless and dangerous.

Watch the emotions but don't own them. They can teach you something, so don't ignore them, but they are not you. They are just emotional track of the movie you live in. Love, as creative power, does not exist in the mind, but the mind in it. However, the reflections, the lesser emotions do.

The lesser emotions such as hate, fear, lust, anger, desire and so on, as well as some of the better emotions like joy, peace, contentment, surprise, and pleasant expectation, are all just refractions, reflections, and distortions of the impersonal love. Love, not the noun we set in our mind and try to define and dissect, but love as verb: love in action, love as connection. This love is the essence; the Absolute if you will.

These emotions are part of the whole when it comes to realizing the truth. We all know, even the most cynical among us, the truth is outside the reaches of the mind. So we must seek elsewhere.

When you feel something, rather than dismissing it, ignoring it, or using the mind to block it, open your heart to it. Remove the subject and object, and remain in the verb. As you examine the functioning of the emotion, its relationship to love or the lack thereof, will become apparent. When you do this with love as creative power, you find that you are nothing less than that indescribable movement.

The Lord's Prayer as Advaita Meditation

Of the two places in the Bible where the Lord's Prayer appears, I have chosen Matthew 6: 5-7, as it is used in the context of the Sermon on the Mount. This sermon, outlining much of Jesus' teaching, describes the kind of attitude necessary for salvation/awakening.

The prayer, far from being a prayer of petition although some of that is included, is a meditation on the Absolute, the unlimited potential.

As you look at the prayer, go deeply into the meaning. You will find a meditation of our relationship with God/Absolute, and a method, a framework for *realizing* that.

Our Father, who art in heaven,
Hallowed be thy name.

One of the most important points here is the use of the term, father, for God. And perhaps, as important, is that it is our Father; not Christ's alone, but our Father. All of us are brothers and sisters to Christ, and sons and daughters of the Absolute. The use of the term father shows a familial closeness: God/Absolute as creator and protector. But sometimes Jesus used the word Abba. Abba means father but goes further in that it translates as daddy or another affectionate child-like name. This shows the connection to God/Absolute is love.

When God/Absolute is seen in heaven, this is a way of expressing the internal nature of God/Absolute. In Luke 17, Jesus tells us that the kingdom of heaven is "within you". He then states that even the name of God/Absolute is holy.

Thy Kingdom come,
thy will be done,
on earth as it is in heaven.

We already know the kingdom is within and this is our opening to it: thy will be done. Not mine. No, I am just acceptance. Then of course the exterior (earth), will be like unto the interior (heaven).

25

Give us this day our daily bread.
And forgive us our trespasses,
as we forgive those who trespass against us.

Asking for daily bread is a prayer of petition, but a little one. And it is necessary to be aware that asking for our daily bread, our necessary sustenance, may be asking for pain and suffering. Pain and suffering, as well as actual daily bread, bring healing and strength for this journey to daddy.

Forgiveness is not something people in Advaita think about much unless it is in the context of karma. And this is what is addressed here. *"And forgive us our trespasses, as we forgive those who trespass against us."* As we practice forgiveness, so our bad karma is lessened.

Most of us will admit selfishness from time to time. This selfishness is inherent in the I. This, at least, is a trespass. Sin, as used by Christ, is really ignorance. *"Father, forgive them, for they know not what they do."* We are called to love God/Absolute with all our hearts, all our soul, and all our mind. This is the prayer, the meditation: that our trespasses (ignorance) be forgiven as we use our hearts, souls, and minds to love.

The use of the heart or soul to love is not hard to imagine, for this is where we place love, but to love with all our mind: This is a meditation in itself!

And lead us not into temptation,
but deliver us from evil.
For thine is the kingdom, the power and the glory,
for ever and ever, Amen

Lead us not into temptation – the mind, temptation itself! But is it evil?

If evil is described as that which leads away from the truth, then the mind is the thing! It is hard to place blame on an object which is only a bag of ideas, pictures and phantoms. But without intent, it stands in the way. Just as a bleeding man was able to say from a cross, "Father forgive them for they know not what they do," we must forgive our minds, and perhaps mind as an idea as well. We need to learn to watch our thoughts pass. They are harmless unless you grab hold of them. Eventually, when seen for what they are they will disappear altogether. When the bag is empty, and fearless earnestness is present, love will fill the mind, heart and soul.

For ever and ever. Kingdom, power, and glory belong to the Absolute. *This is unlimited potential*. Amen.

This well-known prayer is not only a wonderful bhakti prayer/meditation, but a feast and challenge for the mind to find itself, forgive itself, and rest quietly in itself until it is filled with love.

Unlimited Potentiality and the Circle of Love

Ever since the discovery of spirituality in childhood and even during my young adult, and high school years as an agnostic, I have valued universal love.

I returned to Christianity as a result of reading *The Cloud of Unknowing*. The Cloud is a mystical Christian instruction on how to yoke with God in contemplation. It is all about love. The Cloud instructs one to hide the mind behind a cloud of unknowing, and penetrate the unknowing with "little arrows of love". Basically, silence the mind, and be open with and to love.

As a Christian growing up, the statement of Paul, the Apostle, that "God is love" was not lost on me, but the profundity of this statement eluded me. As I passed into the non-dual teachings of Advaita, I began to wonder about "God" and myself. For a number of years, I held an intellectual understanding of unicity, oneness, and the I Am. But years of Christian practice, both in and out of the monastery, had left me with a longing for a "God" that I now had to dismiss as being only in the mind.

This longing, love actually, was manifest as a response to life that said "God" to me everywhere. The sky, the forest, and the desert would bring me to tears. Just the beauty, the stillness and the complex simplicity were overwhelming. The work I did also took on a different feel. The people I worked with, the developmentally disabled, were full of love and often brought tears to my eyes in their simple lives and acceptance. Again, this made me dwell on "God", the Absolute. I kept asking myself: why did I feel love? I knew intellectually that I was one with everything and that "God" was an illusion. So why love? How can there be love between two phantoms in the mind?

Without going into the whole story here, I experienced an awakening that intuitively showed me that yes indeed, there is no "God", and furthermore there is no "me". There is just love. That connection, that love, is all there is. And that is what we are. I experience this in my life always. All is observable as an unfolding of unlimited potentiality, ever moving, the changeable changeless.

Love is quiet and still despite of its dynamic quality. We must be quiet and still to *be* it. But most important is our need to share it. I am not talking about sharing with a lover, but this can be part of it. Our personal love for a partner is not, nor should it ever be, a block to our awareness or our ability to recognize our existence as love. But that love we have for a lover must be pure, not lustful or selfish. It must be a nurturing ground for our greater love.

Love needs to be put into practice. Not just in spiritual practice, but in our dealings with all of the manifestations, including inanimate objects, however base.

When the religious community I was co-founder of at Lincoln Cathedral was just in its beginning stages, the Dean of Lincoln asked me to write the rule for the community. This was a great privilege. But after leaving the community, and more than a decade of Advaita studies combined with the above experience, I rewrote the rule for the Community of the Living Sacrifice into a small book entitled *Community of One*. This book examines the rule for a Christian religious community in terms of Advaita. It was an attempt to describe a life of a seeker of truth and the "Advaita of Christ".

In the chapter on the Eucharist, I detail what I refer to as "the Eucharistic circle of love". Love is all there is. It is an unfolding movement. In the book, I recall a lesson I learned from my birth father. He was a journeyman electrician and I remember his explanation of electricity. He described it as a flow. From the source of power, the electricity flows through the wires to the device to be charged or activated. A complete circuit is necessary. Remove one wire, one connection, and there is not only no power, there is no electricity. The electricity exists in potential, but there is no flow.

In my book, I use the Eucharist as my practice, but this can apply to any practice as long as it is a practice that shuts down the *you*, and opens you to *love*. In the Eucharistic example, we have love, as shown in the sacrifice on the cross, which flows to the communicant by his *real* and *deep* participation in this practice, and then to the world in the form of loving action or loving stillness. If we do not participate in the practice, or we do not go out and share that love with the world, there is no flow. But not only is there no flow, there is love only in potential, not realized.

Love is what we *are*. If practices alone are all we do, there is no flow of love: the circle is broken. If we try to do for others without the practice of centering in some way, we will not be able to sustain our efforts as there is no flow of love; the circle is again being broken. Love remains potential, but requires flow.

So to recap: love is what you are. Love is the connection, *without subject or object*. Subject and object appear when the connection is present. Practice clears the way to the opening required for us to *be* love. Once we realize love is our true nature, we must *act* on it. If love is what we are, then love is what we do.

Complete the Circle, be the love.

The Cloud of Unknowing

After reading *The Cloud of Unknowing*, a 14th-century English spiritual work, my life changed forever, eventually slipping away to a quiet peace. There were many steps and missteps along the way, but it started there, with *The Cloud*.

The Cloud of Unknowing was written, it is believed, by an English priest or monk from the East Midlands during the 14th century. Shortly after reading this small book, in the amazing wonder of the living Absolute, after dedicating my life to the search for God, I was called to service work at Lincoln Cathedral, in the English East Midlands.

Completely unaware of *The Cloud's* origins, my partner and I began our religious community there.

The Cloud of Unknowing is a surprise to many who stumble upon it, as I did in the late 1970s. Not being raised Catholic, I had never heard of this book before or had any contact with Christian mysticism. It was a revelation to me. Not just the content but the discovery that Western culture had produced, in one of the most backward times in history, a book of such profound understanding of the mystical.

Our simple priest or monk recommends putting knowledge behind *a cloud of unknowing*, and waiting with great love on the grace of God. He recommends, both playfully and in great earnest, to be coy with God, not letting him know of our hidden desire:

"So beware of behaving wildly like some animal, and learn to love God with quiet, eager joy, at rest in body and soul. Remember your manners, and wait humbly upon our Lord's will. Do not snatch at it like some famished dog, however much you hunger for it. If I may use a funny example, I would suggest you do all you can to check your great and ungoverned spiritual urge; as though you were altogether unwilling that he should know how very glad you would be to see him, to have him, to feel him." The Cloud of Unknowing, Chapter 46

Just as new-age gurus teach of release from sorrow at Satsang, our little contemplative writes of acceptance of sorrow as a way of not only releasing sorrow but of escaping the I Am:

"Everyone has something to sorrow over, but none more than he who knows and feels that he is. All other sorrow in comparison with this is a travesty of the real thing. For he experiences true sorrow, who knows and feels not only what he is, but that he is. Let him who has never felt this sorrow be sorry indeed, for he does not yet know what perfect sorrow is. Such sorrow, when we have it, cleanses the soul not only of sin (ignorance), but also of the suffering its sin (ignorance) has produced. And it makes the soul ready to receive that joy which is such that it takes from man all awareness of his own existence." The Cloud of Unknowing, Chapter 44

In one of life's little paradoxes, it took Nisargadatta Maharaj to burn into my heart and soul the truth that was present in *The Cloud of Unknowing*. It is often some contact with the exotic, or at least different, to shake us out of our learned responses to stimulation. Ramana, Nisargadatta, and Advaita itself gave new life and images to things just waiting to be discovered. This is why so many Westerners, particularly Christians, find new hope in Eastern belief systems as they break the images of crucifixion, resurrection, and other ideas that have lost all real meaning to most Christians. Without an understanding of the spiritual element behind these appearances, these are just meaningless and bizarre beliefs. While Hinduism has its share of the bizarre, Westerners often bypass these features to concentrate on the heart of what they conceive of as the essence.

Hinduism and Christianity are full of rituals that appear meaningless, not just to outsiders, but often to the ones practicing them. Westerners often see the meaning behind foreign religions because they are not caught up in the bizarreness of the ritual, as it has no learned, emotional meaning. The learned, emotional meaning behind many of the Christian Church's rituals is only the external performance, and the spiritual meaning is often lost.

The Cloud of Unknowing tells us that the Church has had a mystical side for a long time and that Christ's message was about so much more than virgin births, crucifixion, and resurrection. Christ taught Advaita, and *The Cloud of Unknowing* presents as clear a picture of both truth and the path to it as is presented in any text:

"So crush all knowledge and experience of all forms of created things, and of yourself above all. For it is on your own self-knowledge and experience that the knowledge and experience of everything else depend. Alongside this self-regard, everything else is quickly forgotten. For if you will take the trouble to test it, you will find that when all other things and activities have been forgotten (even your own) there still remains between you and God the stark awareness of your own existence. And this awareness, too, must go, before you experience contemplation in its perfection." The Cloud of Unknowing, Chapter 43

As I said above, it took Nisargadatta Maharaj entering the dream to ultimately *get* it here. His words were pure truth to me. Pure love flowed from every word. Maharaj taught me the importance of the I Am, and the need to abide there while *waiting for transportation* beyond the mind. But when the transportation came, it came in the formlessness of *the Cloud*.

The Cloud of Unknowing, with its emphasis on love and devotion, prepares the soul/seeker, for the openness required for being absorbed into the truth. All must be removed, even the I Am. This requires selfless, impersonal love to step beyond the I Am. Be that and accept the invitation!

Yajna: Worship in Sacrifice

"Yajna: (Sanskrit) worship, sacrifice. One of the most central Hindu concepts – sacrifice and surrender through acts of worship, inner and outer.

1) A form of ritual worship especially prevalent in Vedic times in which oblations, ghee, grains, spices and exotic woods are offered into a fire according to scriptural injunctions while special mantras are chanted. The element fire, Agni, is revered as the divine messenger who carries offerings and prayers to the Gods. The ancient Veda Brahmanas and the Shrauta Shastras describe various types of yajna rites, some so elaborate as to require hundreds of priests, whose powerful chanting resounds for miles. These major yajnas are performed in large, open-air structures called yagashala. Domestic yajnas, prescribed in the Grihya Shastras, are performed in the family compound or courtyard. Yajna requires four components, none of which may be omitted: dravya, sacrificial substances; tyaga, the spirit of sacrificing all to God; devata, the celestial beings who receive the sacrifice; and mantra, the empowering word or chant."[1]

I found it interesting that yajna means both worship *and* sacrifice. This is similar to the seminal Christian Rite, the Eucharist, in that it involves ritual sacrifice. While it is true, one involves only oblations of rich and expensive earthly substances, when the other involves the re-enactment of human sacrifice; but as rituals they are sacrificial.

One of the four components above is the spirit of sacrificing all to God. This spirit is essential. Obviously, the thing being sacrificed (oblations/Jesus' life, i.e., sacrificial substances) is there in ritual worship and the empowering words of the mantras or Eucharistic prayers. The celestial beings or the being of Christ or God, all these

---

[1] While searching for the source that Bill did not provide, I came across the following: Hinduism's Online-Lexicon: https://www.shiavault.com/books/hinduism-s-online-lexicon-a-z-dictionary/chapters/24-y/ (3.4.2023)

"things" are held together in the grip of the spirit of sacrificing all to God.

This spirit of sacrifice is none other than our true nature, universal love. But let's look at the nature of sacrifice.

Burning some wood, no matter how precious, or ritual sacrifice of bread and wine will not give us the reality of sacrifice we need to understand. Our lives need to be informed by these rituals. The spirit of these rituals must inspire our hearts and hands (our sacrificial substance), the empowering words of "Thy will be done," and the thousands upon thousands of celestial beings in the faces of the poor and helpless who are with us always; all moving together in this ritual worship we call life. All held together in *the spirit of sacrificing all to God.*

Sacrificing all means real sacrifice: a sacrifice of time, a sacrifice of convenience, a sacrifice of position or popularity, perhaps even sacrifice of respect. Those who seek social justice often lose respect from those in power. The truth can isolate you from your friends, community, and station in life. Will you sacrifice *all*? To give, to give unselfishly to others without need or desire for even recognition, requires being the fulfiller of need without attachment. In this state you can be overflowing with God's love, as you *are* God's love personified, giving without a trace of want or desire.

Love through sacrifice flows through being and *is* being. When there is flow there is no subject/object. Be the love. Be the sacrifice. Complete the circuit with outstretched hands.

The Bhakti of Nisargadatta Maharaj

"Sometimes I feel I am everything, I call that love. Sometimes I feel I am nothing, I call that wisdom. Between love and wisdom, my life continuously flows." Nisargadatta Maharaj

Nisargadatta clearly saw that ultimately, he was the wisdom of *nothing*. But, just as, dare I say wise, was his ability to see that he was the love that is *everything*.

Many Neo-Advaitins concentrate only on the "Sometimes I feel I am nothing..." and neglect the feeling of being everything. Neo-Advaitins also talk down practice or technique and scoff at worship. While it is true, practice, technique, and often worship too, fall off as one progresses. They do not need to and often don't. Anyone who has read Nisargadatta's small early work, *Self-Knowledge and Self-Realization*, will understand that Nisargadatta had a very worshipful side. He was very devotional until the end of his life. He chanted every day. When asked why he did this he explained that his guru asked him to do it before he died and that he always had, and the body gets used to things, and there was no harm.

When it comes to practice, Nisargadatta recommended abiding in the I Am, as his teacher before him had done. This was all that was required for Nisargadatta to realize the highest truth. But Nisargadatta had been learning since his youth and had been practicing bhakti for years before he met his final guru. Neo-Advaitins talk of instant awareness. Simply by hearing a word, or being in the presence of a well-known guru, one can be transported to immediate understanding. Years of preparation, meditation, study, prayer, if you will, are not necessary in Neo-Advaita. Just follow the teacher's words as Nisargadatta did. Even after years of preparation, and meeting his ultimate guru, Nisargadatta took three years to realize. Now, I realize three years is not a long time. But it was *not* instant, and certainly *not* without preparation.

Nisargadatta spoke many times about the *need for earnestness*. Earnestness is defined as seriousness or zealousness. This is not unlike worship and devotion. It is certainly more than simply abiding in the I Am, but going beyond to that which is unknown.

Nisargadatta is right to start with the I Am. For we must understand this, get a good grip on it before we venture beyond the mind. But the I Am is *of* and *in* the mind. It is the highest truth the mind can understand.

While working on this I Am thought, *with earnestness*, there will also be a need to open yourself to others. Just as we learn to be open to emotions and thoughts without resistance or judgment, we watch others without judgment or hanging on. We see their needs and we fulfil them, just as we breath, without thought. This comes slowly to some and needs to be made a practice. We do this, not to be do-gooders, but to complement the I Am practice. For seeing to others acknowledges their reality too, which gives life to the connection of love. This connection takes us beyond mind.

Love has been relegated to the world of emotion for the most part. Sure, we make it the best emotion, but still, it remains with hate, fear, desire, anger, and lust!

When Nisargadatta, or Shankara, or any of the masters speak of love it is not the emotion, but interchangeable with the Absolute, God, or the ultimate understanding. We must understand this. When we see ourselves and the whole of the manifestation as no-thing, a void, we sell out to the mind in its ultimate grab. The mind says, "I have taken you to the ultimate, and it is not conceivable by me, so it does not exist." But this is a lie. Beyond the mind, prior to consciousness, lies the nameless wonder. This is why the I Am practice leads only to the *edge* of the mind. This is why bhakti is so essential to realizing the truth. Without the sadhana of service, whether to a "God", or to mankind, or the earth, you are not prepared to open like the flower to the grace of the sun in its time.

I will leave you with this thought:

Do not conceive of yourself as a noun, but as a verb. A noun is a person, place, or thing. A verb is an action, or being. When we love God, the Absolute, or another, and we know that we and God or another are mind-stuff, simply non-existent nouns, then we realize we are the verb of love that appears to be between the two. Love is all that exists. No me, no God, just the love. Love in action is everything.

"Sometimes I feel I am everything, I call that love."

Don't Mistake Success in Practice for Awareness

I think one of the pitfalls of practices is that the practices become ends in themselves or worse still, substitutes for the end result.

This applies to all practices that are external or internal, silent or active. Ultimately, practices are useless for finding truth. But one would be foolish to avoid practices in the early stages. Most practices are designed to calm the mind. Some are designed to stimulate the mind, and point it in a useful direction. But none is an end in itself.

I have meditated and engaged in contemplative prayer for many years. This was not time wasted or spent in delusion, at least not for the most part! Time spent at the Eucharist, likewise was very useful. Contemplating these mysteries quiets the mind and opens the heart. But they do not lead to the ultimate truth.

Nisargadatta's I Am is a supreme practice. But it leads only to consciousness. Now I don't mean to discount consciousness. It is a wonderful state. But we seek the pearl of great price, union with God.

All of this practice is beneficial because it quiets the mind or opens the mind to useful pointers. But there is an additional pitfall in practice and that is this very thing: this quieting of the mind. The mind needs to be quiet, empty of everything, particularly you. When we reach this state of quietness where we see that we are the observer, then, and only then can we find our way to being observing. But we must not mistake this quietness of practice for awareness, which is dynamic.

I'm a simple guy, so I use simple analogies. One of my favorites is the observing of the verb rather than the noun. This has been dismissed as simplistic. Words are words it is said. This is true, and we all understand the inadequacy of words. But words are part of the functioning of the One, so we need not discount them, or else resort to silence. By using this simplistic analogy, I attempt to point out the difference in being a static noun or an active verb. We are not a thing. We are life itself, ever changeless and dynamically changing.

I did not mean to go into that again, but I wanted to point out that *observing* is what is happening, rather than there being an observer or an observed. It is not just semantics. Meditate on it.

In the Christian Church, practices from the Eucharist to contemplative prayer are designed to quiet the mind and eventually eliminate the you. This is done, so that the mind and body will be open to the grace of God. There is no controlling this grace. We can only be open to it by quieting the body and the mind. In the East, I believe, practices are used in a similar way, be it meditation or some form of yoga. All of these practices result in a quiet mind and an awareness of consciousness. But at some point the mind, with all of its consciousness (noun), must move to the place of consciousness (verb) without the I Am.

This is how we get stuck. We mistake the *quiet*, the *nothingness* and the *emptiness* we find in our practice to be the ultimate, the Absolute. We love this quiet. We love to imagine this quiet, this freedom from mind, is the awakening. We rest in the I Am, unconcerned that there is still an "I". The idea of an "I" is a noun, a thing. We long for awareness, not as a noun to hold on to, but as a verb, to be.

Dwelling in quietness or consciousness, no matter how wonderful, is only for practice. If we imagine a quietness, a stillness, or an emptiness, the mind is happy to oblige with one from our imagination or from the memory of our practice. But the *awakening* is not something we can get our minds around. It is not a thing. No "I", no "self", but the ever-flowing love.

The Fear of Love

We often hear about the play between love and fear. How one can't *see* love because it is hidden by fear, or that *true love drives out all fear* and all the other clichés. But when love itself becomes the object of fear, we have a *big* problem.

I would have to say that this applies to all types of love, even those deemed inferior like romantic love. Romantic love, when it becomes devotion, can bring one out of oneself, and can work toward freedom. The thing to beware of is *desire*. Desire arises from the "me", the next step from the "I" thought. Desire wants what the "I" wants, not necessarily what the situation calls for. Pure love knows the situation *and the response.*

But the word love itself is often the reason for fear. We use words like "self" to describe our personal self, our personality and our person-hood if you will. And again, we move from the personal to the universal by referring to the Self (Capital "S") as God, awareness, truth, or whatever lofty idea the mind contrives. Why not just call it *love?*

We answer that *love* is just another word for the *indescribable* and that we all think differently about the word, and that the "*Self*", "God", and "the Absolute" must be nirguna: totally without attributes. But we all have a passing acquaintance with love. To deny this is almost as foolish as to deny the I Am.

It is true that we all have a different mind concept of love. And there are different concepts we tend to agree on like romantic love, familial love, and Agape or universal love. But intuitively we all know something of love, or at least sadly, the lack of it. Love is the *is-ness*, the being itself. *It* is what started you on this search, sustains you on this search, *and leads you to itself.* Call it what you like, but never deny it draws you, and that its existence is more real than the hand at the end of each arm. We must not fear this draw, this love.

Our attraction for another person is maybe too easy an example of love and too easily misunderstood. So let's use the beauty of a single tree in a forest. We regard the tree as a thing of beauty, created by God for our use, our pleasure, and adding to our atmosphere. We regard it with awe for its beauty, with thankfulness for its usefulness, and with love in its *is-ness*. This is God's *is-ness*. This is the *is-ness* of the Self.

If we now go about dismantling the mind-stuff, we find that first, only the I Am remains of our illusory personal "self". We then, having discovered the observer see that the concept of "God" rests solely in the mind and needs to be discarded along with the personal self. Of course, along with "God" and the personal self goes the tree, and all images that appear to the mind. Does this result in an empty mind, a spiritual silence, a death to the tree? Not at all.

When the images of self, "God", awakening, and even the image of the simple tree are removed, we *see* the movement, the unfolding of the whole. We see love as it *connects* and creates the points of connection instantly without time. We need not make love a concept in the mind. We just have to let go of the mind long enough to let *the real* shine in on itself. The love we feel. The love we manifest, becomes *alive* in the light of this love that we *are*.

Love God. Love the manifestation. Celebrate your oneness with them. See that *only the love is real*. This is your self, not a new self or a *"super"* you, but *your original being as love*.

Eat Your Vegetables First, Enlightenment for Dessert!

As a boy, my older brother would often be made to go without dessert because he refused to eat certain foods, often vegetables. I, on the other hand, never had this problem. I always (well nearly!) ate what was put before me. The difference was not that I liked everything, but that I had learned a little truth: sweet things have more sweetness after the lesser things were out of the way. I have found that this applies to life, and spirituality as life.

One of the reasons many children dislike, even despise certain vegetables and other adult foods, is that their taste buds are still developing and are not very subtle. This means tastes are stronger, and strong tastes are even stronger. How does this apply to spirituality?

Many Neo-Advaita teachers, particularly in the West, teach a version of Advaita or non-duality which is strong or absolute. This is a teaching that says there is no practice necessary, for who is to practice? It is a teaching that tells you that you are already awakened even though the seeker feels that anyone can see that he or she clearly is not, or they would understand this confusing teaching!

Some are ready for this stark teaching. Those that are ready to hear that no practice is necessary are the ones with years of practice, for only they will understand what is meant. The only persons who will have any understanding of *already awakened* are those who understand awakening as an experience. To expect spiritual beginners to understand these concepts without a foundation in the practice of some method of centering or in Christian terms, recollection, is like asking a child to eat foods he has not developed a taste for and in fact finds repugnant. Before any understanding can begin, remembering who you are, this beginning mental understanding of the I Am is necessary. Even with one such as Nisargadatta Maharaj, three years were needed for him to realize the words of his guru. And this was after a lifetime of spiritual curiosity and devotion. When one looks at the teachings of Nisargadatta

Maharaj, one must also look at the *life* of Nisargadatta Maharaj, which is as much of the teaching as anything he said.

In Maharaj's later years, he stuck very much to the basics, as his times of availability due to illness were shorter, and he wanted to cover the absolute ground. But in his earlier life and in his early teaching, he often engaged in worship and advised others to do so as well. He once deflated a woman that thought she had it all down. She was telling everyone how there was no practice or worship to perform, and that we were already free. When asked by Maharaj in his little mezzanine room what she understood, she replied that she knew she was the Absolute and that all was one. Maharaj told her to go and engage in devotion and chanting. She couldn't believe it. But Maharaj knew what she needed. A seed will not grow well in the unprepared ground. The I Am, the absolute nature of things, are concepts that can grow in only a prepared mind. In an unprepared mind, glimpses of the truth can be confusing, perhaps even detrimental or dangerous. Nisargadatta warned that his teaching would burn away all you conceive yourself to be. This can be psychologically and spiritually a very dangerous ground without the proper *settlement* in who you really are. A true teacher will not lead you into confusion but into clarity. A true teacher knows where you are spiritually. He knows whether you need devotion or emptying, or whether it is time *to get on with it* and take that final step into nothingness/everythingness.

Hymn to the Absolute

When Eleanor Farjeon wrote *Morning has Broken* in 1931, she probably had no idea it would become a big hit in the 1970s. When Cat Stevens (later Yosuf Islam) recorded the tune in the 70s, I thought it had a nice lyric, very pretty. But I did not catch the deeper meaning until sometime later when I heard it sung as a hymn.

I love the last five words of the song that speaks of recreation.[2] This use of the word *recreation* has always delighted me in its wonderful exploitation of both common meanings of that word. Words, stumbling blocks that they are, can sometimes point to some clarity.

It is often asked: *why* the creation? Not how and when, but *why*? And the answer is there, in that song/hymn: *God's recreation*! And this is in both the sense that God is recreating as in playing, relaxing, being himself, but also in the sense that God is re-creating, beginning anew!

This *re-creation* is a wonderful part of the unfolding of the whole. Granted, God and creation are ideas and concepts, nothing but thoughts. But thoughts exist, if not in an individual way as my thoughts or your thoughts, but as thoughts that float past like clouds with droplets of *ideas* instead of water. This unfolding, this re-creation, unlike the "new day" of the song, happens every second. The whole universe is recreated with every blink of an eye. The wonder of this is staggering. Just like beginning again, as it *is* beginning again. Re-creating, every second, this wonderful show. No past. No future. Just the unfolding present. The Absolute amusing itself with continuous creation; God's re-creation of the new day!

---

[2] last verse of *Morning has Broken*:
Mine is the sunlight,
Mine is the morning,
Born of the one light
Eden saw play;
Praise with elation,
Praise every morning,
God's re-creation
Of the new day.
https://allpoetry.com/Morning-Has-Broken (05.04.2023)

Living Non-Duality

One of my favorite photographs is of a young monk meditating under the stairs of his monastery. It reminds me of my longing to be a monk, and my desire to hide myself away.

Regardless of what some may say, this longing, this *calling* if you will, is very necessary to the beginning of a journey that lasts a lifetime, and even more so to sustain such an undertaking. It is a kind of madness by worldly standards, as it must be an obsession, a life-consuming endeavor. Anything short of absolute earnestness will not take you to that which you seek.

So much talk goes back and forth regarding non-duality. On the forums, Facebook and other social networks, there are so many who challenge others' awareness or enlightenment. The practices are challenged, and refuted/approved on and on. Westerners will quote Eastern teachers and insist on their superiority to Western teachers. Neo-Advaita will be attacked or praised in turn. Talk. We all understand that words cannot present the truth, but we continue to talk. It's as if we believe that if we stop talking about *it,* it will slip away. Even though we understand *it* cannot be grasped, we continue to grab with our minds by keeping it there, keeping it alive with talk.

Before I sought religious community, there was a formation that called me to community. An understanding had developed that the world had nothing to offer but distraction. An understanding that one thing, and one thing only, was worthy of pursuit: that which was God, that which was real. This required not just a change of thought, but a change of life. A new understanding requires a new life that makes it *live*. In a Christian religious community there is a *way* of life. This is established by the rule for the community.

It fell upon me to write the *Rule for the Community of the Living Sacrifice*. This rule was based on tradition, but also based on the life my partner and I had lived for over a dozen years, and included a lot of psychology and encounter group influences. Later, after leaving the community, I re-wrote the rule and looked at it for consistency in Advaita/Christian thought. This study is one that anyone moving from one system to another would be well advised to make. My understanding was greatly enhanced by honestly and fearlessly examining my Christian faith in view of the absolute understanding of Advaita.

Regardless of the studies we make of our faiths or Advaita, or any philosophy, it's what happens *next* that count. We all see the Sunday Christians, or even more often the Easter and Christmas Christians who show up for church, but that's it. Once they leave the pew, they go about their lives based on other criteria altogether. The same seems could be said of the non-dualists as well. The difference would be that the non-dualists run against their principles even when practicing them! Non-dualists will go to Satsangs and watch a well-known guru humiliate or embarrass a seeker, thinking they are superior to the one who uses *"I"* too much, or who does not know *"who asks the question?"*

When we judge the spirituality of others without being asked, we are engaging in ego only. If someone comes to you and asks honestly for your advice regarding spirituality, that is the time to give them your advice. If you write or make blogs about spirituality, by all means, write your experiences, discoveries, and opinions as honestly and clearly as you want or can. But if someone is not seeking an answer, but stating their own opinion or experiences, that is not the time for corrections or criticism. As long as you feel an urge to inject your unsolicited critical opinion into someone's spiritual writing, you can trust that you are *not* in a position to do so! We all love to engage in discussion of these things, but when it becomes demeaning and one-ups-man-ship, the point is lost along with compassion. Just as a Christian who goes to church on Sundays and sins all week, a non-dualist who is always looking for division in argument and thought, is not living up to his or her ideals.

As a Christian, or as a non-dualist (if you perceive a difference!), living the life is the real test. Living the life in integrity is the way to see if you are progressing or not. You can learn all the words: enlightenment, awareness, manifestation. You can learn and understand Eastern and Western philosophy. You can ask, *"Who am I?"* until you are blue in the face. But if you do not live a life of integrity that demonstrates non-duality, you will convince no one. One of the biggest questions and puzzles many on the path have is in finding a *real* guru. This same criterion can be used here: does the guru walk the walk as well as talk the talk? If a guru's life is not the living out of his teaching, his life is false, and the teaching is questionable.

Non-duality is the opening to life and love. It is in fact *being* love. This is, by any standard, a daunting task for a person. But as your natural state, it is easy as it is as you are. The person however needs to be *hidden under the stairs*. We need to do so much more than talk and read about non-dualism, we need to live it. That will mean different things to different people, but the absolute conviction must be there, as well as a fearless determination to be satisfied with nothing less. Every movement of our life must reflect this. Our actions, our words, and our thoughts must be such that they are no longer seen as our actions, words, and thoughts, but movements in line with the stillness we are. Non-duality is for so much more than talking, no matter how stimulating or edifying. Live non-duality, and there will be no need for words. Love will say it all.

Enlightenment and Mental Illness

One of the things spiritual teachers and seekers alike need to remember is that many people searching for spiritual development are trying to escape from lives that seem like nothing but trouble and strife. This frequently means people who society regards as mentally ill.

I once saw on a spiritual website the question, "How do you tell the difference between enlightenment and mental illness?" It is true that some forms of schizophrenia result in a kind of inability to differentiate between one's own existence and those of others, and a kind of *no-self*-perception is held. This may indeed be enlightenment, and if it causes no pain or behavioral problems may go unnoticed. But if a person, by living this out, comes to the attention of the authorities, they will often be thought mentally ill and in need of psychological help. The fact is, there may be no difference between enlightenment and mental illness.

All my life, I have lived with what is known as Asperger's syndrome. Now, Asperger's is not a mental illness. It is in the autistic spectrum, but if undiagnosed it is often misdiagnosed as mental illness. Asperger's, like most autism spectrum conditions, causes social problems: inability to make friends, socially inappropriate behavior, obsessive interests in one or sometimes two eccentric pursuits. My obsession has always been God and spiritual interests, even as a child. Asperger's was not unknown when I was a child, but it was not an accepted condition until the 1990s. So few psychologists and psychiatrists knew much, if anything, about it. I did not find out about it until I was over sixty, so struggled with it unknown, all my life. Despite of the struggle, or more likely because of it, I developed spiritually more than any other aspect of my personality. In recent years studies have been done with people on the autism spectrum, regarding spirituality, with fascinating results. Having worked with autistic people I have witnessed many unexpected spiritual insights.

It is important to understand that spiritual insight can be misinterpreted as mental Illness by those who are uninformed. I have seen many autistic, mentally ill, and others treated rather than listened to. It is so easy to label all who are different as disturbed or mentally ill, rather than think that they may have a special insight or be open to the real. A perfect example is the great avatar Ramakrishna. Ramakrishna did not act in a conventional way. He saw visions. He jumped and shouted during worship, and even became monkey-like during his Hanuman period. By today's Western standards, Ramakrishna would be considered mentally ill, maybe to the point of hospitalization!

Again, I would cite Ramana Maharshi. In his teens, he viewed his own death, was awakened by the experience, and went silent. He was lost in meditation for some time. If others had not looked after him, he could have died. This would seem like mental illness in the West, even by the standards of his own time.

Having read interviews of a number of enlightened teachers, I have found that many have experienced mental illness, or had alcohol or drug problems. Even without illness or substance abuse, many have had troubled lives with addictions to a variety of unhealthy behaviors. These teachers very often found that a crisis or a life-shaking event brought about their awakening. This is something they and all of us must keep in our minds, especially if we presume to teach.

As teachers, we need to be aware that for many spirituality is an escape. We must see that some seekers may indeed be mentally ill. I read just today about a young woman who sees herself as enlightened. She has reached an intellectual understanding that she does not exist, and sees herself as one with God. She expresses that she thinks she is God. She seems to believe this and sees herself as fully in control. This is the problem with telling seekers that "you already are enlightened."

Spiritual beginners are just starting out on a journey that many do not understand. The compulsion to seek comes before any understanding. To tell such a seeker that they are God or that "you are already awakened", as Papaji used to do, is very dangerous. Another well-known teacher told a seeker who was happily married, that there "is no doer," and no sense of responsibility for our actions. This confused the seeker who went about behaving as he chose, engaging in sexual affairs, feeling that he had no need to worry, as there "is no doer." He lost his wife and suffered a breakdown. A true teacher will know who is serious, who is after self-enhancement, and who is mentally ill. The teaching will be tailored to the seeker.

The important thing to remember is that enlightened behavior is not always normal behavior. Those who follow their own drummer are often outcast. Look at the Christ. He lived the truth and came smack up against authority. Today we may not crucify the Christ, but he would surely land in a psychiatric facility! As teachers, we have to have compassion. If your reason for teaching is anything other than compassion, then you may not be a real teacher. A great description of the incarnation of the Christ is that God loved mankind so much, that he became the object of his love: man. Just as a person realizes that they are love (the Absolute) and then is confronted with the enormity of living that out, a teacher must realize that the call to teach requires him to *be* compassion and to recognize each seeker for who they are and what they need. Mental illness and realization often go hand in hand. It takes compassion to see the difference when there is one.

Sound Effects, Conditioning, and Pavlov's Dogs

As a teenager in the late 1950s, I was just in time for the surge in interest in hi-fi and stereo equipment and sound. Stereo was everything and sound effects records were a big favorite of my older brother and me. There were albums with animal sounds, doors opening, race cars, and almost everything you could imagine. One I remember particularly was called *Steam Railways under Thundering Skies*. This album would conjure up images of trains under dark evening skies, threatening clouds and driving rain. It was entertaining to close your eyes and imagine being at the scene. It was fascinating to think that this flat black piece of vinyl could produce stimuli that in turn produced thought in the form of memory.

Memory thoughts contain every conditioned thought we have had since we were told we were a boy or a girl, or that the sky is blue. We have a mother and father thought, and the story begins: the story of us. And in very short order, the slightest stimuli bring up thoughts from the *memory world*. Many stimuli bring up both pleasant and unpleasant thoughts. Something as simple as the whiff of turkey roasting may send your mind to Christmas and a tree, or a beloved toy that Santa had brought. But it may also dredge up Uncle Charlie's drunken rage at the commercialism of Christmas or your brother breaking your new train set. All this just from a whiff of turkey!

We are surrounded by stimuli that a life in this world has conditioned to a defined reaction. Some stimuli make us joyful, and others sad, or even depressed. We have little control over the stimuli. It is part of the unfolding of life. But we can change our attitude about the thoughts the stimuli bring up. The smell of the turkey could be simply just the smell of the turkey without all the added baggage.

It is important to keep in mind that everything appears in consciousness, from your personal self to whatever image you hold of God. These are all thoughts that appear in consciousness, just reflections of reality. The memory thoughts are of the same substance as these, being conditioned thoughts that you have learned. Just as an infant eventually perceives a divide between its "I" and the mother, the world and all its objects arise. All it takes is the mind instructing a *you* it has created out of its total misunderstanding of what it is. The *assumed subject* must realize it is simply another *object* and that the true subject is unknowable to the assumed subject.

Some events cause transitory pain. There is hunger. There is war. We cannot dismiss the realities of this world, no matter how illusory. Pain that happens at the moment has to be and is dealt with at the moment, be it physical or emotional. It may be well dealt with or poorly dealt with, but there is a response to the stimuli. The response is either a response in line with the moment or it is a response from memory, or perhaps a response from both. Learning in advance how to respond to a physical emergency makes sense and will give one the ability to overcome the panic response, but learned responses to emotional pain can create false images of others and the world. A drunken Uncle Charlie and some bad memory thoughts, and you live the pain every holiday season. The event, having arisen in thought, holds the same pain thought every time you *entertain* it. And entertain is the right word, for you *invite it in and let it have its way.*

That is the key. In finding what is real, discrimination of thought must be a habit. Just as the daily routine of life requires habit, so that it is not a distraction, the useless thoughts and troubling memories need to be politely escorted to the door. They don't need to be given the bum's rush but politely ignored so they leave of their own accord. The best way is to try not to invite them in the first place. At the first notice of stimuli, the first whiff of turkey, simply become aware of turkey. Expand it to dressing, if you dare; but at the first sign of embarrassment at memories of Uncle Charlie or sadness over past disappointments or losses, see those thoughts as what they are, past memories telling a story. Toothless villains vanishing into dust.

Not unlike Pavlov's Dogs, the sound of a bell like the smell of a turkey or the recorded sounds of a thunderstorm, can bring up memories so real we *feel* the emotions and often physical sensations associated with them. In fact, just as the bell is rung or a seed of consciousness arises, the whole manifestation arises with it. The important thing to embrace is the sound, the smell, and the wonder,

53

not the illusive memory thoughts that arise with them. Do not name them, simply be with them in love.

Non-Duality, Poverty, and the Cross

I wrote in a blog recently regarding the charging of money for spiritual teaching. In that blog, I pointed out that the spiritual teacher may need to learn to embrace poverty. Without bringing up all that again, a question was asked regarding poverty as a virtue. While I may not categorize poverty itself as a virtue, the total acceptance of it, should it come, is a most welcome attitude on the spiritual search.

A point that can't be made too often is that to *be* awareness, a life must be led that embraces the freedom and the acceptance of whatever that brings. No matter your religion or philosophical system, or total lack of either, what these things work in your life is what is felt. You cannot say you are free if you still have concerns over worldly security. Lest you think that this is simply a Western, Christian concept coming from a former monk, let me quote from the senior lecturer in Religious Studies at Victoria University of Wellington, New Zealand, Kapil N. Tiwari. In his book, *Dimensions of Renunciation in Advaita Vedanta*, Mr. Tiwari writes[3]:

"Renunciation as linked with uncovering Jnana results in turning the concern of man away from external things to the essential inner nature by accomplishing (that by) which everything else is accomplished. Jnana and renunciation take place simultaneously as one of the Upanishads (the Brhadaranyaka) says:

'Verily, after they have found this soul, the Brahmanas cease from desiring children, from desiring possessions, from desiring the world, and wander about as beggars.'"

Sankara bases his whole philosophy on this foundation. He quotes the following texts to support the above contention:

"The knower of Brahman attains freedom from all fear. When all desires occupying his heart, fall off entirely, then indeed, does the mortal become immortal."

---

[3] Tiwari, Kapil N.: Dimensions of Renunciation in Advatia Vedanta, Delhi: Motilal Banarsidass, 1977

Reason itself declares that the less there is to distract, the more the heart, soul, and mind can dwell in the present awareness. But we fool ourselves. We think we can entertain distractions. Just as I was saying that teachers need to free themselves of the need to ask for donations, the seeker must not fool themselves in terms of thoughts of security. The non-dual teaching requires living it out, not just philosophical discourse, meditation or study. The life you have, the life you see before you *is the awareness* if you are really willing to *see* it. This takes conviction. Not just a positive attitude, but a willingness to lay down everything and follow. So many stop at the intellectual understanding. They get to that place of *nebulous clarity,* that place where the only next step is the step off the cliff into the unknown. They know what is required; but the mind comes in and tells them that there is nothing there, that they must keep searching, find a new guru, read a different text, or any number of other reasons not to take that step, that act of total love that will bring them home.

In the Gospel of Matthew, we find this idea played out between Jesus and the wealthy young man:

Matthew 19:

[16] And, behold, one came and said unto him, Good Master, what good thing shall I do that I may have eternal life?

[17] And he said unto him, Why callest thou me good? There is none good but one, that is, God: but if thou wilt enter into life, keep the commandments.

[18] He saith unto him, Which? Jesus said, Thou shalt do no murder, Thou shalt not commit adultery, Thou shalt not steal, Thou shalt not bear false witness,

[19] Honour thy father and thy mother; and, Thou shalt love thy neighbour as thyself.

[20] The young man saith unto him, All these things have I kept from my youth up: what lack I yet?

[21] Jesus said unto him, If thou wilt be perfect, go and sell that thou hast, and give to the poor, and thou shalt have treasure in heaven, and come and follow me.

²² But when the young man heard that saying, he went away sorrowful: for he had great possessions.

²³ Then said Jesus unto his disciples, Verily I say unto you, That a rich man shall hardly enter into the kingdom of heaven.

²⁴ And again I say unto you, It is easier for a camel to go through the eye of a needle, than for a rich man to enter into the kingdom of God.

²⁵ When his disciples heard it, they were exceedingly amazed, saying, Who then can be saved?

²⁶ But Jesus beheld them, and said unto them, With men this is impossible; but with God all things are possible.

"But when the young man heard that saying, he went away sorrowful: for he had great possessions." This is really at the heart of the problem. We have things we don't want to let go of. Not just possessions, or even security (although how many have even done that?), but the need for the mind to have control. We have to face the fact that all we believe ourselves to be must be offered up. We are momentary waves in a universal ocean. We must be willing to give up our wave-ness in order to *be* the ocean. All this takes, is earnestness, that serious, single-minded, whole-hearted, unwavering willingness. That is surrender.

That brings me to the final part of the title of this note: the cross. Many people have asked me in view of Advaita, non-duality or awareness, how does the cross fit in. Many are aware that Christ taught a form of non-dual awareness, but do not see the meaning or purpose of the crucifixion in any Advaita sense. Whether one is a believer or not, the cross is significant in that it points to surrender. Whether for a Christian or an Advaitin, surrender is the key that opens the door to understanding. When the mind had reached its limit of understanding and surrenders to the heart, a whole new unspoken understanding floods the open mind and heart. The cross speaks of complete surrender, acceptance of fear, acceptance of death. The letting go needed in Advaita is no less. Surrender to this death of the mind, and resurrect to the freedom you have always had.

Renunciation, the cross we must bear. To be open to all, we must be free of concern for tomorrow. In response to my note on spiritual teachers, I was told that *this* was why they needed to charge for teaching. My response was that this view shows no trust in the unfolding. To trust in the unfolding is to be part of it. Renunciation frees us, not what we have laid aside. Our peace must not depend on well-laid plans, but on a willingness to surrender unto death. Non-duality requires more than talk, but a willingness to give up all we hold for all we are.

The Empty Vessel Catches the Rain: Non-Duality and Christian Contemplation

True Christian contemplation is often misrepresented, and to bring non-dual teachings into it would seem a precarious idea at least. Experience, however, has shown otherwise. An understanding of what contemplation means, in historic Christian terms and what it means to you as a seeker, either in non-duality or as a Christian, is essential.

In historic Christian terms, contemplation differs from the Christian idea of meditation in one very important way. In meditation, we think on one event or idea from the life of Christ, or a passage from the Bible, or another sacred text. We dwell on this thought and discover meaning. This is, of course, all in the mind in non-dual terms.

In the self-inquiry of non-duality we do much the same thing. We look at ourselves. We dwell in the I Am until we see that our existence is all we can account for. Dwelling in the I Am leads to the uncovery of the impermanence of the manifestation, and our own story dissolves. This is not unlike Christian contemplation.

The difference in Christian contemplation from both non-dual self-inquiry and Christian meditation is that Christian contemplation is a dwelling in *no thought*. From the Desert Fathers to the present day, methodologies have been constructed on how to *do* contemplation. But true contemplation is not *done*, it simply happens. Contemplation can come to one who is not studied in it at all, for true contemplation is a movement of grace. One can try to make oneself receptive, by living a life free of desire, but the nature of grace follows no rules. It neither punishes nor rewards, but flows with love only. The reason a monk or nun leaves the world of desire behind is not to run away from life, but to meet the unknown head-on. The idea is to empty out all that is the not real, the egoic mind, as it were. For only in an empty, unattached mind will contemplation come. This is the goal of contemplation if it is described as having a goal. For true contemplation has no goal apart from wanting to *be* with "God" or the Absolute.

59

This *wanting*, this is the *earnestness* of Nisargadatta Maharaj. This is a single-minded longing, not to know, but to be. Just as love, by its being, creates you to love, you must return the love by letting go of the *you* and returning to the source. In the wordless silence of contemplation, there is communion with the source. Knowledge is acquired through this silent communion, though it is not knowledge with words or concepts, but the knowledge of the heart.

The organized Church promotes contemplation among its clergy and monastics and to a lesser degree its laity, but limits it by only allowing the insights or revelations that conform with Church doctrine or belief, thereby taking the heart out of any serious inquiry. Contemplation, if it is to be a useful practice, needs to be seen as free from any doctrinal restraint or it will simply reflect the mind that is controlling it. The changes that are the *fruits* of contemplation will occur only when unrestrained, and only when they are *consciously unspoken*.

Love, "God", the Absolute, whatever concept you like, informs, or to use a Christian term, *indwells,* and separation vanishes. But this is only *available* to *be*. There is no explaining it to yourself or others. It is real. It leaves no questions, as the questioner is absorbed, and it changes your life. It becomes your life! This is the important part: no matter if you are in a monastery or practicing non-dual self-inquiry, the teaching must be part of life, and not an escape from it.

As stated above, contemplation is not a practice as such, but a way of being. Brother Lawrence of the Resurrection in his quaint, simple way spoke in his *Practice of the Presence of God* about "turning his pancake in its pan for the love of God." This willingness to *stay in the moment,* this *earnestness* that was so insisted upon by Nisargadatta Maharaj, is the essence of contemplation. The contemplative monk, the self-inquiring non-dualist, is not negating life. They are not indulging in self-punishment or self- annihilation. They are becoming empty vessels. Being open to all possibilities: taking no stand, being *no-thing*, they are free to be everything. The empty vessel catches the rain.

What Are You Looking For?
Seeking Without the Seeker

The reasons for seeking are many but much seeking is done to *get something* or *get somewhere*, not simply for its own sake or for love's own sake.

So many seekers in non-duality come from other spiritual places where they felt let down or unfulfilled. Many come from mainstream churches whose rules or unbelievable dogma made no sense. Some are rejecting belief altogether, and looking for an intellectual understanding that fits with their intellectual development. Non-duality has become a favorite of the educated spiritual crowd, with proponents appearing on Oprah, and doing Satsangs all over the world. Enlightenment has become the crown on the head of a complete education. Notwithstanding, the understanding that the mind cannot grasp enlightenment, endless discourse ensues about self and no self, present awareness, and all the rest of the non-duality speak. But educational self-improvement is not the only reason so many seek non-dual teachings.

Just recently, I heard a spiritual teacher say that pain or suffering is often the reason for people to be drawn to non-duality. This may be the case with some. It may be the case with many. If this is so, it is a shame as awareness or enlightenment is not a *cure*. Those who seek comfort or a better life in non-duality should realize right from the start that non-dual teaching does not bring improvement, it simply brings *clarity*.

There is so much mingling of psychology and non-dual teaching, particularly in the West, that it might be a good idea to look into where the two meet or dovetail with each other. Self-help programs, life coaches, substance-abuse programs, in addition to psychologists and psychiatrists, abound here in the West. Psychological exploration can be very useful, both as therapeutic recollection and as self-inquiry. But psychological techniques should be left to those trained in that field, and no free-form psychological experimentation should be attempted by a non-dual teacher unless they have studied and know the results well. Certain psychological methods, like group therapy, can be very useful in self-inquiry. But when the group therapy methods are used as Satsang or a sort of hot seat group session, this can be a problem.

There are places where non-dual teachings and psychology merge, but care must be taken to understand the differences. Clinical depression is a perfect example. It is recognized that many, not all, depressions have a chemical component. Solve the chemical imbalance and the mood changes, simple body chemistry. Sufferers of clinical depression are treated with chemical substitutes and counseled that the depression is the result of chemistry, and has no real cause. The depressed person learns that he or she is not the body and that the feelings of loss or sadness, and other signs of depression are only caused by chemicals and are not real events. This can result in the sufferer having a complete experience of his or herself as being not the body/mind, but something that can *look* at itself. But the depression, the chemical imbalance, goes away only with medication. From personal experience with this kind of depression, I can tell you it is quite fascinating to watch this depression as an observer; watching as pain, like any other thought float by. Not confusing it as a feeling needing a response, but the simple chemical process of pain thought. This process, this *I am not the depression*, is a psychological process not unlike the beginnings of non-dual understanding.

The problem with both this desire for self-improvement psychologically and educationally, is that the desire for an improving oneself is a selfish desire. Selfish desire does not lead to non-duality, even if that selfish desire is for non-duality.

The only reason to be a seeker is that you are called to be a seeker. There is no choice. The seeker who loves "God" and goes in search for him or her, without thought of a heaven or hell, is the one possessed with the earnestness Nisargadatta spoke of. Of course, there is no need to love a "God" or an image of a god specifically, but *there must be love*: love of wisdom, love of truth, or simply love itself. No other goal will take you out of yourself, will allow the *you* to die. The self-improvement of the mind is only enhancing the mind, self-image, and ego. The self-improvement of your happiness level or learning methods to hide your pain, only give temporary solace to a still existent *you*. Only when you are lost in seeking that which you are, that which draws you to itself, will you be absorbed into that which you seek. Only when both sought and seeker are absorbed in seeking is there non-duality.

Only selfless love will *be* selfless love. If we seek truth, reality, love, or any other name you like, we must vibrate with a love so strong that we want only that. If we seek intellectual wisdom, we can find it, but it is not love. It is just more thoughts. If we seek emotional security or personal self-improvement, we might find it temporarily in some practice or group of Satsang supporters. But that which is sought with love without fear, *or with the acceptance of fear*, is that which *is*. Seeking only with fervent love, without thought of intellectual reward, accepting confusion or depression as part of the unfolding, will open you to the flow of grace that love is. Seek only to answer that call. Let the seeker vanish into the seeking. Let yourself vanish into life!

Advent, Incarnation, and Non-Duality

One of the things frequently missed by those who have moved their spiritual search from organized religion to non-dual inquiry is the regular celebrations and holy days. Advent and Christmas maybe two of the ones most missed.

Now, of course, many still celebrate Christmas as a secular holiday, but the spiritual meaning of the birth of Jesus is often lost in the teachings of non-duality. It is ok to have office parties, enjoy Santa, presents, and all the festivities, but spiritual meaning? Never, not in an Abrahamic religion! Too much duality! But maybe...?

An Advent season does not go by that I do not think of the former Anglican Bishop of Durham, the controversial David Jenkins. Bishop Jenkins was controversial right from the start. He later went on to be very progressive and after retirement was one of the first Bishops in Britain to bless a gay marriage. But even before his appointment as Bishop, he held controversial views on the resurrection, and our purpose here: the birth of Jesus.

Bishop Jenkins held the view that the virgin birth was very possibly written after the fact by those wishing to emphasize the spiritual quality of the event. In one of his most controversial statements, he stated: *"I wouldn't put it past God to arrange a virgin birth if he wanted, but I very much doubt that he would."*

This, and other statements by Bishop Jenkins caused so much dissent when he was appointed Bishop of Durham, that the fire at York Minster three days after his consecration was said, by some, to be God's judgment on the Church of England for appointing him. Looking deeply into the bishop's writings, however, I found one of the most spiritual (even in non-dual terms) descriptions of the incarnation I have ever heard.

In the *Brompton Lectures* of 1966, on the Incarnation, Professor Jenkins (as he was then) presented a clear concept on how the incarnation of Christ came about and the nature of Christ and "God":

"...the actual nature of this Christ confirmed and re-defined the nature, activity and power of this God as being rightly understood primarily as love of a particular and distinctive kind. This love was the self-giving, identifying and involved love demonstrated by Jesus and commended by him through both example and commandment. It was so distinctive in its total self-identification with the loved that it was necessary to develop a little used word, agape, to refer to this love and so distinguish it from such types of love as those involved in ordinary friendship or ordinary sexual relationships which could be (although they need not be) self-centered."

It is so easy to see that this agape, this self-identifying love, becomes the Christ, by simply loving and identifying with man. Love *becomes* man in order to love, and in this particular story, to bring love to man who has forgotten his true nature.

If you understand that Jesus, the man, was filled with *Christ Consciousness*, and saw others as brothers and sisters (himself neither better or different from them) you understand that incarnation is the story of us all. When Jesus taught the disciples how to pray, he said, "Our father," not my father. The Christ clearly saw that all of us come into existence by an act of love: not a physical act of procreation, but a movement of love itself, or "God", or the Absolute. This love, so *"totally self-identifying with the loved,"* becomes *you*.

Once you understand this you understand why this *pull* you feel toward safety, toward permanence, is a result of identifying as the loved or the lover, rather than the love itself. This is what creates the feeling of separation. Just as the Absolute (which is everything in One) allows itself to be you for a short time, it is absolutely necessary for you to *live that out* by being *it* eternally. This is the purpose of non-duality, if there is one: to live out that *oneness*. To live for understanding, and an acceptance of lack of understanding; to surrender to what is, *accepting that it is love working* and doing the best with what you are given. Practical advice, not beautifully spiritual, but this incarnation business is nothing if not practical.

Advent reminds us of the birth of the Christ. Not a past event, but an ongoing universal incarnation. It is incarnation itself. Not just the

65

baby Jesus, but the baby *you and I*. The birth of love this day and all days, celebrated in this story of birth, life and death, Jesus' and ours. No matter what your religion, belief system, or philosophy there is no reason, why you cannot enjoy the beauty and spirituality of Christmas. *Celebrate incarnation*, that wonderful, terrifying, and exhilarating experience we all share. The Advent season and Christmas are celebrations of the birth of love, a timeless event re-created each day. This season of joy is more than just camaraderie, commercial enterprise, or even brotherhood. It is a time to reflect on our very being, *our incarnation of love.* O come, O come, Emmanuel!

Noel: A Spiritual Children's Book for Christmas

I wanted to recommend a children's book for Christmas called *Noel*. It was written by Romeo Muller, illustrated by Bill A. Langley, and published in 1993 by Little Golden Books. It was previously made into an animated television Christmas special of the same title by Pacific Animation Corporation.

I find it appealing because, rather than the usual Christmas themes, it is about love being our nature and the liberation of death. This may seem an overly serious topic for children, but the story is so lovely, and the ending so joyous, that children will be delighted.

The story is about a Christmas ornament named Noel. Noel is born in a glass-blower's shop, and right at the moment Noel is being made the glass blower hears his only daughter is going to have a baby and he cries with joy.

It was Noel's good fortune that one of those tears of joy bounced off Herman's cheek, trickled down his glassblower's pipe, and fell with a tinkling sound inside Noel. It became the small ornament's happiness.

Noel and the box of eleven other ornaments are bought by a family with children, and Noel experiences his first Christmas. At the end of the season, the tree is taken down and Noel with his companion ornaments are stored in the attic. But season after season Noel and the others are returned to the tree for Christmas.

As the years go by, the children grow up. The parents grow old and move away from the house, and the ornaments are left alone in the attic.

Noel and the rest of the dozen were left in the attic to become faded and chipped and a thing called forgotten.

Could everything be over?

Nothing is ever truly over when one has a happiness. And so one happy day, years later a new family moved in. The new family finds the ornaments in the attic, and decides to put them on their tree.

And then there was a thing called a miracle.

For now, that Noel's old glass body was gone, his happiness, the thing that *really* was Noel, was released. Like a merry little comet, it rose from the floor, bounced around the room, then flew up through the chimney and into the Christmas dawn.

I tend to agree with Nirsargadatta's view about teaching children about religion or spirituality: *"Leave the children alone!"* But this book has so much truth in it, and so much love, that it is just what children need to hear, and could start a very interesting (and challenging) discussion.

Living on Love Alone:
Confessions of a Spiritual Teacher

As I was re-working my Facebook page for the new layout, I found that a wave of honesty flowed over me. As I was putting in the information regarding education, I thought I would write something about that, as many seekers might like to hear what a teacher of non-duality might have to say in this regard.

My partner and I were asked by the Dean of Lincoln Cathedral to form a religious community in Lincoln, England in the 1980s. This was in itself a miracle, as between the two of us, we have not even one high school diploma.

Now I know it says on my profile that I studied at the College of Marin, and this is true, but I only attended one semester having passed the entrance examination after dropping out of high school without graduating. I spent the last part of my senior high school year in a psychiatric hospital due to Asperger's syndrome, which being largely unknown in the 1960s, went undiagnosed. I studied teaching at college as I loved learning, but I was an emotional wreck in my teens and early adult life, so the social life at school was hell.

I was always interested in spirituality, even from my earliest days, and a sense of *oneness* was always there in some nebulous form. Growing up as a Christian, I had no doubt that "God" was with me always. The awakening I experienced in my late forties was just a natural occurrence in a process that had begun at birth. Of course, I had studied Advaita as taught by Ramana Maharshi and Nisargadatta Maharaj, but their teaching only confirmed what was already present, and my awakening was that I had been living an awakened life all along. As an Aspergian child and young adult, I had learned to be the observer. I was, and still am, a very shy person. Silence was my way of life.

And while I hardly ever talked, I watched and listened. I observed that love was the only thing that mattered, and if I relied on that alone with perfect trust, life was good.

My partner and I have literally lived our 43 years together on love alone. We worked in San Francisco's Tenderloin district, and not only made a successful living in dangerous circumstances but managed to make a difference in others' lives. When we joined the Church, we continued to work for the poor and homeless. When we had the opportunity to travel to England in the 1980s, we sold all our possessions and trusted in God to see us through. When we were asked to form a new religious community, we were neither surprised nor confounded, even though we had no formal training or education in such an endeavor. Our work involved caring for and counseling former psychiatric patients being released from one of the most terrible psychiatric hospitals I have ever encountered. We also took in people sent to us by the local probation service and ex-prisoners. We never flinched. We trusted in love only, and we were amazingly successful. Living on love alone, trusting it only, not only allowed us to reach out in the dark to anyone, it laid the ground for understanding. And I guess this is the point of this piece.

Many who come to non-dual seeking come from educated backgrounds. As I have stated before, many look at enlightenment as a crown to a good education. But what is in your mind does not lead to the truth. In some, perhaps many circumstances, education can be a stumbling block to awareness. I have been a real advocate for the simple seekers. People like Brother Lawrence of the Resurrection, a simple monk, shoemaker and cook, who was responsible for *The Practice of the Presence of God,* a small book of oneness that is a classic of Christian mysticism. Or St. Therese of Lisieux, whose *The Story of a Soul* is a testimony of a life of love in action. Or look at Ramana Maharshi, or Nisargadatta Maharaj, or even the Christ. Simple earnestness, simple love. These lead to understanding. These lead to truth. You can study under well-educated people. You can read all the spiritual literature you can lay your hands on. But living a life of service, trust and love is what takes you to the Absolute. To be in "God's" presence, to *be* God's love, is the Absolute. You can't learn it. You can only *live it.*

Christmas: The Incarnation of Love

Christmas is a holiday that many of us love as children but may lose sight of as we grow older. Of course, Christmas is a Christian holiday, as much as others have attempted to appropriate it for commercial reasons, it remains a Christian holiday. As a Christian holiday, it has taken on the trappings of the religion it springs from. There is the Annunciation, the virgin birth, the shepherds, the wise men, and all the rest of it. All these *stories* can be traced back to earlier *stories*, from earlier times, and it becomes tempting to dismiss the whole celebration as simply more myth. This temptation might seem even more appropriate to those in the non-dual community.

If we are experiencing oneness, or attempting to do so, we could do worse than looking into this incarnation story of the babe born in a manger.

Like the babe born on the night we celebrate as special or *holy*, our nativity, our life began as a vulnerable babe as well. Thrust into a world that appears as soon as we perceive ourselves as *separate*. Innocence complete in itself, but born with, or should I say born *as* the misperception of separation. Love itself, born always, but fearful of an *imagined* separation.

In spite of the grown Christ Child's assurances of eternity, we want to *cling* to him, hold him up as *special*: God's only son. He must be better, perfect, good! "Why do you call me good?" he asked, "No one is good, save God alone." The Christ called us his brothers and sisters. He begins the Lord's Prayer with "Our Father." God, who is love itself, is the father of us all. Love creates, becomes through incarnation. *Our* incarnation brings love into the world just as the incarnation of love we celebrate at Christmas perpetually brings love and light into a dark world.

Just as there never seems to be room at the inn, love seems often to go unrecognized. Just as the make-do qualities of a stable reveal the beauty of the surrounding life, our life and attempts at love shine above the momentary hates and discord that appear to surround us. Christmas this day and all days, sanctified or not, are celebrations of the *extraordinary ordinariness*. The birth of love this day, this Christmas Day, is a celebration of incarnation, yours, mine, and Christ's. All born together, beyond time, in the wonderful Absolute.

Accept the invitation to realize incarnation, this season and always.

December 26ᵗʰ: The Turning Point of Commitment

On the 26th of December, I often hear people talk about the letdown on the day after Christmas. The build-up to Christmas, which used to start after Thanksgiving when I was a kid, but now begins before the Jack-o-lanterns are put away, often leaves people with a disappointed or somehow, *non-complete* feeling. This reminds me of the letdown feeling seekers often have when they have a spiritual experience or a moment of awareness that does not last.

The practices we engage in or the meditations we follow religiously, or whatever lifestyle we adopt to develop spiritually, like the preparations and build-up to Christmas are really the *life* we seek as it were. The goodwill, the camaraderie we feel in the holiday season, is the *purpose* of the season! The hectic shopping, the decorating, the *single-minded* pursuit of a happy holiday, for ourselves and others are what give life to the season.

In spiritual practice or spiritual life, we do much the same. We seek to develop ourselves, to be closer to God and one another. When in our practice or life we have a Christmas moment, a moment of awareness and peace, we want to hold on to it. But it, like Christmas day itself, moves on. It is not diminished, just moved into memory, that dwelling place of phantoms, both good and bad (you choose, it's your memory!). But these movements, both Christmas and spiritual experiences need not come and go.

Every year, during the holiday season, I, like millions of others, watch Dickens's *Christmas Carol*. Every year we watch Ebenezer Scrooge change from a wretched old sinner to a changed and generous good citizen who keeps Christmas well every year. We know this story as well as the biblical accounts of Christ's birth. How often do we say at this time of year, how we wish it could be like this all the year through? But do we even try to make the simple changes it would take to make those things happen? In our spiritual life, *do we seek without ceasing*? Do we give *all*? Do we practice with the *earnestness* Nisargadatta asked for?

73

December 26th is a great day to test your commitment to what you seek. Is Christmas over? Many I have met in the Church do not even put up their Christmas trees until Christmas Eve. That is the day the birth of Christ is celebrated. And the tree is left up until Epiphany, the celebration of the arrival of the wise men. The story of these men from other faiths who came to worship the birth of love, speaks to the spread of the love. Not just around the world, but around the heart. Christmas day is not the end, but just the beginning. Every day is and can be experienced as a new day, a new beginning. No matter what memory tells you yesterday was, today is now, unfolding like a Christmas morning.

One of the things I used to tell my spiritual advisers when I was in the Church, was that I had come to look upon death as being like Christmas. All of life is the fun, the decorating, the celebrating, waiting for the big event. In Christian terms, this was the afterlife, the being with Christ. But upon realizing the afterlife is really the *ever-life*, one sees that it's Christmas every day. Sure, it's not happy every day. Not every Christmas is a happy one. But that's the point. Christmas is in the living. The slogging along from one island of bliss to another. Lots of mud in between, but one drop of bliss and you're hooked. When both life and death can be looked at as Christmas, even when the pocketbooks are empty or the dog has knocked down the Christmas tree, *the living remains the Christmas*.

Spiritual experiences come and go, just as Christmas. But the effect is more than simply a memory. They are an assurance from grace. Just as this Christmas holiday holds promise if we let the life-changing possibilities of a Scrooge affect our lives into a commitment to make every day *the most wonderful day of the year*, our spiritual lives can be turned on a dime and in an instant, of total commitment and earnestness.

Let December 26th be the turning point of commitment. Being one requires only stopping being anything else.

The Child Behind the Mask

When I was about 22 years old, I had the most extraordinary experience. I was having trouble with depression, and in the middle of a confusing identity crisis, I found myself, at that early age, longing for my childhood. The whole social/sexual thing was something I was totally unprepared for, and the seemingly simpler time of my youth seemed like an alien world. I found myself asking: "What happened to the child? What happened to the child?"

In the depths of that longing, a longing of wanting to be clean again, the child I had been appeared before me and engaged in a silent dialog with my soul. There was a silent sharing of sadness over the loss of innocence, but also an understanding that this dream child was just that, a dream, and always had been! I was also made aware that this child was not me, was *never* me. For here I was, conversing with the child I was, a child who lives only in memory: a *dream* child.

This experience went on for some time. I can't say for sure how long; but there was a tendency to not want the child to go, as I was learning, *uncovering* so much. But like all experiences that come, it went. It left a permanent impression however. I had long believed myself not to be the body, but here I could see that I also was not this memory child. I was observing this child, just as I observed my observing self, and could plainly see they both lived in memory. The child, created from past memory, the present man, created from instant recollection memory. Yes, *we make it up as we go along.*

The dream child is not entirely fictitious. It is what remains in memory of the original spark, the comfort of constant awareness. Once the infant emerges from the womb, and shortly thereafter transforms I Am-ness into a separation from everything else, self-protection begins.

The first mask is the I Am-ness itself. From there it is mask after mask. Always the child is trying on new masks: a Mommy mask, a Daddy Mask, a good boy/girl mask, a bad boy/girl mask. And the masks don't go away just because there is a *new* mask. Think how many people go through several different sets of masks as they are presented with different situations. Some will regress to infantile behavior. Infantile, defensive behavior in an adult can be a frightening thing. It is the kind of behavior that leads, ultimately, to war. But the fear of the child, the primal fear of separation and alienation, is hidden under masks. So many masks hide us from ourselves and others.

When I was in the monastery, I had already had years of psychiatric inquiry. I had been to some pretty dark and scary places in my soul and held no illusion of my holiness. In the formation of the monk, there is further breaking down of the ego, whatever that is. But let it be sufficient to say that by the time one has gone through the kind of inquiry into one's soul those two practices lead to one has few corners in which to hide. When I left the monastery, I told people I felt like I was walking around without my skin. A monastery is a safe place to go skinless. In fact, that is one of the main purposes of religious community. In a community, masks must be removed one by one, until the original face is all that shows.

I have found that the dream child has the frightened separated I Am at its heart. It is this child that lives deep inside us all. It seeks the memory of the *spark*, the completeness of awareness, but it will not take off that last mask: the mask of I Am. Instead of taking off that last mask, it puts on more masks for protection, so by the time adulthood is reached, the spark is hidden under masks of teacher, businessman, lover, wife, mother, seeker. The dream child still cries for union under all the masks, even its own. But the letting go of the masks needs to recognize the fear of this child and lead it back, mask by mask, so it has the fearlessness to let go of the final I Am mask.

To find this dream child takes all the courage one can find. To face your true self, which is what the dream child actually is, is often to face ugliness. We like to see children as sweet, innocent little beings, untouched by violence or greed or any of the sins we see in ourselves. But the fact is, anyone who has observed a preschool playground knows that small children can be extremely selfish and violent in expressing their selfishness. Once one has the sense of I Am-ness and has yet to learn to use the masks, self-protective behavior is what you will get. We all are selfish. Some more than others. It all depends on

76

the degree of fear or trust. Some dream children have more masks than others.

Remember that your wife, husband, boss, teacher, child has a dream child. Their behavior, no matter how adult, will be based on the fear or confidence of that dream child. If you come to recognize your dream child and its fears, you will go a long way in understanding the bad things others seem to do. When we can see each other as scared children simply trying to get home, perhaps we can give sympathy, instead of enmity. When you begin to realize that your self-protective behavior comes from the longing for safety of the dream child, you can understand how you can go to the source, the spark beyond the I Am, and find your original face. Remove the job mask. Remove the man or woman mask. Remove the adult/child mask. Finally, grit your teeth, and remove the I Am mask. Being remains.

The Child Inside:
The Practice of Observing the Child

I recently put up a blog/note titled *The Child Behind the Mask*. This child, which we labeled the *dream child*, lives in us all, as both the ideal and the frightened little child that will go to any length to protect itself.

The ideal, this concept of a *pure* beginning is largely fiction. Sure, there is hidden in memory a vision of completeness, a remembrance of being without desire or fear, but it is a distortion. It is a distortion because it is the vision of a *me* having a remembrance of a *me* without desire and fear. The innocent child we remember ourselves to be is already corrupted by the simple appearance of its separateness. This recognition of separateness leads directly to the *frightened little child*, and its subsequent behavior.

This recognition of separateness, which many psychologists feel takes place by two years old, has already had its precursor in the birth itself. This sudden eviction from the comfort and *self-enclosed* safety of the womb is the common experience of mankind and animal kind alike.

In *The Child Behind the Mask*, I stated:

"Remember that your wife, husband, boss, teacher, child has a dream child. Their behavior, no matter how adult, will be based on the fear or confidence of that dream child. If you come to recognize your dream child and its fears, you will go a long way in understanding the bad things others seem to do. When we can see each other as scared children simply trying to get home, perhaps we can give sympathy, instead of enmity. When you begin to realize that your self-protective behavior comes from the longing for safety of the dream child, you can understand how you can go to the source, the spark beyond the I Am and find your original face."

Recognizing your dream child is the beginning of the process. Then the fun begins! When you begin to see that behind all the masks you wear, there is this frightened little child who struggles for survival, you can not only calm the frightened child but see the child in others as well.

As a child who grew up with undiagnosed Asperger's Syndrome, I have had plenty of time to develop coping mechanisms in my dealings with others and the outside world. Chief among these of course is the understanding that there are no others or an outside world that is any different than the inside world. But beyond that bit of philosophy, that the mind spins very well, I have developed practical ways of coping with everyday relationships. *Observing the child* is one such method.

Most of us, no matter how sophisticated, follow patterns of behavior learned as children (often very young children), that cater to our desires and fears. We move naturally toward love, but when our sense of separateness distorts that flow, desire and fear take over. All the emotions arise from this distortion of our natural flow toward love. This is easy to see in children, as they have yet to develop and put on the masks of subtlety. The emphasis on *me* and *mine* among children lives very much on the surface. As we grow older, and more masks become available to us through education, experience, and practice, we hide the me and the mine under more socially acceptable poses like authority, chain of command, or fear of insubordination. As adults, whole populations of people are held captive to ideas and ideals by the social standards far more than threats of physical coercion. The purpose of *observing the child* is to uncover the frightened, often angry child within all we meet, so we can meet them on equal terms.

The masks are no more than poses taken to protect the child inside. By looking beyond the masks, the superficial, the skin of protection, one can observe the *man behind the curtain*, or more appropriately here, *the child behind the curtain*. By seeing your spouse or your boss as the child that lives inside of them, you can see what desire or fear they operate from. By observing the child, you uncover the heart of what makes some people so fearful and angry. Anger is almost always a reaction to fear. By looking at your boss or spouse as the little child within, you are looking at the center of their being, the place where love dwells. The child believes it has learned how to protect itself against feeling pain, but what it has learned is how to hide from love.

Due to the primal experience of birth and the idea of separateness that stems eventually from it, we are always seeking love or trying to get along without it. Many feel that love is elusive and not reliable. They will point to war, or murder, or child abuse. They will say that these things prove that the world is crazy, follows no rules, and that love is just another thing that happens. But anger, murder, even war are distortions of love. If the child reaches out in love and learns that parents are cruel, he will learn self-protection very quickly. If the child is given *things* instead of love, he will grow to value things and see love as a pipe dream, always out of reach. Every selfish, self-protective act is a distortion of love. It has to be, as all there is, is love. The child inside will always act in the interest of love, either in reality or in a distortion thereof. By observing yourself and others as children, you are getting beyond the masks, even beyond the *dream children* themselves, back to your original face.

The next time the boss starts being rude or aggressive, look at him or her and return them to the period in their life when this behavior might have seemed more appropriate. Think of them as the frightened child this behavior rightly belongs to. You can only do this when you are ready to do the same to your own behavior. When you feel angry over events over which you have no control (which is really all the time!) or when you feel jealous or slighted, look at your own dream child. Only when you can remove that last mask, the *I Am mask*, are you free from this dream child mask. When *all* masks are gone, even the belief in the innocence you once were, then the other dream children will reveal themselves in their vulnerability and no longer be a threat or a bother but simply frightened children struggling to get protection from a lack of love while swimming in a sea of it.

We are all children playing at life. Only when we can see each other as such and understand that we are all subject at times to the dream child, that longing for love, together with the feeling that it is always out of reach, we can see our predicament is the same. Only when we can stop seeking love, go beyond the I Am of the dream child, and realize ourselves *as* love can we see others as love as well.

The Absolute: Life as It Is, Even the Sad Bits!

I was recently in a comment thread on Facebook. My comment did not have to do with the subject of the thread itself, but in response to a comment made by the author of the thread, which was only egos are sad.

I took exception to this and responded with the shortest verse in the Bible: *"Jesus wept."* Jesus, of course, in this context, was responding to the news that his dear friend Lazarus was dead. Now, Jesus knew that in a short time, he would raise his friend, so his sadness was out of compassion for Lazarus' sisters, Mary and Martha, and for the mourners gathered there. This is compassion *in action. There is sadness*. There need be no Mary, Martha, or even Jesus to be sad and weep, for there *is* sadness.

There is *only love*. Sadness lives and arises within love. Here, I am not talking about a love that is the opposite of hate or fear. That is the emotion of love, and a mere shadow of the Absolute, which is love itself. The Absolute is what you are. The Absolute contains all potential, is all potential. It is not a thing, but an unfolding.

In the comments in this Facebook thread, it was said that:

"The natural state of the reality of you as God created you is pure joy – ever-increasing joy without limit."

"Love and joy are the same thing."

"If you are love/joy then you cannot be sad."

If we accept that love and the Absolute are the same and that this is the only reality, then saying that joy is the only natural state of reality is limiting the Absolute to what the mind conceives of as joy. The bliss of the Absolute is only experienced by being it. Nisargadatta Maharaj expressed it this way:

"There is in you the core of being which is beyond analysis, beyond the mind. You can know it in action only. Express it in daily life and its light will grow ever brighter."

Living the life you have, this *expression* you see all around you is the only way to *be* the Absolute. Just as the Christ recognized his divinity, he also recognized his humanness. This is not duality, but a merging that has already taken place. To say that humanness or sadness are not part of the functioning of the Absolute is to say there is something apart from the Absolute or separate from it.

Another comment in the Facebook thread stated:

"The Absolute doesn't contain opposites."

The Absolute contains everything, including opposites. Where else would they arise from? You might answer that they arise from the mind, but is not the mind functioning within the Absolute? The same commenter went on to say:

"When you are loving, are you not joyful? When you are joyful, are you not loving? The same is not true of despair and joy. You are not joyful in despair."

Love indeed brings joy. Joyfulness, however, does not necessarily mean *universal love*. It could even mean *selfish desire*. In despair, there is no love seen, but love is what sustains during sadness, which may arise, even in universal love. Sadness and human behavior were experienced by the Christ. He lived his humanity to the cross. He never ran from it but accepted it. His life was not always joyful, but always in touch with love. The parent who loses sleep over a sick child, or the elderly couple watching one another slowly fade in abilities and vitality, experience love as the reality they are in. Sadness and death are inevitable, but they arise and live within love, the Absolute.

Life is as it is. Accepting all that arises, letting the illusory go its way, not by chasing it off or denying the pain, but by open acceptance, is living a life of love. If we wait for perfection, or an end to sadness, ideas that live only in the mind, then we are waiting on a non-existent future for something that is unfolding *right now!*

Life is already perfect. The pain is often the love beckoning. To tell people, especially seekers, that there is a reward of perfection and perfect bliss when life is already perfect is to send them to look for a dream, not to awaken them out of one. Life with all of its painful illusions is a perfect seamless thread. All one needs do is see through the illusions, stop seeking perfection, and *realize* its presence, even in apparent sadness and death. Stop dividing the *real* from the *illusion*, and accept all as life.

Life as it is. Isn't it wonderful!

The Finger Pointing at the Moon: Could It Be Me?

The image of the *finger pointing at the moon* is such a well-known Zen image as to be almost cliché. The image is often used to differentiate the teacher from the teaching, or the image from the substance.

The *person* we imagine ourselves to be is the *true finger* on which we fixate. This person seems to point to potential, rather than realizing itself as an expression of that potential. All persons arise from that potential and are expressions of it.

While we must not mistake the finger for the moon, we must not discount the finger altogether. The finger is an expression of potential and contained *within it*. The person, the life, the illusion or maya all function within love: the creative potential. Life, with all its joys *and* sadness, is an *expression* of the ever-unfolding potential that is love.

Just as we come to be aware that the finger is an expression of the moon, we come to realize that we, and that other finger (God) are expressions of love, and find oneness lost in it.

Love without an Object:
Non-Duality in Action

While we cannot *know* another's enlightenment or their pain, with unconditional love, we can be one with it.

Love is open and responds before the need even arises. When my partner and I were in the religious community, we were asked by the Lincolnshire Probation Department to take in probationers that had been deemed hopeless. The Probation Department had given up on a number of offenders who did not seem to respond to anything.

My partner and I, as I have said before, do not have one High School diploma between the two of us. While we both have gone through some counseling and a lot of real-life situations ourselves, we were not trained in psychology apart from a few college courses of mine. Now we found ourselves living with, and counseling a thief, an arsonist, two child molesters, and a rapist, among others.

Now remember, we were two gay men, allowed to take vows and form a religious community in the Anglican Church at a time when the Anglican Church was even more anti-gay than it is today. This was grace, nothing less, and we knew that gratitude demanded unconditional sacrifice. Our community was all about unconditional love. We had based our community in part on the writings of Jean Vanier, the founder of L'Arche Communities, communities set up for the committed faithful to live with the developmentally disabled. We opened our doors to anyone and everyone. We provided a home, cooked meals, and saw to the physical and spiritual needs of all the members of the community. No matter what a person's past had been, no matter what they had done, they were treated with love and respect.

Our community followed a daily course of contemplative prayer and the Eucharist. These gave us the grace to know what to say and do. Not by following doctrine or some practice, but like the oneness of Advaita, by removing the *me* from the equation. If you remove the *me*, and see the *other* as simply an *expression* of love in movement, then only love is left to be experienced.

We cannot know another's suffering and pain, just as we cannot judge another's spirituality or enlightenment. But we know of pain and suffering, just as we know of spirit and enlightenment. When a person reaches out a hand for help, we do not know what they suffer, only that they suffer, and that alone calls us to action. If we are tuned in to love, unconditional love, the love will meet itself and the flow of love will bring awareness that resolution is taking place.

When you realize you are love, nothing else, and nothing less, you realize the magnitude of that responsibility. That realization also removes any doubt that you can realize that responsibility. You just act, not a personal action, but a movement in the flow of love. For the realization of love to happen, there must be an absent *me* and the awareness that the *other* is not separate, but a manifestation of love itself.

We can talk about non-duality or Advaita at Satsangs and meetings. We can learn the words and even have some spiritual experiences, but until we give ourselves away in service to love itself, we are playing intellectual games and supporting a *me* seeking enlightenment. If you find a teacher who does not give his or her teachings away for free, out of love, or offer some service beyond their teaching for pay, you would be better off going to a homeless shelter or a battered woman's shelter to offer your service. For love *asks for nothing but demands much*. We learn more from service and open love than we can from any teacher. Advaita, non-duality, require love in action.

"I am telling you again: You are the all-pervading, all-transcending reality. Behave accordingly: think, feel, and act in harmony with the whole, and the actual experience of what I say will dawn upon you in no time. No effort is needed. Have faith and act on it."
Nisargadatta Maharaj

Realization, Awareness and Enlightenment

These three terms for an awakening: awareness, enlightenment, and realization are all used to describe the indescribable *state* of *uncovery* we often describe ourselves as seeking. Of these, I have come to accept realization as the most apt.

Awareness and enlightenment both seem to involve a future happening: "I am not aware now, but seek awareness", or "I am un-enlightened, but will become enlightened." While realization simply means that I observe *the unreal as real and the real as unreal*. A simple slip of the mind!

What is the meaning of realization anyway? It is to arrive at the understanding that there is substance, meaning, particularly without mental understanding. We are talking of an *acceptance of living for the unseen*, inexpressible, but clearly understood. It is impossible to explain to both others and yourself, but clearly written in the heart with a conviction that is both peaceful and absolute.

To realize yourself as love, not an intellectual understanding, but to make it real, is that which you seek. It is not a future event. *It is now.* All you need is absolute conviction. You are not moving mountains here, just *turning your view*. See yourself, not as the seen: body/mind, story, past, future, but as the unseen: loving, experiencing, living for the real. Absolute conviction is the secret ingredient. Absolute conviction makes the real that already is, real as experience and in experience. Live the love and it is true. Extend your hand in trust, and your actions become *real* actions. Don't dismiss the seen, as it is a reflection of the unseen. Don't fall into the trap of separation of the seen from the unseen. Just observe them as they are. They are all part of the functioning of the whole.

If you want realization, reach out with absolute conviction and absolute courage. It is *with* you always. Embrace it.

You are love, make it real!

Service: Completing the Circle of Love

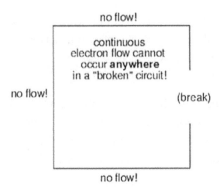

So much is written in non-duality regarding practice or method, and about how there is no practice or method possible as there is *no one* to practice or follow a method. This, while true in the Absolute, is of little to no help to a seeker (...and yes, I understand, there is *no seeker* either!).

I once wrote that while I realize that we are only players in a play, I do not see a script of destiny, but unlimited potential being lived out in the instant. Predestination, this idea that *everything is ok*, or *"It's all working out according to God's plan"* is all mind-stuff. Predestination occurs only in time, one of the mind's favorite organizers. Unlimited, unformed potential unfolds not in time, but all at once. Past, present, and future occur instantly and simultaneously. It is only when the mind organizes them that they separated, leaving the present *now* with no more reality than the others, once it is *named*.

So, we understand that *we* are a *verb,* the flow itself, not subjects or objects but the unfolding. While we cannot affect the play, we find ourselves flowing in by practice or any known method, we can do our best not to impede the flow.

So how do we do that? By showing no resistance.

My Father was an electrician all his working life. When I was a small boy, he described to me his understanding of electricity. He had a great and mystical understanding of electricity that I carry with me to this day. He described electricity as potential energy, existent all around us as potential, but only realized when the circuit is complete with all the necessary elements. The really intriguing thing to me was the idea that there is no flow when the circuit is incomplete. But more than that, without a complete circuit, there is no electricity! The flow of the unfolding of the universe is no different.

When I wrote the rule for the Community of the Living Sacrifice, I used the example of the electrical circuit as an example of how the love flows from the Eucharist through the participant and into the world. I referred to this as *the Eucharistic circle of love*. This, however, can be applied to any spiritual practice, and can also be applied to *involved conscious living*. By this, I mean any way you have of *grounding yourself to the truth*. Any way you have of staying in the *flow*.

The power in our circuit comes from our source and our connection to it. This is contemplation, or self-inquiry, or whatever method opens you up and reduces your resistance.

Now comes the important part: *service*. Once we are *flowing* with the *source power*, that is, *being the source power*, we must complete the circuit by sharing the source power with others and the world. If we don't complete the circuit, there is only love *in potential*, not the flow of love in action.

Are *we* important to this process? We have been taught by many non-dualists that we are unimportant, have no need for action or practice, and are illusions separate from reality, whatever that means in a non-dual sense! But our importance to the complete circuit is essential.

When we understand that we are the free-flowing potential of life, not the wires of the circuit or the various devices along the way, but the movement of the power itself, we can open up and stop all resistance. This requires no practice but a simple surrender. A surrender so complete that you become as a pure platinum connector and the flow is so unimpeded that love has no different face than yours.

The Possibility of Possibility:
The Unlimited Potential that You Are

I remember a sermon heard long ago on Good Friday in Lincoln Cathedral. The priest spoke of a small church in the English East Midlands that possessed a stone altar so ancient that a female tourist commented that the dark and somber chamber, especially the altar, made it look like a place of human sacrifice. The priest went on to point out the faith that the Church indeed sees this altar, this place of worship as a place of sacrifice. It was this sermon that inspired the future name of the religious community my partner and I founded: The Community of the Living Sacrifice.

The Eucharist, the Holy Mass, is the great sacrifice of the Church. Many in the Church have a difficult time seeing this rite of the Church as a *real* sacrifice. So it is not surprising that those in the non-dual community, who often believe that no practice is the best practice, would look askance at the usefulness of the Eucharist. But the Eucharist can be one of the great openings to the understanding without words.

Those who attend churches that see the Eucharist or Mass as a symbol or a remembrance get very little out of the rite, apart from the small "c" communion of recollection with their fellow worshipers. When I was a boy, I was a Presbyterian. Our church had communion once or twice a year and used Welch's grape juice and Wonder bread. This considerably reduced the mystery this held for me. The only mystery left was the fact that I was too young to participate, and by this time I was old enough, I was lost in agnosticism. But, however, you look at the Eucharist, there is little sacrifice in passive participation in a Church ritual. So what *truth* can be found in the Eucharist?

If we see Christ as *Christ Consciousness*, we can understand that the spirit that moves us and *is* us is the same spirit that moves the Christ. That power of incarnation incarnates *us*, as well as the Christ and all of the manifestations. The Eucharist is no less than the full participation in that Christ Consciousness, as well as a celebration of

92

unified oneness. This participation requires sacrifice and *all we are*, if the sacrifice is to be complete.

The belief in transubstantiation is an accepted idea in the Roman Catholic Church. Not being a Roman Catholic, I have no real understanding of their interpretation of this mystery. I do hold however, that bread and wine do substantially change into the body and blood of Christ. I believe this is essential for the participant in the Eucharist to get the full benefit.

We all understand that bread, wine, body, and blood are all mind-stuff: simply images on a screen of the mind. The *substance* of them all is the same: the Absolute. There is no need to transubstantiate the objects as they start, are, and finish as the same substance. The sacrifice we encounter here is the sacrifice of the mind. Reason, the traitor to the truth, must not just be suspended, but killed. We tell ourselves that the bread and wine *are* the body and blood of Christ because we want to be swallowed up in this mystery. Christ and us; dying on the cross, outside of time, dying to the mind, lost in the reality of the *one substance*.

This is a sacrifice only to the extent that the participant makes real, i.e., *realizes* themselves in the mystery. This is where *earnestness*, one of Nisargadatta's most often-used words, comes in. The earnestness makes the bread and wine, and the body and blood of one substance. The earnestness makes the unseen real, and the seen becomes one substance in light of the unseen. Earnestness *is* sacrifice. The willing sacrifice of the known for the unknown, the seen for the unseen, is the sacrifice required by earnestness. Courage is required for earnestness, because it requires *action first, assurance after*. The assurance is in the action, not separate from it. This brings us to the circle of love.

As we have said elsewhere, love exists all around and through us, as a state of potential. Like electricity, love requires a complete circuit. We get our *power* from our communion with the Christ Consciousness, or the Absolute. We do this by attending the Eucharist, mediation, self-inquiry, or Satsangs with souls who inspire us *out of ourselves*. We then become instruments in the circle of love.

But for the love in potential to become realized, we must share it through service. This is all one act, one movement. Absorption in the real, becoming one with, and *in* love, and sharing the love by *being* it. This act of trust, sacrifice, if you will, requires the trust to live as *if* you understand. *As if you are realized.*

So much in non-duality is written by advanced teachers for advanced seekers and is therefore written in the most absolute way. This is how we get the no seeker, no person, nothing to do points of view. And of course, we will once again say, yes, in the Absolute, these statements are true. But what must we cover with the beginning seeker? Telling him or her that they don't exist, and should stop seeking, might just be met with some resistance!

It is sufficient to suggest that the seeker looks to see what can be found of substance in the ideas one has about oneself. Upon meditating on these questions, the uncovery of the lack of substance beyond the ideas themselves opens the possibility of possibility: that which is unlimited potential. That unlimited potential is what I refer to as love.

That is the first thing to teach: love is the unlimited potential that you are! You are not a person, you are not the other. You are not even God. You are the pure spirit of God, with no God being necessary, the idea of God coming only as an afterthought in time. And here is the second point to teach: time is simply a way the mind uses to organize ideas into a sequence.

So much emphasis is placed in New Age thought on the *now*. But the *now* most think of, is a *middle* place in time, falling in between past and future. I just like to say *everything happens at once*. For if you consider it, past and future are all in the mind, and thoughts occur in the *now*, even thoughts of past and future. In fact, thoughts of the present, the now, are also thoughts, once they have happened and been considered. Only unconscious awareness *happening* is love: unlimited potential. Earnestness in understanding, without knowledge, that you *are the movement of love itself* and the constant removal of time as an ultimate reality, are the places to start.

This *earnestness,* a word often used by Nisargadatta Maharaj, is really the key to the door of awareness. Seek and ye shall find. So much emphasis is placed on humor in the West, that any guru who wants a good following, feels it necessary to be a bit of a comedian. While humor has a place in spirituality, humor often becomes more important to the followers of a feel-good guru than his earnestness. Earnestness is defined in the dictionary as *seriousness.* It does not mean for this to be in contrast to humor, simply that earnestness is not unlike devotion, even worship. This is why an attitude toward bhakti is necessary for a beginning seeker. For only with a single-minded, single-hearted concentration, can one become love and live outside of time.

Eucharist: Non-Duality and the Circle of Love

You understand intellectually, that you are one substance with all there is, *that you are the movement of love itself*. But the mind cannot comprehend what that means or what that is. The mere attempt at explanation only starts to lead away from reality. This is why we must first act *as if* we really *believed*, because in that *act of trust* in the real, *the unseen,* we step off the cliff, through the looking glass, into the real, *as the real is the act itself.*

The real does not live in the thinking about the act, before or after, but only in the act itself. Just as in our acceptance of the reality of the substance of bread and wine and its ability to *share* our sacrifices with those of the Christ, as one substance, we come to understand the courage needed for true *earnestness*. Earnestness is the need to let go of all beliefs, seen and unseen, and trust in *substance* itself, *even before the substance is realized.* For in that trust, that intuitive understanding of the unseen, when *acted upon*, is *realization in action.*

Negative Space as the Lighted Screen

In art, the concept of negative space is used to cause an object, a shape, to stand out against the background. This often results in the negative space becoming the subject of the art, rather than the recognizable shape, be it familiar or abstract.

In spirituality, this concept is sometimes used to present the objects of manifestation as they appear against a backdrop of *nothingness*. This has been described by some sages as being like a motion picture screen upon which pure light is projected. The mind, as represented by the film casts images, shadows if you will, on the screen. The screen remains unaffected, always bathed in pure light, no matter how distorted it appears to the mind, which clings to certain *shadows* and judges them as acceptable or unacceptable. This analogy has a number of failings, even though it does accurately mention the interference of the mind.

The main problem with the screen, film, light analogy is the fact that in reality the screen and light are one and the same, and are not passive at all, but alive with projection and reflection. The film, this bag of thoughts we take for the mind, is what distorts the flow into objects. The lighted screen, the Absolute, is always there as negative space, but neither passive nor negative, but alive with simultaneous *projection* and *reflection*: unlimited potential.

Within this unlimited potential, which is love, is caring, compassion, acting, and all of the verbs we experience. It is the mind that creates out of memory, *nouns*: us and those cared for, us and those toward whom we have compassion. The mind also attributes all *action* to us, or to be about us. The mind takes all of the flow of the lighted screen, all the movement of projection and reflection, and personalizes it to the "me", the I Am.

It is the dynamic of the screen that is alive: the projection and reflection. We must see beyond the mind, which can only *interpret* this *still movement*, this *unfolding* as objects in motion. This is why we call it *negative* space as it is not available to the mind even though it is neither negative nor passive, but movement: unlimited potential itself.

To return to art, students are often taught to recognize negative space in a drawing by copying a drawing upside-down. This allows them to see just the shapes, without the mind turning them into recognizable objects. This is what we must do in our hearts and minds when it comes to the spiritual. If we concentrate on the moments between thoughts, rather than the thoughts themselves, we are looking at the negative space, the *still movement* that flows as unlimited potential. This unlimited potential is love itself, the space we all occupy.

When we live with the conviction that the lighted screen is self-functioning and needs no "me" or "God", or any other shadows, we can rest and let it be as it is: love without lovers, life without end. Seeing this negative space as the *subject* of the art, and all the *objects* as only existing to draw attention to that fact opens us to true seeing and pure action.

Sweet Biscuits and Unconditional Love

Back in the days when I was in the religious community, we ran a home for those who had no other home or needed a place to feel safe. We made a home for former psychiatric patients, ex-prisoners, and people on probation, as well as those who were simply lost and seeking something. One of the things we considered essential, however simple, was the *never-empty biscuit tin*.

For those who are Americans and some others, the term biscuit refers to what you commonly think of as cookies, not the hot bread-like item one spreads with butter and jam. You might ask yourself, "How can *cookies* be a part of any religious community's *essential* activities?"

When an individual or a group of individuals get together with the idea of helping, they need to constantly keep in mind what helping means in any given situation. We know what *we* want. We know what *we think* others need, no matter how wrong our ideas may be. We cannot know completely what another person needs, only that they need. We struggle every day, just to understand what we think we need. Offering help to another requires stepping far enough from ourselves to see what is needed. This requires absolute commitment. Not commitment to help, but simply *absolute commitment*. The only thing you can offer openly and honestly is love itself.

Our community offered a prepared breakfast, supplies for a self-prepared lunch, and a full supper. This is what you would offer anyone you were looking after. But this is an obligation.

Sure, meals convey love very well. They nurture and satisfy up to a point, but they are necessary survival. Providing meals may be interpreted as simply seeing to it that no one gets sick, and does not become a burden or problem. Conveying love requires more.

When I was a boy, and would do something that got me sent to bed without dessert, or if I was angry and locked myself in my room all day, the great release came when my mother or father would come and bring me a bit of something, a cookie, or a piece of cake. I remember many times breaking down and eating the sweet treat through bitter tears of sorrow and remorse, making the treat seem like the physical embodiment of love and forgiveness. Something extra, something that is *not required* conveys the idea that "I care" or "we care". This is so important to the poor, whether poor in finances or spirit.

The placing of a biscuit tin that was never allowed to go empty and was always available to everyone, while seemingly un-necessary, was a boost to the spirit. It was a way to say "you're important", not just as a human being, but as a *loveable* human being. The poor, no matter what makes them poor, struggle to get even the simplest needs met and are mostly very grateful for whatever they receive. But to go beyond that, to make available an *extra*, even something as simple as a cookie, says. "Yes, I love you. I want you to have not only what you need, but something lovely, something fun."

We grow up in a society that complains about entitlements and taxes. We will begrudgingly allow that we, as a society, need to provide for the public welfare. But we also want to guard against *abuse* by the poor. We believe in tough love, a term invented to label abuse of power, revenge, and brain washing as some kind of helpful procedure. You add *tough* to love, and the love vanishes. So many in our society have grown up with no love. Tough love has been applied to every situation. Beatings, deprivation, the idea of *the giving and withdrawing of love*, are what produce school bullies, and later, corporate thieves without any moral or societal conscience.

We cannot help the poor while making them feel we are only doing it grudgingly or out of obligation. This is counterproductive. We are so afraid of being taken advantage of that we give our love only cautiously, which is not love at all. Love is only love when it is given freely, without caution, without fear of our being taken advantage of. Tough love is conditional love. Love with fear or concern is conditional. Unconditional love requires giving without concern for results.

Unconditional love requires simply being. And in that being, the realization that the *other* is also *being*, not separate, but the same universal being. All we can know is that they need love. We cannot know what they, as individuals need specifically, but we know they need love. We must give them what they need. After we have given all we can and the needs are met, go one step further. Offer them a cookie.

Ash Wednesday: A Non-Dual Perspective

Ash Wednesday may seem a strange day to those in non-dual circles, as the church concentrates so much on sin. Sin seems a strange idea in a world where *everything is perfect*, but the organized church sees sin as the reason or need for religion. In organized religion, the spiritual side of the faith is often made subservient to the moral side of the faith. The church in the Lenten season becomes all about repentance and sacrifice, with the idea that *Christ died for our sins*, and his death and resurrection is responsible for our redemption.

Sacrifice is indeed an important part of understanding our place in all of this, but repentance has to come from a real place of understanding, not simply an idea of our sin. Sin is simply ignorance, not some laundry list of morality that varies from culture to culture, or person to person. We need to remember that the Christ, while on the cross, said: *"Father forgive them, for they know not what they do."* Forgive them their lack of understanding, their ignorance.

As I have often said of Nisargadatta Maharaj, *how* he lived his life is as much, or more of the teaching than his words which were, after all, just words. This is also true of The Christ. His message, interpreted over centuries in words of different languages, becomes distorted. Rather than the message of removing ignorance and pointing to the always present moment of God's love in action that the Christ, and all of us, are *incarnated* as, the message has become one of fallen nature and a need for a redeemer.

The Christ referred to God as *"our Father"*, not simply his alone. We are all sons of God, born for holiness. The Christ's death on the cross is a demonstration of the kind of sacrifice necessary to claim victory over ignorance. Our life, as spirit (being) lives on, with or without the body. The sacrifice of the Christ tells us that we must be willing to let go of the body/mind and all its attachments. We must sacrifice all we imagine ourselves to be, for all we are. But this is not done as an act of will. As stated above, this must come from a place of real understanding, *realization* if you will.

This brings us back to Ash Wednesday. On Ash Wednesday, the celebrant at the Mass places the ashes, often made from the burned palm crosses of last Palm Sunday, in the sign of the cross, on the foreheads of the communicants. This is done with the words: "...*for dust thou art, and unto dust thou shalt return.*" This is really the key to Ash Wednesday. This statement, that we are but dust and destined to return to dust is very humbling if we see the truth in it. We are not sinners in some moral sense. We are in ignorance of our true nature. Our true nature, *as individuals*, is *dust*. We may intellectually understand that our true nature is the flow of love appearing as *this*, but until this is realized (made a wordless conviction), we must see the dust.

Ramana Maharshi's awakening came after a vision of his own death with the conviction that he was not the body and would not die with it. This is the message of Ash Wednesday.

"...*for dust thou art, and unto dust thou shalt return.*" This rite reminds us that our human nature, our individuality, is nothing more permanent than dust. We meditate on this throughout the Lenten season. This is the preparation we make for Easter, this realization of our nature as mortal while living in a swirl of immortality. We prepare and meditate on the sacrifice of The Christ, the cross, and the resurrection. We see the Christ Consciousness rise above the death of Jesus the man, to remain the ever-present Absolute. It is by seeing ourselves as dying on the cross with Jesus, that allows us to understand that life does not die, only dust gets blown by the wind. It is our *minds* that must die. Bede Griffiths, a Benedictine monk who lived in India, experienced a stroke, which he described as "*a death of the mind.*" This opened a deepening sense of overwhelming love that never left him.

Above I stated that repentance has to come from a real place of understanding, not simply some sense of sin and guilt. This understanding comes from an awareness of our personal nature, our *self*, as impermanent. We are ashes. We are dust. We are mortal. Once we realize we are impermanent, the importance we hold ourselves in vanishes. In its place is the conviction that, while we as the small "s" self are impermanent, what remains is the capital "S"

Self, which is permanency itself. The imposition of the ashes and the subsequent meditation on its significance reveals that we, impermanent phantoms, are a reflection, an appearance of the permanent, the universal. Sacrifice pride and become ashes, dust. Prepare to crucify the mind, so to be resurrected in the heart.

My Life in the Clouds:
An Awakening to Love

Realizing that one is told these days not to talk of spiritual experiences and also realizing that I have seldom paid much attention to what one is told not to do, I am going to talk about a couple of my experiences.

I have been going to write this for a while but have hesitated, not just for the above reason, but because I have thought that my experience might be seen as silly by many who look for big, earth-shaking experiences. I grew up with a great sense of understanding that something was *going on* that most did not understand, but recognized in the back of their souls. I was told about God but had a sense that nobody really knew about him. I always felt that if God was all they said he was, we should hold him in our minds first of all things. It was clear as a child that this was not the case with most people, even those who talked about him a good deal.

I found a friend in God and carried him around with me. I had no doubt that the kingdom of heaven was, as Jesus said, within me. I learned a game on my own in which I could ask a question, and then open a random page in the Bible, and find an answer. No one but me was aware of this. I am a very shy person and was an even shyer child. My life was a very secret one. Even my parents knew little of my personal, secret life. When I reached my teens, I became more and more agnostic. This happened because I began to question everything. This happened because one day my high school American History teacher was out sick, and the teacher who taught Philosophy took the class for one day. He talked of Descartes, and at once a whole new world opened up for me. People actually *thought*! They actually *thought about thinking*! How wonderful that was. And although I still felt that there was something beyond myself, within myself, God became a casualty of reason.

I lived as an agnostic from my middle teens until my early thirties when a transformation of sorts took place. I had read and studied philosophy, the occult, and some Eastern philosophy during that period, but nothing affected me in my soul until I picked up a copy of *The Cloud of Unknowing*. That little book on Christian mysticism changed my life. This happened to be my thirty-third year, and I realized that this was the same year of life that the Christ was crucified.

During this time, I had my first significant spiritual experience. While sitting in a darkened room in deep contemplation, I was given a vision of the crucified Christ. This was not some wonderful crucifix or glorious vision but the presentation of a dirty, bleeding, dying man. All the pain was revealed, all the suffering was felt first-hand as I stood before the cross. This was the answer, this sacrifice. This was what I was called to do, and it was frightening. I was prepared to give my life also, but I had been with my partner for twelve years by that time and did not want to separate from him.

So I sought spiritual counseling from an Episcopal priest. This led to reading much Thomas Merton and to make a long story short, led eventually to the formation of the religious community my partner and I began in Lincoln, England. As I have said elsewhere, the Church of England was not prepared for two gay men to begin a religious community at that time. Even though we had the support of the Dean and Chapter of Lincoln Cathedral and the Bishop of Lincoln, the community was forced to close and our home for lost people was closed.

This tragedy was devastating and pushed me away from the established church. Even before the community was destroyed, I had begun to read about Ramakrishna, and later Ramana Maharshi. I loved the eccentricities of Ramakrishna, but Ramana captivated me, and gave me answers not found since reading *The Cloud of Unknowing*.

When we returned to the United States, I found Nisargadatta Maharaj's *I Am That* in the library while looking for books on Ramana, and I fell in love. After reading all I could find on Nisargadatta, and much of Ramesh Balsekar's writing, I felt that the intellectual understanding was there, but I missed the love that I had found in my return to Christianity.

All my life I have experienced waves of love and gratitude that would come over me and bring me to tears. This would be caused by almost anything: a baby's laugh, a beautiful sunset, anything. Now, with the idea of *oneness* firmly in my mind, I began to wonder, how can I feel love when there is only one. God, at this time, had become a reference only. Nisargadatta referred to God occasionally, but I had no sense that he believed in God, but just used the term for convenience. Still, the feeling was there in me. How can I love God when no such being exists outside of my mind?

This troubled me. One day, while working as an apartment manager, I was sitting in my truck waiting for my partner who was shopping. There had just been a rain storm and the clouds were breaking up and it was wonderfully beautiful. My eyes filled with tears as a wave of love flowed through me. But this time, instead of the troubling doubt or questions that God and I are separate, the conviction that I was the love overwhelmed me and has never left me since. I realized that there was no God, no me, just this *connection*. The space between thoughts of God and I was love in all its flow, all its creative movement, and I am that.

From *The Cloud of Unknowing* to the cloud of understanding, I had come full circle. Ten years after this experience, I wrote this all down in a book in which I re-wrote *the Rule for the Community of the Living Sacrifice* in view of this new understanding. Now ten years after that, I have crawled onto Facebook, and have started to share.

Living "As If"

Questioner: "What made you so dispassionate?"

Nisargadatta Maharaj: "Nothing in particular. It so happened that I trusted my Guru. He told me I am nothing but myself and I believed him. Trusting him, I behaved accordingly and ceased caring for what was not me, nor mine." I Am That

The above quotation from *I Am That*, expresses one of the most important points in Nisargadatta Maharaj's teaching. Nisargadatta's teacher, Siddharameshwar Maharaj, told him to abide in the I Am and behave accordingly. Nisargadatta trusted the words of his teacher. In Nisargadatta's teaching, he passes on the words of his teacher and tells us that *if we believe him, and behave accordingly*, we will realize the Self as well. He goes on to say that if we don't believe him, we should abide in the I Am until we see what we are not.

It is clear that Nisargadatta did not get instant awareness, but lived out the teaching of his teacher on trust alone until the final understanding. Nisargadatta lived and behaved *as if* he already had the understanding. This is a very important point that is often missed. Nisargadatta *trusted* (believed) first, and lived as if he were already awakened.

Intellectual understanding comes to many of us quickly. We can see the truth in the I Am, and we can understand the concepts in the mind concerning non-dual awareness, but we have not *realized* it. To *realize* something is to make it *real*. This means to make it a part of us, to *be it*. Nisargadatta had spent many years in spiritual search before meeting his final teacher. Much of this involved bhakti, devotion. This mindset, soul-set, if you will, allowed Nisargadatta to trust his teacher. He recognized Siddharameshwar Maharaj as one *entering his dream: a true guru*. This allowed Nisargadatta to trust his teacher absolutely. This trust, faith, if I can use that term, allowed him to live out the teaching in his daily life.

This living out of the teaching is no different in any spiritual system. If one has faith in Christ, one can walk the path to the cross, with the confidence that the Christ has overcome death. Just as Nisargadatta could see that Siddharameshwar Maharaj lived a life of oneness, we can see that Nisargadatta, Jesus, Ramana Maharshi all lived out their teachings. This indeed, is the true test of a teacher: do they walk the walk? I have often pointed out that Nisargadatta's life was as important, if not much more important a part of his teaching than his words. All true teachers are their teaching personified. But which came first, the understanding or the life?

We can see in the case of Nisargadatta, trust came first, followed by understanding. Ramana trusted sufficiently to engage thoughts of death, the courage to delve deeply into the I Am, without knowing the result. Even Christ, in the Garden of Gethsemane, expressed doubts but went to the cross on faith. All of these actions took courage. They took living *as if* the understanding were already there. Behaving accordingly comes first because it is almost always required as a first step. I say *almost always*, as it may be possible to become aware spontaneously, but I have not witnessed it.

When I say to *live as if*, I do not mean to pretend. Far too much pretending takes place in spirituality. I mean to accept the intellectual understanding and live *as if it were realized*. This takes trust, faith. It takes trust in the teacher, and trust in yourself. This *living accordingly* is so important. Trust, faith opens up the heart. To live in the heart, as well as in the mind, is the basis of understanding. One of Nisargadatta's most famous sayings was *"When I see that I am nothing, that is wisdom, when I see that I am everything, that is love, between the two my life continually flows."* This melding of heart and mind is at the center of any spiritual teaching. Trust requires one other factor: courage.

When we talk of courage in a spiritual context, we come to sacrifice. Sacrifice requires giving something up. In Christ's case, giving up required the whole nine yards: the sacrifice of his life. In the case of Nisargadatta the sacrifice was one of will. Nisargadatta took his guru at his word. He subjugated his will to that of his trusted teacher. The close observation of ourselves that is required in self-inquiry involves sacrifice if it is done honestly. The willingness to let go of the *story of me* is, in its way, a sacrifice of our lives. And this sacrifice must come first. Once we realize that we are love itself and that nothing can harm or diminish that which we truly are, the sacrifice has already been made. The small self is dead, and we live as the Self. No more fear or harm can come to us. It is the *before,* the living out of the teaching that requires courage and trust.

So we *are* required to *do* something. Teachers that say that *there is nothing to do* or there is *no one* to do anything, misread the texts and the teachings. We are required to live out the teaching, the understanding. We are required to *live accordingly as if* the understanding is present. When teachers fall from grace, ego, sexual dalliances, hypocrisy or whatever failings are seen. It has been said they fall under the influence of *the shadow* or some hidden trait that they transfer onto others. This is simply fancy talk for failing to live accordingly. We are required to sacrifice our desires for acceptance. Love is already perfect. It is our distortions and perversions of love that appear as imperfections. Our acceptance of others must be absolute. If we put our story of them before the truth, we only see our story, not who they really are: love in action. In living *as if* (living accordingly), we step off the cliff into the unknown. We do this every day.

We do not just talk about non-duality. We live its reality every day. If I believe that you and I are *not two* then that is how I will treat you. When asked what were the greatest commandments, the Christ said *"to love the lord, thy God, with all thy heart, all thy mind and all the soul, and the second is like unto it; to love thy neighbor as thy self."* Love God completely, with all at your disposal, and love your neighbor as your *"self"*. This is living accordingly: Loving God, yourself and like unto that, your neighbor, as one. When this is seen with absolute clarity, the understanding is alive, real and realized. Until that realization, live *as if* that were your reality.

Work Out Your Enlightenment with Fear and Trembling

In response to a recent post about living out non-duality, I received a few messages regarding peoples' attempts at understanding, but expressing that they felt that they fell short or that they did not have perfect understanding. I think this may be one of the most common misconceptions of awareness or enlightenment.

The concept of perfection is simply another concept that must be gone beyond. This concept, however, may be one of the hardest to kill, as many of the non-dual teachers believe it as well.

While no teacher, guru, or spiritual master has been perfect, many seekers as well as teachers try to convince others, and worse themselves, that they are.

Nisargadatta Maharaj, who I look to as one of my most important teachers, is well known to have had a very fiery temper. Although, a man of infinite compassion, he would regularly throw out persons who he saw as insincere. This was especially true of the followers of Osho, who would arrive at his little mezzanine room in their saffron robes. Nisargadatta's tolerance for this sort of thing was very low. Many see temper and anger as imperfection, which in the ultimate understanding no doubt is, but Nisargadatta was human as well as enlightened. This humanness is often overlooked by teachers of spirituality who fail to see the relative as well as the absolute. In the case of Jesus Christ, we see an even better example.

The Church sees Jesus Christ as being both fully divine and fully human. His humanness, however, is often ignored or excuses are made for it. In the book of Mark, we read the story of Jesus coming upon a fig tree, and being hungry, he hopes to get some figs from it. Upon finding that the tree has no figs, even though it is not the time for figs, Jesus shrivels up the tree in anger. The Church attempts to explain this human reaction by making the tree a metaphor for Israel, and its lack of bearing fruit. The fact that it was not the time for figs is ignored. This denial of Jesus' humanness is an attempt to make

Jesus perfect, both in humanity and divinity, even though the story's purpose is to show his human nature. Again, in the same chapter, we see Jesus lose his temper at the money changers and merchants in the Temple of Jerusalem. Righteous indignation, no doubt, but also fully human. Perhaps the most important story of Jesus' humanity is the passion in the Garden of Gethsemane, when he asks to be relieved of the crucifixion but submits to God's will. Jesus reveals a divine being with both doubts and anger, fully divine and fully human.

In non-duality, we often insist that our gurus and teachers live a blissful life of perfect understanding. Any imperfections we notice are occasions for finger-pointing or accusations of fraud. Ramana Maharshi is often looked at as the ideal enlightened sage. And yet, upon close and honest observation, we see a man who struggled to keep his ashram in the control of his family. He spoke of awakening as being universal, yet followed the traditional separation of caste, insisting that Brahmins not sit at meals with lower casts in his ashram. Although Ramana saw his true nature, he tolerated veneration and even worship with his disciples frequently singing hymns to him, *in his presence*. Any of these things in a modern or Western teacher, we would label *ego*! But Ramana was human.

Much of what is today considered Neo-Advaita, had its start with HWL Poonja (Papaji). Papaji would often tell people that they were already enlightened. This of course was part of his teaching method and true on the absolute level, but he often failed to make this clear and sent some of them off to teach. He later said that none of these teachers were even partially enlightened. He often gave seekers spiritual experiences, which he later dismissed as false experiences. Asked why he gave people false experiences, he answered, "to get the leeches off my back." None of this looks like perfection, but Papaji was human.

If Jesus, Nisargadatta, Ramana, and Papaji were subject to human faults and weaknesses, how are we to become perfect? To expect to rise above or beyond humans while abiding in the flesh is unrealistic. We can experience the divine within ourselves, but the body is weak. The Christ said, "Watch and pray, that ye enter not into temptation: the spirit indeed is willing, but the flesh is weak." Our perfection is an uphill struggle. Enlightenment is an ongoing unfolding that happens in the *now*. Enlightenment is not an event that happens and then goes on as a past experience, but a working out.

The Apostle Paul tells us to "work out your own salvation with fear and trembling, for God is at work in you, both to will and to work in for his good pleasure." Constant action and effort are required. *Effortless effort*, as they say in non-dual circles, is the key to enlightenment. I read of teachers who will tell you that their enlightenment happened in such and such a year or at such and such an event, like it was in the past, and they are now living it always. But we know that there is only now, only this. Awareness and enlightenment are either working out now, at this moment, or not at all.

If you have ever been on a diet, you know that it is difficult to stick to one. One of the best pieces of advice when dieting is to stick to it. Even if you backslide and go off the diet for a day, the advice is to go back to the diet the next day and not be discouraged. This is also good advice on the spiritual search. Keep seeking, even when you have "*found*" something. What you seek is the road you are on. Work out your enlightenment with fear and trembling. Live every day in the *present*, not in some past enlightenment experience. Enlightenment is unfolding, not static. You can experience your true nature, but the body/mind continues until its end. The humanness, the body/mind is not separate from the reality; use it to work out present awareness.

The body/mind is like a wheel rolling downhill. It rolls until the momentum gives out, or it runs into something, and then it stops. As long as it's rolling, we are meant to see beyond it: *to work out our salvation*. If we stop it, or the working out, we stagnate or backslide. Perfection is not a state. It is the action of life itself. Perfection is in the *being*, not something that is finished or complete. We need to constantly remind ourselves that, although we are perfect and divine, we are also inseparably human. We are not only human beings, we are *humans* being.

113

Mr. Rogers, Me, and Remembering Non-Dual Awareness

"The child is in me still, and sometimes not so still." Fred Rogers

I have recently put up some quotes on Facebook from Fred Rogers. If anyone doesn't know who Fred Rogers was, he was an ordained Presbyterian Minister that had a television show for children called Mr. Rogers Neighborhood as his ministry. Since his passing, his show is on Public Television only once and a while, but I never miss it. Fred did not talk about religion, or mention God, but talked about simple human relations in terms a child could understand.

I have found that children are often capable of understanding great spiritual truths. As we begin or continue the spiritual search, we often find that we are looking back at a time of simplicity that we remember from our childhood. The story is told of a three-year-old who has just had a new baby in the house. One day the parents found the three-year-old curled up in the baby's crib, with the newborn. "What are you doing?" the child was asked. "I was just sitting with the baby", the child said. "I was trying to remember. I had forgotten so much."

We, on the spiritual search, also discover that we have forgotten so much. As children, we live and love and swim in freedom. As we become older, we long for a different kind of freedom, one we imagine will be of our own making. As adults, we begin to rely on our education, our acquired knowledge. The intuitive response we once had as children is buried under self-imposed wisdom. I think one of the factors that leads many seekers after spiritual understanding is that call to remember because we sense that we have forgotten so much. This seeking often stems from a fear that comes to all adults at some point. As children, we are protected by our parents. We are free of worry about the simple daily needs and cares that are so much a part of adult life. We long, if we are honest, for that simpler time of no care or responsibility. We remember the comfort of our parents or teachers as a safe haven, even if our childhood was not the best. We see the protection provided by these

114

guardians as the reason we felt safe, not recognizing that it was our spontaneous love and joy in life that was our true savior. When we feel that it was the guardians that made us safe, we often look for spiritual teachers that will give us some prescribed plan or method. We look to a *father* God, whom we can trust, or a guru who we see as encompassing all truth.

When I first returned to the Church, I took a Lenten class in the *Jesus Prayer*. This is a form of meditative prayer using the mantra, "Lord Jesus, have mercy upon me, a sinner." We were however asked to contemplate on it and to come up with our own personal mantra. Mine became "Father, my Friend, I love you." The "father" part was there because this was how the Christ had described God. The Christ used the word *Abba* frequently, which means not simply father, but something like *daddy*. This was the closeness that the Christ wanted to convey. God is not just the creator, but loving daddy: our father. The "my friend" part of the mantra was because I felt that close. God knew me, understood me, loved me. And the "I love you" part conveyed my return of that feeling. Of course, this all belonged to an *imagined* God. One I did not yet understand, but longed to.

After the discovery of Advaita (non-duality), which was not really a discovery, as I had a sense of oneness even as a child, I began to seek the realization of that understanding. The child in me recognized that I had *forgotten so much*, and I began to understand intuitively that love was my true nature, and I began again to live, love, and swim in freedom. This freedom is life itself. It is giving freely, as a little child. It is standing in awe of a beautiful sunset, as a little child. It is letting the tears flow, in happiness or sadness, as a little child. Yes, there can be sadness, even in freedom. It is the acceptance that makes it whole, holy.

When I watch Mr. Rogers' Neighborhood, and I hear him talk or sing about "*The mad that you feel*", or "*You have to do it, do it, do it,*" I remember the *forgotten so much*. One of Mr. Rogers' compositions that says it all is, "*There Are Many Ways (To say I Love You)*." This is at the heart of the realized person. Not great words, or mystical experiences, but the living out the *many ways*. If your teacher sets him or herself apart or views themselves as somehow on a different level than you, then they are seeing separation where none exists. Realization tells you that you *are love*. There is no need to *be loved*, only to share it freely. When you and the other see that you are both love itself, you and the other become secondary to the love *that you are*.

Fred always began his show with the song. "It's a Beautiful Day for a Neighbor" and ended the show with the song, "It's Such a Good Feeling (to know you're alive)." Wonderful neighbors, joy in living is what enlightenment and awareness are all about. If you make it any more complicated than that, you need to get back to *the forgotten so much*.

Imaginary Horses and Spiritual Experiences

When my brother and I were small, we would often play at cowboys. Sometimes we were on the same side, and sometimes we were sworn enemies. One of the things my mother always talked about, well into our middle age, was how we would argue over imaginary horses.

We would argue over who's was the fastest, who's was the strongest, who's was the smartest, and all the rest of it. Sometimes it would even come to blows! "You insulted my horse;" "Them's fightin' words." It's incredible how much trouble can be caused by two boys arguing over imaginary horses! We, in non-duality circles, can be no less destructive and, dare I say, childish in defense of our verbal and written descriptions of enlightenment, awareness, the Absolute, or perhaps worse, spiritual experiences.

We are waves in the same ocean, if I may use a tired old metaphor, but waves are just the same, some tall, and some shorter. No judgment, just appearances anyway. The point is, each wave is part of the unlimited potential unfolding. Each will have a slightly different view when expressed in words or even thought. The oneness, the love, is only actively present when it is *silently, wordlessly* present *in the heart*. So we are all liars!

We all look at the same object, but we see it out of different windows. "By golly, the view is different from here, you must be wrong!" All this talk about authentic experiences, as opposed to, I guess inauthentic experiences, or authentic awakening as opposed to continuing to sleep, or whatever is the opposite of awakening, is simply judging one experience against another. To argue over the differing experiences may be something for philosophers and academics to entertain themselves with, but if we seek realization, we need to go beyond even the division of authentic and inauthentic. The moment we take a position, we invite its opposite.

I never tire of hearing the spiritual experiences of others. As I said, it's like seeing out of a different window, and perhaps getting a different take on the always present view. One of the things that pushed me away from the organized church was its tendency to want to limit the spirit. Oh, spiritual experiences were fine, as long as they did not contradict Church doctrine or someone's interpretation of the Bible. This denial of the active, present movement of the Holy Spirit, and its ability to continue to create, inform and incarnate, is a denial of all that the Christ stood for. When we allow our minds to commandeer a personal understanding or awakening experience, and it becomes a doctrine or position where we say, "This must be your experience as well or it is not an authentic experience," we deny the possibility of movement to the spirit which is freedom itself.

To argue, or even give much philosophical discussion to other's awakening, or other's spiritual experiences, is like arguing over the qualities of an imaginary horse: *it's all made up* in the first place, and you can keep changing your story as you go along. The only horse worth talking about is a real one. But in the spiritual realm, where do you, and even more important, *how* do you seek the real deal?

Well, the Bible says, you can tell a tree by its fruits. Now, I realize that I just questioned interpretations from the Bible in the last paragraph, but this is quite a good tool for discernment. I think that love is at the heart of understanding. This is most definitely a position on my part, as this is how *"I"* talk about what *"I"* see out of my window. I cannot see out your window, or know your view, but I know what you are looking at. *"I"* can imagine what you see, just as *"I"* imagine what *"I"* see, but neither will be the truth. Perhaps what I report or some other reporter tells you will resonate with you. If so, this is fine. But if a teacher, guru, or spiritual leader tells you that you must have a particular kind of experience, or in other words, if he has a faster, smarter, stronger horse, then you need to look at two things: is there love here? (Do you see the honesty and integrity of love?), and are you free to work out your own struggle as a wave becoming aware that your horse is imaginary.

It's the teachers that continue to argue the qualities of the horse, instead of enjoying the tales of the views from all the windows, that will take up a position at one window only, and tell you that their view and their horse is the best. But we must let them do this. It's not worth troubling over imaginary horses.

Living Accordingly: Life as Practice

„You cannot be half a saint.
You must be a whole saint or no saint at all."

Therese of Lisieux

When St. Therese wrote those words, she was not declaring herself a saint or saying that we can become saints, but pointing out that we must strive to reach the top of the mountain and not be satisfied with halfway up. In spirituality, there can be no half-way measures.

Therese of Lisieux knew from an early age that loving God, either through direct worship or through service to others, had to be a whole-hearted endeavor. She gave her life very early to the singular worship and service to God. But it's not only Christian saints who recognize that full devotion to the task at hand, that the seeking, the longing for closeness to the source, is what is required. Similar to Paul's call in Philippians 2 to *"...work out your salvation with fear and trembling; for it is God who is at work in you"*, the Buddha said, *"Be a lamp unto yourself. Work out your liberation with diligence."* Diligence, like Nisargadatta Maharaj's often-used word, *earnestness*, is at the heart of the spiritual search and a constant in the Spiritual Life.

What does earnestness in the spiritual life mean? What does it mean to *"work out your salvation with fear and trembling?"* Earnestness and diligence are both words that speak of constant, serious attention. That's all. This sounds simple until you look closely at another passage from the Bible, Mark 12:

"The first of all the commandments is, Hear, O Israel; The Lord our God is one Lord: 30 And thou shalt love the Lord thy God with all thy heart, and with all thy soul, and with all thy mind, and with all thy strength: this is the first commandment. 31 And the second is like, namely this, Thou shalt love thy neighbor as thyself. There is none other commandment greater than these."

All thy heart, All thy soul, All thy mind, All thy strength; that's it. That's what is required for salvation or liberation.; Loving God in thyself and in thy neighbor, and consequently in all things, sentient or otherwise.

The "fear and trembling" mentioned in Paul's letter refers to the inability of the mind to understand the workings of the heart. I go into this in another blog, *Nebulous Clarity*. To put it simply, nebulous clarity refers to the state of acceptance of understanding without the ability to articulate it to others or yourself. This *living without understanding* is the heart of sacrifice and acceptance. It is here, in the fear and trembling, that the conviction is tested. Do you live and move with the conviction that you are love itself? Can you let the mind live in fear and trembling long enough for it to trust the heart? This is where earnestness and fearlessness come in. Single-minded attention to the reality that you are is essential.

The Buddha, Nisargadatta Maharaj, and Saint Therese had many things in common, but among the foremost was their single-minded attention to reality that they were. They did this, not by simply meditating and engaging in recollection or prayer, but by living a life that was an integrated whole with their spiritual understanding. Your spiritual life cannot be a separate life from your daily life. Just as Therese says, "You cannot be half a saint", you can't be half in and half out of the spiritual life. You are either in it or not. The lives of these three saints of spirituality were a living testimony to their words. They all were of different faiths or paths, but they were one in devotion, *earnestness*, if you will forgive me one more time!

Living a life in non-duality does not require leaving behind the life you have. That would be duality. What is required is integration. No matter how non-spiritual your life may seem, the Absolute, God's love is all around you, flows through you, is you, and is available at all times and in all things. Brother Lawrence of the Resurrection, a Carmelite monk, is described in his famous work *The Practice of the Presence of God* as having an aversion to kitchen work, but he used his work as a way of loving the Lord:

"So, likewise, in his work in the kitchen (to which he had, at first, a great aversion), having accustomed himself to do everything there for the love of God and asking for His grace to do his work well, he

had found everything easy during the fifteen years he had been employed there. He was very well pleased with the post he was now in. Yet, he was as ready to quit that as the former, since he tried to please God by doing little things for the love of Him in any work he did. With him, the set times of prayer were no different from other times. He retired to pray according to the directions of his superior, but he did not need such retirement nor ask for it because his greatest labor did not divert him from God."

Living the truth, living as if we believe what the sages tell us is a great start. Nisargadatta says: "*If you trust me, believe when I tell you that you are the pure awareness that illumines consciousness and its infinite content. Realize this and live accordingly.*" Live accordingly!

This little statement, almost tacked on at the end, contains the method, the practice recommended by Nisargadatta. He goes on to state that if you don't believe him, you should engage in self-inquiry and the I Am. But the "live accordingly" remains. Whether you trust the Guru or find yourself on your own, living out the realization is the realization.

A life of sacrifice need not be a life of pain or suffering, although that too will come, but it is a life of rejection of personal wants and desires in favor of universal love. It is living in acceptance of nebulous clarity, and constant service to the reality that is beyond your mind's conception. The courage to live "as if" you understand, "as if" you always are ready, always in the flow, is what is required for that understanding and even for that courage to happen. For the potential energy, love, to flow, there must be a connection to the truth, and a means to express it. The truth is in the expression, as that is all that exists in reality. We must give all we have. We must disappear as must the other, be it God, man, or world. All that matters is the expression: the loving, the living.

Enlightenment: In Sorrow and In Joy

At the end of St. Therese of Lisieux's autobiography, *The Story of a Soul* is this description of her passing where she laments, she does not wish to lessen her suffering, her eyes alight with supernatural joy as she passes:

"At a few moments past seven when she knew the end had come, she said calmly, 'I do not wish to suffer less. Oh, how I love Him! My God, I love thee.' Gazing beyond the statue of Mary beside her bed, her eyes alight with a supernatural joy, she died."

This may be a somewhat dramatized version of the actual happening, but it conveys what was intended: being in love, dying in love.

Why do we seek? Or, perhaps a better question, what *compels* us to seek? For to go after an illusive quarry like enlightenment requires a compulsion. But can it be a quarry? When what we seek is ultimately, intimately ourselves and the path we follow, this cannot be a quarry, but fascination itself.

I have said many times that my spiritual search began when I was a very small child and I realized that if God was who they said he was, he warranted my undivided attention. This is what Therese expressed on her deathbed, "Oh, how I love Him." This is not some wish for relief, in fact, she said, "I do not wish to suffer less." Therese simply wanted to love her God. She did not even ask for peace of mind. She wanted nothing but to love. This is what the Christ referred to as the pearl of great price.

The pearl of great price is not an object of desire, or even a wish for peace, but a burning to be in love. This burning is the earnestness spoken of by Nisargadatta Maharaj. It is a burning for enlightenment. It is not a burning for the fruits of enlightenment, like bliss or peace of mind, but *a burning for love itself*. It is this burning that leads to awakening because it is awakening. This is why I talk of movement and unfolding. Creative love beckons, compels, and fulfills. All as one movement, love calls us to seek, and sustains us on the way to ultimate fulfillment in understanding. This may appear to happen all at once or appear over time. The appearance is secondary to the ultimate fulfillment of the movement. The important part is the devotion.

The devotion needs to be there right at the beginning. If we start out with a desire for something, be it wealth, happiness, or simple peace of mind, we will not be able to be open to the devotion (read love) necessary for our task. This is what sacrifice and surrender are all about. We need to be able to say with Therese, "I do not wish to suffer less." Our hearts, minds, and souls need to be on the pearl of great price, which is love itself. Being in love. Dying in love.

This is the heart of earnestness; to love without desire, or want for the simplest thing, but to love. It is only through this agape kind of love that sufficient earnestness can be lived. It comes around to the circle of love that I so often talk about. Love, in its creative self-indulgence, calls us to seek, sustains our search, and leads us to fulfillment in itself.

The seeking and the sustenance are part and parcel of the fulfillment which is inherent in the whole flow. Our purpose in this is to not only cooperate with it (surrender) but to actively, whole-heartedly, live it, in sorrow or in joy.

Light in the Darkness: Watching the Sunrise

In medieval times, there was a widespread belief that light was the purest form of God's power: his essence. This is reflected in the wonder of the stained glass-windows of the great cathedrals.

In many ancient and modern tribes, there is a tradition of sitting in meditation during the sunrise and sunset. The power of the sunrise and sunset is unmistakable in scientific or primitive terms.

> *"Each dawn, in the sunrise, I am gratitude.*
> *Each eve, in the sunset, I am trust."*

The sunrise, bringing today's promise, is another occasion for gratitude and boundless joy. The sunset brings rest in the trust that if tomorrow never comes, the light still never goes out.

And this is it; what we seek – this light that never goes out. Whether we conceive of ourselves as wrapped in light, or lost in the embrace of God, there is a wonder to this light. Gratitude and trust need to be our only practice and prayer.

To paraphrase the Bible, *"the light shown in the darkness, but the darkness perceived it not."*

This perceiving *not* of that which is all around us; this light, this awareness, is at the heart of the confusion of mankind. But the answer is also right before us. It is the practice of gratitude and prayer. Whether you actually sit and watch the sunrise or sunset regularly (which I highly recommend!), or you are moved by the swirling patterns of stained glass reflected on the floors of cathedrals or temples, it is worth taking the time each day to re-connect with grateful, trusting, wordless prayer. For the moment you are lost in gratitude, in silent connection, you are bathed in the light, and no darkness is left to perceive it not.

The Facebook Bus: Spirit Tour

I recently wrote a piece in which I talked about all the various teachers and seekers as being like faces looking at the same object out of different windows. Playing with this idea, I began to think about our contact here on Facebook. I got to thinking about what a gift we are given with this technology. Taking up the window metaphor, I began to see us all; all the Facebook seekers, philosophers, and would-be teachers, touring in a grand bus, all enjoying the same sights, but from a slightly different window.

The exciting part is that each one in turn takes the time to explain their particular view from their particular window. Of course, occasionally someone will report a view that is so unusual or so mundane that there are scoffers. "Oh, you didn't really see that, it's an illusion." "Oh, that's just the egos in the back of the bus, don't listen to them." But for the most part, we enjoy the various reports. As we tour our world here on the Facebook Bus Spirit Tour, we encounter so many different ideas, from so many different places. Each window has a slightly varied angle, as each viewer has a slightly different perspective. We hear from Christians, Hindus, Jews, and non-dualists, both "neo" and old school. We hear the philosophical atheist and the fundamentalist Bible-thumpers. All ride the same bus, all take the same tour.

We can hear of spirit guides dictating books. We can hear of austerities and sacrifices. We can hear of monasteries and ashrams. We can hear of simply leading the life. All the windows offer not only differing views but differing interpretations of those views. Our bus begins to take on aspects of a circus train. But that's alright because all we have to do is get ready for the show. "Window thirteen reports of lasting awareness." "Window five's view is clouded with maya, cleaning needed!" But the ride is exciting and new. We are pioneers in our sharing of spiritual experiences in this medium The Satsang, the gathering around the guru's feet, has given way to open daily sharing of spiritual insights and ultimately, love. Not that our Facebook Bus Spirit Tour is a replacement for Satsangs or personal contact, but it is a way for some of us to share who otherwise may not meet any of you.

I have been on YouTube for quite a while doing my outreach to gay youth. *The Cowboy Monk's Corral*. I found that while many write off online communications, much important contact can happen there. There can be what Mr. Rogers used to call on his TV Show, "important talk". I enjoy and learn from so many different windows both here on Facebook and on other sites, that I value it as a real part of my life. I don't divide my online life from my real life. I enjoy telling you about the view from my window as we ride the tour bus. I hope I am respectful of your view and your vision, and that others are as well. For now, we can share, seeker and teacher alike. No flowers needed, no soft music, no postures, just us in our computer chair window seats reporting the lovely or terrifying view as the tour goes on.

I Am Here!

I was asked, "If love is the basis of everything, how does it result in the manifestation?" And the follow-up question was, "How do acts and feelings of selfishness arise out of love?"

The second question is easier to answer than the first. Attempting to explain the first question involves a translation from the silent language of the heart to the wordy babble of the mind. My answer has always been to explain the circle of love. The circle of love is based on the principle of an electrical circuit. An open electrical circuit has electricity in potential, but not in actuality. All the necessary qualities are there; the power source, the connectors, the various devices, but the power flows only when there is a complete circuit.

This is why service is so important to any spiritual practice. The power source, love, or God's love if you wish, is manifested as the world, as us. It does this by just *being*. It is the nature of love, the Absolute, to manifest for its own expression. This means when there is an expression of love, there is manifest a means of expression. We are the source that flows through the circuit of love as well as the devices along the circuit, having been created as devices solely for the purpose of loving. It is clear. Our purpose is to enjoy ourselves, each other and the world. The problem is, we don't. and that brings us to the second question.

If all there is, is love, how do selfish acts and feelings arise? A darn good question. Nisargadatta suggested that a seeker looks into themselves because he was aware that only by seeing how hollow a concept anything but the I Am is would bring us to that point: this awareness that we love ourselves. This is the I Am you know. This is an acknowledgment of love. "I am here, as the Who cried from Horton's flower. I am here. I am recognized. This recognition is love calling and answering. The problem arises with the degree of the size of the "I", or ego that arises with the I am. You see the "am" part is fine. That "am" is simple awareness. It's that oft-inflated "I" that will distort and pervert the appearance of the pure expression of love into

127

fear and jealousy and even hate. A strong "I" wants and is conditioned to want, separation.

All I's suffer from some degree of self-love, strong enough at least to keep a *personal* image alive. But most live in that image of the story much, or all of the time. When the "I" is seen as separate, there is going to be some degree of selfishness. Now, as we all know, some degree of self-love is always present and should be. But any degree of self-regard beyond self-respect can lead to further separation.

If we feel that we are separate, that we are alone and *need* love, we are going to demand love in our very behavior. Instead of loving freely in a world made of love, we are going to restrict and demand love for our "I" alone. The "I" wants to keep it, hold it, possess it, and selfishness is born. And from that distortion to further perversion until the ultimate conclusion is reached. The "I" must live at all costs, even at the cost of other "I's". This is how love appears to twist into selfishness, fear, and hate.

The pull of the "I" is strong. This is why sacrifice, renunciation and service are recommended. While sacrifice, renunciation, and service may seem unpleasant endeavors, they put you right into the center of joy. For once the fascination with the "I" is gone, everything else, including the "I" can be enjoyed in their fullness and freedom.

Awakening Out of Madness

By the time I was nine, I was seeing a psychiatrist weekly. It was not until my early 60s that I came to the conclusion that I had experienced Asperger's Syndrome all my life, and had never even heard the word before. Although self-diagnosed, my childhood and youth showed me that this nearly unknown condition that had been a terror to my youth had also been a boon to my spiritual development.

The occasion for seeing the psychiatrist at such an early age was a sudden fear of going to school that I could not understand. I loved school as a child. I loved to learn. But the social side of school, even in the early grades, was terrifying to me. Initially, it was recommended to my parents to force me to go. So there were long scenes of me having been locked out until I came home after school, crying at the door and begging to be let in. The terror of going to school was so bad, it ruined my other time as well because I would be thinking about it nearly all the time.

Finally, it was decided to get me a home teacher and see a psychiatrist for therapy. The trips to the psychiatrist were a great relief from the terror of school.

I consider it lucky to have had the opportunity to look deeply into myself at such an early age. To be able to do self-inquiry at such an early age was wonderfully liberating. It was discovered that I was above average intelligence, as many Asperger's folks are, but my social inability was taking up so much of my waking hours that I had little time for anything else. But, in any event, I do not want this to be my life's story, I want to make the point that those of us who have had the occasion to look deeply into ourselves, our behavior, and our life from *the outside* have had, perhaps, a leg up.

I often find it hard to discuss my awakening experience because, in most ways, it seems I have always been awake. One of the aspects of Asperger's Syndrome is an obsession, or at least a strong interest in some field of study or hobby. These interests can sometimes be off-beat or esoteric. Mine was always spirituality. I lived in a world apart as a child. Not a sad world, but a world filled with love and light. By the time I had spent a year or two in school, I was terrorized to the point I would hide all day rather than face speaking to someone. But besides all this madness there was an abiding trust at first in God, but then eventually just trust. Yes, even in the agnostic period of my teens and early twenties I lived my life on trust. So it is difficult talking about a single experience as an awakening, as I have been largely awakened, even in the throes of apparent madness.

Seeing a psychiatrist at nine nipped in the bud a lot of dodges and rationalizations that many of us go through as we grow. Many of us wear some sort of mask much of, if not all of our lives, never realizing it is these very masks that hide the true self that we so desperately seek. When you see madness all around you from the start, it is easy to reject it for a peace you see less clearly, but no less real. This is why, in so many cases, people, particularly "normal people" seem to have such a struggle grasping the nettle and doing what is necessary. Often it literally requires a life-changing event": a death, a birth, a descent into madness, something that shakes you out of your "normal" view of yourself. Earnestness, that drive that pulls and pushes in turns, comes from a surrender to that place of peace that sees less clearly but knows the real. The safe quiet place of nothingness is rejected until the sights, sounds, and voices of the mad world drive you to earnestness.

As I struggled out of my childhood, I had found enough *others*, some struggling themselves, others helping the struggling ones, but both coming from a position of unconditional love. It is these to whom we want to turn for pointers. Those who have escaped all the madness and live in the peace of love never ending.

The Key to the Door

For those who find the non-dual path appealing, the danger of dryness often becomes an issue. Those of us who have an intellectual leaning will often try to find answers in the mind long after the mind's usefulness is spent. The question as to why we do this, especially in the West, requires us to look a bit at the position we come from.

Many of us on the spiritual path of non-duality in whatever form it takes, come to it from some other faith or spiritual background. Many come from a Christian background that they found unsatisfying or terrifying in turn, looking for something with fewer rules or more personal freedom or participation. It took me over thirty years to discover that the Christian Church had a mystical, non-dual side. I have always believed that the pull of other forms of spirituality is often based on their otherness.

If you are brought up in a Christian Church or any other spiritual system that has ritualized practices or beliefs, those practices and beliefs become, at first, charged with meaning. Later they become less important, particularly when we observe uncomplimentary clergy or congregational behavior that indicates a lack of belief if not downright hypocrisy. But apart from the hypocrisy, we begin to lose interest in the same stories we have heard over and over. We forget that the stories are spiritual pointers and start making them into history, or worse, law! Under these circumstances, it is not surprising that a *religion of the mind* might become popular.

When we delve into Eastern spirituality, this *religion of the mind*, many exciting images arise. Not only new stories, new Gods, but new words and ideas to expand our knowledge. Even though images in your own spiritual system may point to the same truth, these new, exciting images convey a meaning that has become lost in convention or a lack of attention and earnestness. These new gods we see as much less threatening than the God that could send us to hell! We see them as the symbols they are, instead of a hated, oppressive father figure. We see no need for worship or devotion. We are free to explore reality with the mind! But in our rush to find the truth, we throw the baby out with the bathwater.

This *religion of the mind*, Jnana Yoga, self-inquiry, non-duality however you describe it, has often become a religion that despises religion. By that, I mean that many will not go beyond the mind in their search. They have only scratched the surface of their own religion or belief system, and now want to dive headlong into a new system that will be logical and reasonable. They say faith has nothing to do with it, love has nothing to do with it. There are no questions as to why monks and nuns, Christians, Buddhists, and Hindus sit in silence for long hours, over periods of many years. It is the silent contemplation of love, along with living as love in action, that brings us home.

When I was a monk, and writing the rule for the community, I wrote of spending time before the cross as a way to true knowledge. This can be looked at as a penance to those who neither like stillness nor who fear emptiness. But this is the way to love. We do not sit silently in hopes of getting some new thought or idea. We sit to be silent *in love*. This is not some hippie romantic notion. By opening all that we hold ourselves to be, by becoming empty vessels, we become filled with the indescribable knowledge of love. Meditation on an object or idea is not a spiritual pursuit, it is mind control. Contemplation, on the other hand, is an emptying, a releasing of control. An opening to what is.

We can argue Bhakti vs. Jnana all day. But a combination of the two is vital to any spiritual understanding. No matter how you build your concepts, Western, Eastern, or whatever, living out your spirituality is the only way to be it. The mind can only lead you to the conclusion of words: I am. Stepping into love openly, with the trust and wonder of a little child requires going back to the source, the love itself. The mind leads to the door. The key to the door is love. Without the key, you can't open the door and there is no point to the trip! When we were little children, we sometimes wore a key around our neck so as to not lose it. We need to wear this key of love around our hearts.

Is This What You Want?

I am going to tell you about a couple of my dreams, so I want to begin with a statement about my thoughts on dreams. I have examined dreams from both a psychological and philosophical point of view and have to say that the psychological view seems to be commensurate with my experience. That said, I also have great respect for potential and its ability to do almost anything!

While I believe the manifestation generally follows predictable rules, I do not discount an unpredictability beyond my understanding. If the spirit creates a manifestation, it can certainly arise as a dream.

The two dreams I mentioned were both dreams of Nisargadatta Maharaj. I discovered *I Am That* in 1986 in the San Francisco Public Library. My own copy, a hard-cover Indian edition purchased at Field's bookstore in San Francisco, was purchased a short time later. I have been acquainted with Maharaj for over a quarter of a century. I have not only read *I Am That* several times, but I have also read almost everything by or about him. But that was some years ago. So I was surprised to recently have had two dreams in close succession that featured him, as I had never dreamed of him before. I tell of them because they were a strong impetus to begin writing and talking about non-duality from my own perspective.

Both were short, and the first was the easiest to explain. In the first dream, I was in a room, Nisargadatta was standing in a doorway. In his hands were sacred objects made of plaster from a variety of different faiths. He looked at me and threw the sacred objects on the floor, breaking them into pieces. He looked at me a second time, and the dream was over. An easy dream to decipher, the uselessness of religious dogma, is clear enough. My only question was, why would I have such a dream? I know that already. Why waste a perfectly good encounter with Maharaj on something so basic? But I dismissed it largely until the second dream a few weeks later.

In the second dream, Nisargadatta was again standing in a doorway. As he silently stood there, I approached him and put my hands on his shoulders. We stood face to face, with me staring into those eyes, and tears started to well up in both our eyes. As we stood locked in this silent embrace, there was an unspoken question, "Is this what you want?"

It took me a while to understand that it was meant for me to share my message. That I share this love. It was clear I was not to be a spokesman for him or his message. We were two faces, two expressions. I would not presume to teach as Nisargadatta did. The message was not to worry about my lack of education but write in my simple way as he taught in his. His, or the Absolute's question. "Is this what you want?" meant do you want to be a conduit for this love we now share? I had my experience, my understanding twenty years ago. I had tried to flog a book, but it didn't catch anyone's attention, so I just lived my life.

Being a somewhat introverted, quiet type, I had no desire to teach. But I did have the desire to share with like-minded/-hearted folks. This is why I write and share on Facebook and my blog.

Because *this is what I want*. I want to look into your eyes, figuratively or literally, and share that love, that understanding. Dream or not, psychological or philosophical, I was able to share that moment with Maharaj. I hope to be able to share such a moment with you and in turn ask, "Is this what you want?"

Living Joyfully as Nothing

At one point, when working in homes for the developmentally disabled, my partner and I had to report some abuse that we witnessed. The abusers were our employers, and as we were all living in the same home at the time, this created a difficult and sometimes ridiculous situation.

We tried to ignore the situation until the investigation was completed. But our employers and their relatives would attempt to abuse us verbally whenever we encountered one of them in the hall or on the way to the bathroom.

One day, one of the employer's relatives ran into both my partner and myself in a narrow hallway, and unable to get immediately past, started using abusive language and calling us Laurel and Hardy. Well, unknown to this fellow, my partner and I got great pleasure out of it because Laurel and Hardy were our alter-egos, our heroes, our *realistic* images of ourselves.

It never helps to have a great image of yourself. The lighter the image the less energy is needed to maintain it. This is particularly important in times of stress or adversity. When I was writing the *Rule for the Community of the Living Sacrifice*, and I came to the section on poverty, I wanted to make one point very clear: there's more to poverty than simply going without.

I spoke of accepting, not only the lack of basic necessities but being able to accept the scorn and rejection of others. It is no secret that in our classless society, we are very class-conscious. At one point after returning from England, my partner and I being unable to find work, found ourselves homeless. We were sleeping in our Honda wagon in beautiful Monterey, California, in a Safeway grocery parking lot. After the store closed there was no bathroom. This is something few even think about when it comes to the homeless. But this is one of the indignities the poor face every day.

When we lived in the City, irate citizens would complain mightily if they came upon a phone booth or doorway that had been used as an expedient restroom, without considering that some are denied even so much as a comfortable place to take care of nature's call. This, and other indignities are endured by the poor on a daily, sometimes hourly basis. This was something I wanted to include in the rule. One had not only to endure want but endure abuse.

When we talk non-duality, we are by implication talking service. When we hear of bullying or witness a racial slur, do we stand up? When we see a homeless person, do we remember the good Samaritan or do we think, "That's the guy who had peed in the phone booth." We label people, even some of us in the non-duality community. He's *homeless* like it was a tribe. He's an *illegal* like his whole legitimacy is questioned. Do we stand up, even if it means abusing ourselves? But then, we worry about being labeled ourselves. "He's 'soft' spiritually. He doesn't know who is asking the questions. He dares to question Ramana."

Like Laurel and Hardy, we are all clowns living on a movie set. We can puff ourselves up like Oliver Hardy, or we can practice the humility of Stan Laurel, who sometimes was completely oblivious of his own presence, But, whatever role we play, it must be light. We must see that this body/mind of ours is an oversized suit, a pair of floppy shoes, worthy of laughter. Oh, we can dignify ourselves, put on a three-piece suit and our best hat, but around the corner Laurel and Hardy wait with a bucket of paint. It is so much easier to stop worrying about accomplishments, honors, and labels, both those we seek and those we run from.

If I accept the role of child or buffoon, my eyes are open with wonder and I laugh when I fall on my butt. I see clearly that to take any of these shows we see and participate in too seriously is the most serious mistake we can make. Just as we dislike labels, we need to refrain from labeling ourselves or others. When we accept the lowest place at the table, no one can say, "Go lower." When we live in the conviction that we are everything, we can live joyfully as nothing.

A Hike in the Spring: What a Lesson!

Spring seems to have sprung here in Southern New Mexico. We went for a hike this morning in the open desert near our home. Eddy, our dog, is just starting to find lizards to chase who just as quickly find holes to hide in. It won't be long before he will have to go back on the lead for the danger of rattlesnakes.

While Eddy was attempting to chase lizards, I started to wander off in my mind to the scene of a predator: a coyote, wild cat, fox, or something, chasing a lizard or small mammal. I could easily sense the small animal's fear and the predator's anticipation.

I began to speculate on this scene without words. No flashing teeth, no fur, no claws, just *fear*, but without the word; without the *idea* of fear. And, of course, the hopeful anticipation, also wordless, also idealess. What a lesson.

To see life as wordless, non-conceptual, is to see life as it is. There is no judgment of good or bad between the predator and prey. Even the names predator and prey vanish in the wordless, non-conceptual reality. Momentary fear and anticipation are just playing themselves out, and vanishing into the flow of love/life. Remember that the fear and anticipation are also just reflections of that flow. What a lesson.

As the Spring brings the new leaves to the trees, another lesson is unfolding. Six months ago, the leaves fell. Meditate upon this *without time*. Outside of time the tree grows, comes into leaves and fruits, and loses its fruit and leaves, *all at once*. When we add time as a factor, we can break down this process. Seasons move over time. But, in fact, what we observe is *potential*. Not a potential something, but raw potential itself.

Grasp in your hand the tiny seed of a tree. You hold *potential*. No guarantees. No predestination, but potential. The entire universe is like this seed, full of potential, but with no guaranties apart from the *promise to return to itself*. In the seed of the tree lives the potential for a whole forest of trees. The potential for the universe lies in the seed known as love.

Love, like the seed of the tree, is raw potential. It *grows into everything*. What a lesson.

Whispering Rabbits and the Resonance of the Spirit of Love

When I was a small boy, my mother used to read to me at bedtime from one of the series of Little Golden Books called *The Sleepy Book* by Margaret Wise Brown. In that book is the story of *The Whispering Rabbit*. This story is about a rabbit that is very sleepy, and while yawning, swallows a bee who promptly curls up and goes to sleep in the rabbit's throat. He could only whisper and was still sleepy, so he asks the other animals for help on how to get the bee to wake up and go away.

The only advice he gets is that he should have kept his paw over his mouth when he yawned. Finally, he comes upon the groundhog who tells him to make the littlest noise he can possibly make because the bumblebee doesn't bother about big noises. He is a very little bee and he is only interested in little noises. So the rabbit goes through a series of attempts at small noises.

It was a little click made hundreds of miles away by a bumblebee in an apple tree full of bloom on a mountaintop. It was a very small click of a bee swallowing some honey from an apple blossom. And at that, the bee woke up. What wonderful ideas for a small boy! The sound of a fireman thinking, and quiet as an egg.

Why this is Zen for children and adults too, if they take the time to see it. Margaret Wise Brown was a spiritual teacher, even if she passed as just a gifted children's writer and poet. Whether Ms. Brown knew she was writing spiritually charged words or the revelations lie in the listener, the spirit is alive here.

We who dare to write about spirituality need to have an understanding, spoken or not, that we are but facilitators of the spirit. When we see the power of bees and bunnies, we get a glimpse of how our words might have an impact and how indeed, they are not really our words at all.

I think one of the best constant meditations is on time. While I have great respect for time in the relative world, I try to keep a constant awareness that time is a trick of the mind to organize and explain, and not a reality. As a writer, and a respecter of timelessness, I am aware that you are reading this *right now, as I type it!* You are responding to *that* which has brought about its writing in me. In reality, there is no *you* reading, just as there is no *me* writing. There is just the flow of spirit/love instantly unfolding as a passing on of love.

Above I said that whether Ms. Brown knew it or not, she was passing on not only spiritual information but inviting thoughts that could lead to awakening. This is the point. We have no real control in this realm of spirituality. If we as writers or as readers underestimate the play of the spirit here, we miss the whole deal!

I have written over one hundred blog posts in the last year. Most I wrote with a particular theme, or at least with an idea or direction. But that hasn't stopped readers from misinterpreting a number of them, sometimes taking them in a direction I had never considered. I find this fascinating. How one person can receive an inspiration (to fill with spirit) and the reader (also a receiver) can become inspired, but react or see the inspiration slightly or even entirely differently. How wonderful is that?

If something I write finds resonance with you, it is not the *I* and *you* that are at play, but the inspiration; that infilling spirit that breathes life into this shadow play of you and me. These words are your words. Although they come from a different form, the same spirit that forms the words in my head forms them in yours. You may see the same light as the same color I do, or not. Perhaps you see it with no color. No matter. We communicate because we are communication itself, not two separate communicators.

No matter what you read, remember that time is not a factor. Duality is not a factor. When you read Ramana Maharshi, you are not reading the words of a past Master, but a *living inspiration*. The spirit that enlightens Ramana indwells and lives in you. No time, not one nanosecond, has passed since Ramana spoke and you heard. When you read the Masters, even with hundreds of translations, the spirit unfolds anew, *for the first time*. The smiling eyes of Ramana live in your memory, but the inspiration of Ramana lives in your heart. No, I am not Ramana. I am Ramana's love.

Remember, whether you read Ramana, the Bible, the Upanishads, or *The Sleepy Book*, the inspiration that speaks to the authors is that the living spirit that flows through you, is you. The resonance you feel is not with the writer, although he or she may be a good conduit for you, the *resonance* is with the spirit of love.

Reflections of the Source

When I took this picture, I was fascinated by all the faces one can find in these rocks. It reminded me how, since a small boy, I had been seeing things in other things.

Being a kid who liked to draw, eventually evolving into photography, I had, since an early age been able to see. By seeing, I mean in the sense that the word is used in photography: to be able to find a picture by eliminating chaos. To reduce a picture to its necessary elements. Nothing more, nothing less.

The seeing things in other things I talked about is also part of this seeing, but it's kind of the reverse. Have you ever seen a piece of torn wallpaper that looked like something? A cat or a sofa or who knows what. Or the silhouette of a tree in the twilight? Faces appear, innocent shapes are transformed into terrifying or amusing phantoms.

It is the nature of the mind to take known shapes, colors, and other sensory stimuli and turn them into recognizable objects. While this may be recognized when the rat in the corner of the room turns out to be nothing but a discarded, crumpled newspaper, it is much harder to recognize in the creations it makes of the reflections that it sees.

The mind takes the reflections of the real, the Absolute, and shapes them using memories it has collected all the time. Black/white, good/bad, right/wrong. Even the nuances like shape, size, color, and sex are all memory things. The world swirls and unfolds around us in infinite and unexpected ways, yet we try to confine it to words or familiar images.

When we see animals or faces in torn wallpaper or an abstract pattern on a tile floor, we are experiencing the mind pulling together shapes, colors, and patterns into familiar objects. The mind experiences an oval with two protruding elongated shapes on top, and poof it's a rabbit when it is really a silhouette of a cactus that is shaped kind of like a rabbit.

Beyond the visual, this also applies. When we see a certain look or hear a certain tone of voice, we also make a mental picture from past references to that certain look, tone of voice. This is the point where the relationship becomes distorted. We start putting past experiences and past feelings into a fresh situation that is happening now. We not only do this unconsciously in our daily life, thus rendering everything stale and repetitive, but we intentionally and methodically go about doing this in relationships.

We judge others we meet, based on others we've met. We judge other ideas by ideas we've had. Just as the mind pulls together colors, shapes, and other attributes to create forms, it also takes attitude, prejudice, and past experience and pulls them together into a relationship. From love comes the desire to express itself. The expression, which is *us* and the *other* in relationship, is seized by the mind and made subject to past memories, prejudices, and attitudes. It is a total distortion.

An undistorted mind, an undistorted view, is to see the discarded newspaper in the "rat", and behave accordingly. The practice lies in seeing each day and each relationship as fresh, new, full of potential. Every moment is fresh, don't let the mind hijack it into repetitive mediocrity. Don't get lost in the pictures your mind creates from the reflections. Get fascinated with the *source*. Your fascination will bring you home.

Those Who Return to the Cave:
Spiritual Teachers

I just changed my Facebook profile to read "Teacher" instead of "Spiritual Friend". I did this in response to some recent posts on Facebook regarding teachers. I try not to become part of trends, and my to teacher from spiritual friend was partly due to a trend I saw around me, but the main reason was a degree of reserve that I found unnecessary.

It's been almost a year since I dared to refer to myself as a teacher. Although my teaching has been almost exclusively my writing on the internet, both on Facebook and my blog, I have found a number of my readers enjoy my writing.

As I have said many times, I did not make a decision to teach until twenty years after an awakening experience that was as simple as it was profound. Along with the awakening itself came the compulsion to share and teach. I cannot imagine an awakening without this element, this desire to share it with the whole of creation.

In Plato's famous story, *The Allegory of the Cave*, this is very well illustrated. If you remember, the scene is set deep in a cave where the fire, hidden from view, is the only light.

Prisoners are tied so they must look ahead, and are facing a wall where all they see is the light reflected from the fire, the fire being hidden from view by a low wall. Slaves walk behind the wall, out of view. Each slave holds up a flat wooden figure of an animal, a man, or a tree. All the prisoners see is the reflection of these wooden objects, as their shadows are reflected on the wall. They are seeing shadows of artificial objects.

An occasion arises when one of the prisoners finds his bonds loose, and with great effort, escapes. He finds that once untied, he is weak from being in one position for so long, and that it is necessary to climb out of the cave with great effort. Upon reaching daylight he finds the sun is too strong and he must adjust to it. Once he is adjusted to the new discovery, he begins to remember the others down in the cave. Forgetting the struggle to reach the light, he returns to the cave to tell the others.

He finds that very few even want to listen to his story of the light. Those that do listen, are put off by the story of his struggle, and never mind, *you're interrupting the shadows*!

Plato knew the difficulties of being a teacher. But let me get back to this idea of teacher vs. spiritual friend.

We, in the spiritual community, are all spiritual friends. This is as it should be. We all learn from each other. If a spiritual teacher is not learning daily from moment to moment, then they are living a remembered existence, a remembered awakening, not an ongoing unfolding. There was a time when it was recommended that fathers and sons become buddies. This was thought to bring father and son closer together. It was found that what a son wants from his father is for him to *be his father*! I think ultimately, after all the democratization of everything is gotten over, we will find that a teacher is what we want.

The Christ taught us to pray to our Father. This image of the father is an image that is comforting and corrective at the same time. The teacher has much of this comfort and correction about him as well. The image of the father also has the factor of love. The teacher needs to be recognized as the one who climbed out of the cave and came back to tell you about it. Because he loves you. He has seen the light. He has become the light. He knows it's real. He can't bring it to you and he cannot find words sufficient to make it real for you, but he can tell you he's seen it.

If he's truthful he will tell you that even though it is there, freely available to everyone, it is a life of acceptance and earnestness that will open it to you. All he can do is love you, and like a good father, be patient and steadfast in knowing that you are no different than he. He will return to the cave again and again if necessary, and all he will ever ask from you is earnestness.

Seeking Love Only and Getting Joyfully Lost!

So many times, you hear about the seeker actually seeking something. Truth is sought. Enlightenment is sought. Even something as simple as peace of mind becomes a goal in this search for something.

We read so often of seekers, often deeply troubled, giving up the search. Psychological problems become too much. The search becomes muddied, pointless, and then, just in that moment of failure and surrender there is a breakthrough, an awareness.

This idea that the search itself must end in the disappearance of the seeker is a true one and a confusing one. Intellectually this is not a difficult concept. A non-existent seeker, seeking after that which it already is, is not hard to mentally banish. As long as there is a desired object, however, this is difficult to realize.

Peace of mind is an interesting quarry. It is destroyed in the very seeking. First, you start off with the assumption that you don't have it! This sense of having lost, or worse, having never had peace of mind is troublesome. It is anxiety itself. But it is not, as some would have you believe, the reason for the search.

The search comes from the call of love seeking itself in itself. The call to seek peace of mind, enlightenment, or a cure to psychological problems are usually not sufficient to lead one to awakening. It's true that a search that leads to frustration and an abandonment of the search, or a psychological crisis, may trigger an awakening experience. But it is the seeking after nothing other than the love that is for no other reason than to be near it, to be it, that gives you the *earnestness* necessary.

When we were small, peace of mind could be accomplished by climbing into the arms of a parent or other trusted adult. All we need to do now is to climb into the arms of *what is*. Accepting reality. Not an imposed reality, but a reality we have come to trust. We cannot accept what others say but need to explore our world, our mind, and our heart.

Awakening is not a single act, but a falling in line with what is. You are love loving. To accept that, to live that, is what an enlightened life is all about. You, life, the universe, are all unfolding in this tapestry of Love. Love draws you, not desire for something, even as simple as peace of mind. Seek love only. Only then can the seeker get lost in the search, as the search is the unfolding of love itself.

Teaching with Love and Wisdom

When I started high school, I was looking for the lowest possible common denominator. In my later adolescence, I had briefly been involved in some volunteer work with some great people in nature conservation and caring for wild animals. That fell apart for me however as I drifted into an uncertain puberty. I started high school with an ambition to be an auto mechanic and hide away from society as much as I could.

This all changed in a dramatic way one day, completely by chance, when my U.S. History teacher called in sick. John Curtin, head of the Social Sciences Department and the only teacher of Philosophy at San Rafael High School, came to fill in. Mr. Curtin, not knowing where our regular teacher was in the curriculum, decided to talk philosophy. I had only a brief idea of what philosophy was at that point. My Asperger's, and social ineptitude had placed me up to that point in a lot of remedial English and math classes, so this was a breath of fresh air.

Mr. Curtin talked about Descartes and I was hooked. Not just on Cartesian Doubt, but on Mr. Curtin, philosophy itself. This wonderful, heady feeling that *here* I would find something, here where people actually loved to think. I mean, that's what philosophy means: *to love to think*!

This captivation of mind and heart was the beginning of a love affair that continues to this day.

After the class, I made an appointment with my counselor to see if I could get into Mr. Curtin's Philosophy class for next year, as I had to be a junior or senior to get in.

My counselor was not encouraging as my English grades were low and I needed the teacher's recommendation to take the Philosophy class. The U.S History teacher whose class Mr. Curtin had taken was surprisingly on my side. He astonished me one day when I returned from one of my frequent absences from school. I had written what I considered a pretty average essay on Social Darwinism and apparently, Mr. Abraham liking it more than I, had read it to the class in my absence. He was all for my taking philosophy, showed John Curtin my work and I was in.

John Curtin is responsible for my earliest belief that love and wisdom must accompany each other. My first assignment in the philosophy class was to write an essay on why Socrates was considered a corruptor of youth. I have to admit that after nearly fifty years I am at a loss as to what I wrote regarding Socrates, but I remember what John Curtin wrote on my paper. *"This is one of the most beautiful things I have ever read!"* This is from a man who I idolized. A man who I knew had read many beautiful things. This might have been too much if I had not read on, *"...and some of the worst English I have ever seen."*

John Curtin took his lunch hour every day to help me improve my writing ability. He had me rewrite that essay every day until it was perfect. His love of teaching and love of learning was contagious. I remember being introduced to Bob Dylan, Carl Reiner, and Mel Brooks' 2000 years Old Man and Gregorian Chant in his classroom.

I remember one summer day the class had moved to a small circular seating area outside and the class was all sitting around Mr. Curtin. I was transported in my mind to ancient Greece, and the love of learning and the beauty of that moment has stayed with me. I vowed at that moment that I would be a teacher. I meant then that I wanted to be a secondary school teacher, something that never materialized, but an understanding occurred then that I have always believed; that a teacher needs to transmit love.

A teacher, no matter what is taught, must be a conduit of love in some form. A teacher must convey a love for the subject taught. By love I mean a passion that is visible and felt through the skin. In spirituality this is perhaps doubly important because love is the very subject, the very heart of the teaching. People say they resonate with this or that teacher. This means that they feel that connection that is love. When something in you touches something in me, that is the something that connects us: love. The words of a teacher are important. His pointing is important. But his life, his sharing of his love, is what makes for

149

resonance. A teacher who loves inspires love in you. It is this love that gives the courage to surrender.

A Laughter of the Heart

Nisargadatta Maharaj talked about *earnestness* and *living accordingly* as two of his most important pointers. Abiding in the I Am was his teaching, but this was always followed by earnestness and living accordingly.

Today, with the advancement of the internet, the teachings of the I Am are everywhere. On Facebook, and at Satsangs we have turned the search into a game. It is not a game. It is deadly serious.

The dictionary defines earnestness as 1. serious, zealous, not trifling, ardent 2. seriousness, not joking.

To call the search a game or to make it a game is to turn a serious endeavor into a sport, even a competition. Satsangs have turned into entertainment and the funniest guru becomes the star. Brilliant, rude, and funny gurus are very popular, particularly on Facebook.

I am not saying that the search cannot be fun at times. Life can be a hoot as it is. A good joke is a good joke. I do not take any position regarding the sacred or profane, but I as well as Nisargadatta, see *earnestness* and *living accordingly* as the prerequisites to investigating the I Am.

Not trifling, not joking. This does not mean no fun, no humor. But it does mean more than fun, more than humor. It is no doubt wonderful to go to a Satsang and find laughing good natured people, but does that carry over into your life? Does that prepare you to hold the hand of a dying spouse or child and give comfort? Does it open you to your brother's needs? Many Satsang goers, and I would speculate teachers as well, are seeking peace of mind or the ultimate (whatever the mind imagines that is). Some idea or better understanding (education) is also often sought. In my opinion, these are all trivial reasons to search.

The only reason to search is if there is a call. Not some holy or religious call, but a call to be present with the dying spouse or child. Not to understand, but to be truly present: hand in hand as one. This

151

call is also what allows you to understand the need of others and love them without having to like them.

While we may ask, "Death where is thy sting?" regarding ourselves, losing a loved one is a different story and some laughing jackass of a guru is not going to make that pain vanish by telling you to seek *who is lonely* and that *they are not the body*. Non-duality has to be a part of life as lived, part of a life that recognizes and accepts the reality of life, pain, and all.

The clouds are beautiful, the sun rises every day, and your loved ones die. We need a teacher who can help us see a fresher cloud, a simpler sun, and hold our hand in grief. This requires seriousness, earnestness. Laughter will return, grief will lessen, but only if we *accept its reality*.

We cannot do this by making life a game, no matter how clever or humorous. When we realize that love is not a game, and we accept that grief and pain are part of love, then we can enjoy serious laughter. A laughter of the heart.

Just Think About Something:
A Good Friday Meditation

When I was a small boy, every Good Friday I was always made to stay inside during the three hours. From noon until three o'clock I was obliged to refrain from play and do something quite like draw or color. As I got to be a bit older, maybe around eight or so, I was expected to think about what Good Friday meant during those hours. As Presbyterians, we were not obligated to attend church, but my mother always saw to it that my brother and I were properly respectful during that period.

I guess at about eight or so when I was required to "think", I asked my mother what I should think about. Should I think about Jesus dying on the cross? Should I think about Jesus's life?

Should I think about the coming Easter joy? My mother, not being particularly religious, despite being the daughter of a United Brethren Minister, did not know what to reply. So she said, "Just think about something."

I have to admit that this tradition continues today. Good Friday does not pass that I don't spend at least three hours in meditation about the crucifixion. Now, as a non-dualist, my meditations and thinking are much more centered on the eternal meaning of this horrific event.

I have mentioned previously in my writing somewhere an event that changed my view of the crucifixion. At thirty-three while meditating in a small closet in the dark, I was suddenly presented with a close-up view of Christ on the cross. This was no glorious depiction like some medieval or renaissance sculpture or painting, but a real man hanging, bleeding on a piece of wood. Blood and dirt were everywhere. Excruciating pain was on the face, and horror was in my heart. I was there, at the foot of the cross, experiencing this straightforward example of earnestness.

In the years following my encounter with Ramakrishna's teachings and those of Ramana Maharshi, my sense of time drifted away. I was able to see that past, present, and future are all happening at once.

Any past event is appearing in the *now* that contains all there is. It is past only in appearance as thought, but in reality, happening in this moment of *now*. I am standing at the foot of the cross. Christ is being crucified now. This example of earnestness is in my experience, not unlike my vision of years earlier.

We study scripture, Christian, Hindu, Advaitin, non-dualist, and we are not reading the words of dead teachers or saints from the past, but the continuing emanations of those who wrote and taught. Ever widening, as the expanding waves caused by a single pebble tossed into a stream, the thoughts, actions, and words are unfolding *out of time in the now.*

Jesus on the cross was confirming this time happening at once principle when he began praying the twenty-second psalm, *"My God, My God, why hast thou forsaken me?"* This psalm, this predictor of the event he was now experiencing, and Christ's praying this psalm brings together *past and present* in a way that *opened* for Christ the reality of the future resurrection. Christ lived in the *now* which contains *past, present, and future.*

Christ knew the past was not separate from his life, but appeared as the past in the present moment. He was also able to see that the future is also in the present moment. The awakening that is sought, this resurrection of that which we are, has always been and will always be; it is here *now* in this present moment.

Whether you are a Christian or a Non-dualist (if you perceive a difference), this Good Friday meditate on this understanding of the *now* containing all appearances, past, present, and future. Allow yourself to be drawn into this mystery. Die in *earnestness* along with the Christ, and be resurrected into Christ Consciousness. Your past appears to contain your birth. Your present appears to contain your struggle. Your future appears to promise to awaken. Live them all at once. The promise is fulfilled. *"It is finished!"*

Think about this, or to quote my mother, *"Just think about something."*

And We Are All Love!

Well, Holy Week and Easter Sunday are over for this year. After Thursday, I kept silent on Facebook as I watched friends and strangers alike make light or even laugh at the principal feast of Christianity. Easter baskets, jelly beans, and chocolate bunnies were paraded out as symbols of the beliefs of a train wreck church. Even one friend stated, *"To 99.8 percent of Christians the Easter story is about transcending the fear of utter extinction at death,"* as if he knew the hearts and minds of 99.8 percent of Christians!

But it is okay in intellectual circles to trash Christianity, even at its holiest season. Sure, there were the notes about how the death, crucifixion and resurrection of Christ are symbols of higher spiritual truths. But the events are dismissed as myths. Jesus does appear to have been a historical person, having been mentioned in more than the Bible alone, and crucifixion was the means of death during Jesus' time and many years earlier. These are facts. And indeed, they were and are symbols, just as you and I are symbols of a spirit in action.

Somehow it has become smart to refute Christianity. How clever we are to see through such a tissue-thin religion. The church may have turned the teachings of Christ into a train wreck, but yet tradition has bought us St. John of the Cross, Terese of Avilla, Thomas Merton, and Bede Griffiths. The same people who will refute an actual virgin birth or resurrection will happily talk of blue-light experiences or past lives. We read of karma, gunas, shaktipat gurus as if these are somehow more acceptable to modern brains than incarnation or resurrection. These are *all just words and ideas*. To choose between them is to live in separation.

Somehow, to some people, a pilgrimage to Arunachala or Tiruvannamalai is superior to a pilgrimage to Bethlehem or Jerusalem. Some even worship Arunachala. But we must not worship Christ. Holy sites are only holy in our minds. To separate one from the other as superior is dualism. I can worship a tree, a mountain, or a picture of Ramana or Christ. It is the same.

I don't think it is proper to demean or even make light of another's beliefs, ideas or religion. To do so during that person's holiest of festivals is clearly unwarranted and unwelcome. I am not a believer in anything. I experience the reality firsthand. The truth has *nothing and everything* to do with all the different belief systems and spiritual practices. A Christian can find the truth in their religion, just as well as a non-dualist can. You can get just as hung up with blue light experiences and there is no seeker or doer, as you can on virgin births and the resurrection. The next time you feel drawn to make light of another's faith or you want to clean up their belief system in your terms, it would be good to remember that we are all right, we are all wrong, and we are all love!

Non-Duality and the Other

Our words, our minds see love as something that happens between two persons, things, or objects. The mind interprets love as a connection, a desire, a longing, a need, but the mind insists on another for completion. We love a friend. We love our spouse or life partner. We love God. We love the forest. We love the thought of love. It is always us and the other. This is how the mind conceives love. But this is not what love is or how it works.

Love, in its essence, is all there is. In John's first letter in the New Testament John writes, *"God is love, and he who abides in love, abides in God, and God abides in him."* A bit later, a few verses down, John writes, *"We love, because he first loved us."* I have always loved this *"God is love"*. He doesn't say, God is like love, or God is similar to love, but God *is* love. This is very plain: God *is* love and love *is* God. It is a way of expressing that love is all that the mind can comprehend.

When awakening happens there is the wordless conviction that there is only love. The "I" thought vanishes, as does the "other", leaving only the essence, the love. The creative energy that is love is so dynamic that its unfolding creates *expression*. We and God are not expressions of something, we are *expression* itself. The mind does not understand expression without an object to express or be expressed. This is also true of love. The mind does not understand love without a lover and a loved one, so it conceives (thoughts) the expression between the two. The mind, rather than being an object in reality, is simply made of these thoughts. These thoughts are simply expressions suspended in time, labeled as we see fit, and projected outward.

"God is a concept by which we measure our pain", wrote John Lennon many years ago. This has become a popular idea in modern spiritual circles, particularly Neo-Advaita, or popular non-dualism. We create God in our own image. This is true, but "God" is an expression of love, is love. *"...he who abides in love abides in God, and God abides in him."* To abide in love means to be the expression

157

of love, or so the mind would put it. But you are not the expression of anything, you are *expression itself.* To be expression or to be love is not something the mind can wrap itself around so it conceives objects to be expressions.

This is why it is necessary to silence the mind, this *bag of thoughts* we take as us. It not only wants silencing, but annihilation! When this occurs, we no longer need to conceive ourselves as expressions of love but as expression itself. We no longer need to love God, but simply to *be.* This is not something that can be expressed in words or thought, but only by *being.* We are *being,* we are *isness,* we are love. Once this is realized (wordlessly understood), we can use our bag of thoughts as our servant rather than our master. We can answer hunger, safety, our work, and any number of human functions without disturbing the peace of being.

We can love a God, or a guru, realizing that these are expressions in the mind of expression itself. We can love ourselves as expression: the unfolding of love. As Ramana Maharshi loved his holy mountain as wordless expression, as a Christian loves Christ as expression, as Christ himself loved and trusted God as expression, we can answer the question of *who* is the *you* in "*You were there.*" It is love expressing itself, in itself. It is one!

Keystrokes of Ego, Keystrokes of Love: Spirituality on Facebook

I have written a good deal about how a word or idea written even centuries ago is not an old idea from the past, but a continuing vibration set in motion in the now. I have also put forth the idea that both past and future are part of the *now experience*, having no independent reality.

This means that any text or book we read, even if written by some person long dead, is written for the reader right now. Any impression, insight, or awakening that happens is a result of this widening vibration. The potential that is love is constant and the inspiration that causes the writer to write also causes the reader to read. This all happens at once, time not being a factor.

It is very exciting to know that I pick up the Bible, the Gita, or the Upanishad, and that I am reading new words discovered right now. An idea or set of words may have been around for centuries, but my reading of it is new. Not just new in that I am just discovering it, but new in its passing through the potential that I Am. A tree drops a seed on the ground and there is potential for a new tree. The wind or a bird may move that potential (seed) far afield resulting in a different growth pattern, perhaps a hybrid species. We never know the effect or results of our words or thoughts. Once written they take on a life of their own.

This is something to consider when using social media like Facebook. As much as many of us trivialize what is said online, it starts vibrations that are part of the potential. Communication online is real communication even if it is not face-to-face. I live in a little farmhouse in the Hatch Valley of New Mexico, yet I can communicate with people all over the world. Sure, the communication is different face to face, but no more or less real. People are affected by what I write. I would be naïve to think otherwise. I would love to travel and meet you all face to face, but I do not have that luxury.

In some respects, this online communication is more real than a face-to-face meeting. You don't have to see how old or young I am. You don't have to note that I am almost bald. You don't have to make judgments on my size, mannerism, or if I look spiritual or not. You just experience the vibration of the words. Not my words even, but words given by spirit to spirit. If we have to meet face-to-face in order to communicate, we are requiring a body, something that we are not.

Facebook can be very irritating at times. To really be involved in it requires the reading of notes that maybe you would rather not read. There are people, even in the spiritual community who like to use Facebook to play games and show off their great wit. They claim that what they write should not be taken seriously, but the words and thoughts set up vibrations that the receiver (reader) interprets with the equipment they have at hand. Just as I may read a message in a spiritual book that the writer intended to mean one thing, I may take it as another. So it is with the internet. A Cynical joke suggesting that one should throw oneself in front of a bus may seem harmless to the joker, but an unknown receiver may be taken literally.

If we in the Facebook spiritual community want to convey the truth of spirit, we need to convey nothing but love. Sarcastic, dark humor does not convey love. Cynicism does not convey love. Sarcasm and cynicism are part of ego and one-ups-man-ship. Sure, no one likes to read bliss bunny stuff. Like it or not, spiritual or not, we live in a world of transitory pain and apparent death. No one says to clean it up but to accept it with bitter tears that themselves become transitory. We, who are older, realize that death is the uninvited guy who waits outside the door, not only for us but for the ones we have been given to love. This is why we must convey nothing but love.

My being a teacher and being on Facebook is a relatively new experience for me, as well as my readers. I have been on Facebook for only a short time and have only a small number of readers, but I love every one of them. I will not play with you. I write about love, nothing else. There is no other thing worth writing about. Indeed, there is no other thing. If you write a spiritual status or notes and you are playing with people, being cynical or sarcastic, you are flaunting your ego, not loving. Loving requires the gentleness or exuberance of a child. Loving requires the humility of a child, a humility to be honest and straightforward, even mistaken once in a while. In using words, we open ourselves to error and deception, for truth lies only in silence.

But we must not think what we write is harmless. Those of us who understand the bullies that haunt the internet, the hurt and even suicides that result, understand that to write anything unloving, anything that makes fun of what some hold as sacred is to embark on very shaky ground. To be clever is to live in ego. To be gentle as a child is to live in love.

Nothingness, the Unexplainable, Reality and "Oh give me a break!"

So many are actually actively seeking nothingness that one begins to wonder what is the attraction. We seek to go beyond words and thoughts and envision nothingness as a higher state. We seek escape from the tyranny of words and thoughts, only to exchange it for the tyranny of nothingness. For we forget that nothingness is also a word, a thought. Nothingness is a mind creation, as is Nirguna Brahman, or is-ness or any of the words and ideas we have about the unexplainable.

The unexplainable is just that, unexplainable. Silence is a word we know. Contemplation is a word we know. Reality is a word we know. What *is*, we cannot know, we can only *be*. This is frightening because we want to know. Some will joyously exclaim, "I know nothing", and then proceed to tell you all about it. Of course, they will tell how they have examined all they have believed themselves to be and found nothing of substance. They may even write a book about it. A book about nothing. Give me a break!

I hold a leaf in my hand and see oneness. If I imagine no separation, oneness appears, but it is an imagination of my concept of no separation. Oneness is a concept. Non-duality is a concept requiring the duality of non-duality vs. duality. If I take your hand and tell you I love you, I can imagine us and love. But this is in contrast to alone and indifference, all of which belong to imagination. So what is *real*?

Reality is one of the great concepts that is often ignored. In the non-dual community, we engage in viveka, discrimination. Reality is discriminated from illusion. Illusion is to be ignored or eliminated, so reality will shine forth. We pick and choose one over the other. Yet, we claim all is one. Give me a break!

We will sit in silence attempting to meditate. We engage in contemplation, gently moving thoughts away from our consciousness. We see thoughts as distractions from the thought of silence, and our concept of what silence is. When we achieve silence in our terms or open to a nothingness in our terms, we feel we have made it. We have simply traded one concept or another. Give me a break!

I can experience sadness, and proclaim that it is a ripple in the sea of perfection. I can claim that life is perfect, its imperfections being only illusions. But what is perfection? Is it more *real* a concept than sadness?

Before I get lost in these paradoxes (really dualistic!), let me get to my point. Life is here. We do not know what it is, but we appear to be in it. We can only *be it* by being ourselves. Some of us are pulled by what we are to examine. Most of us who are in the non-dual community, understand Plato's view that "The unexamined life is not worth living". So we examine. But if we take positions of real vs. illusion, or guna vs. nirguna, we are not practicing Advaita, we are refining dualism into new concepts. Give me a break!

We can only live life as it is: paradoxical, confusing, and nebulous. We all understand love or some distorted concept of it. This is not an understanding that is in concepts but in the very heart of things. Our only hope is in flowing along with life as it unfolds before us. Resistance is effort, knowledge, ego. To hold a leaf without judgment, in love without understanding, to say "I love you" with every movement, finding our way as we go, yes, sometimes with *fear and trembling*, is all we have, all there is. Real and illusion, I am that!

Asperger's, Earnestness, and Freedom

I have to give an amount of credit to the fact that I was born with Asperger's Syndrome, that I have been able to be true to my conscience most of my life. It has been an obsession of mine since I was a small boy to follow that which I have perceived to be right, no matter the cost to me personally.

If one has to have an obsession, and most Asperger's people do, I am grateful that mine has been to follow the call of the spirit. I try to keep this in mind when I write about spiritual practice and the spiritual life. I know that I am often somewhat absolutist about living out the teaching of non-duality, but it is the only way I have been given to do it. I know that some teachers find my insistence on not taking money or asking for donations to be an extreme position. I understand their points but have to follow my instincts.

This inability to put the spirit in second place has led both my partner and myself to live very lightly on the ground. We have moved from job to job, home to home, so many times I have lost count. Over a period of forty years or so, we have had maybe thirty-five jobs. Our work has almost always been live-in work, whether managing apartments or working with the developmentally disabled, so we have had to pull up stakes continually. This has given us, over the years, a great sense of freedom, as being broke and homeless no longer has any real fear to it.

Just before we went to England to begin the religious community we founded there, I had a very trying experience with the Episcopal Church in San Francisco that almost soured me on the Church altogether.

After reading *The Cloud of Unknowing* and returning to the Church, I started to attend daily Mass at Grace Cathedral in San Francisco. Once I became known to the clergy there, and they became aware of my maintenance abilities, I was asked to become the Cathedral's first full-time maintenance man. I loved that position. I was able to attend Mass and then go and work on my beloved building. My life became very integrated. My shop was directly below the choir and every morning I could hear the boys from the Cathedral School sing their morning service. My life as a monk had its foundation here, and for a couple of years, I lived in heaven.

This part of my life coincided with the coming of the Reagan administration and the homeless problem his policies brought to the cities of America. The Episcopal Church of California responded to the homeless crises by establishing shelters in a number of churches in San Francisco. Grace Cathedral was one of the churches that participated. The homeless were allowed to sleep in the crypt of the cathedral overnight, and in the morning, sandwiches were handed out as they left for the day. My partner and I were volunteers at the shelter and would hand out the sandwiches before Mass every morning.

Being on San Francisco's Nob Hill, this attraction of the homeless to Grace Cathedral did not go down very well with the wealthy residents of the area. This led to the homeless having to be asked to leave the cathedral as soon as possible after getting their breakfast. When it was found that the homeless would often stay around the cathedral, sometimes even sitting in the sanctuary, the cathedral hired armed guards to send them off. This seemed to me to defeat the purpose of offering shelter, and I was very offended by it. Being who I am, I was very outspoken about it and confronted the clergy about it, to their embarrassment.

One morning, while I was passing through the sanctuary checking lights, I noticed a homeless man sleeping in one of the side pews, completely out of sight. He was very quiet, so even though the Cathedral School was about to have its service, I did not disturb him. Just as the boys had started their service, and as I was returning, I heard a deathly shriek and saw the homeless man who had been sleeping in the pew limp to the center of the sanctuary and kneel at the main altar, pursued by two large armed guards.

The guards grabbed the man and twisted his arm behind his back so that he let out a cry that rang through the cathedral. The boys were aghast, and I ran to the front of the sanctuary and confronted the guards. I told them that it was God's house and that they were to get out of it now! To my amazement and relief, they did as I asked.

The following day I was called to the office of the Dean and fired. I could not believe it. I appealed to the bishop who I knew quite well, also having been employed at the Diocesan House, but he said he had no control over the cathedral affairs. I was allowed to continue to work for the bishop, but my cathedral days were over.

My faith in the caring and integrity of the Church was greatly diminished, and my heart was badly broken. It was a sad moment, but my faith in God, in spirit, continued, and was freed from the confines of the established church. This allowed my partner and I to begin our community with an eye only on the spirit, not concerned about how we would fit in.

This is why I advise everyone to free themselves of things that bind. It is so important to be really free. Following the spirit where it leads you may cost you everything you believe is your life. But to follow the spirit must *be your life*. Every moment, every movement must be for the sake of love. While I have to admit, that Asperger's helps me stay the course, and you might find it more difficult, it is the most important thing. It is the *earnestness* Nisargadatta Maharaj spoke of. It is the light in the eyes and the smile of Ramana Maharshi. It is what you are. To be it, is freedom itself.

*As a footnote, I would like to say that a few years ago, the Dean of Grace Cathedral (not the one who fired me!) apologized to me for the above incident, for which I am very grateful.

Getting Off Your Spiritual Backside

Secretly fearing we will
know the "answer"
only in death
we talk and talk
of knowing the unknowable
explaining the unexplainable
instead of living and loving
That which we are,
have always been,
and will always be.

Yesterday I listened to a young spiritual teacher on the internet radio speaking on Advaita. Later I listened to a well-known teacher with a large following and a huge Sanga. He was asked about how to respond to life under a government he disapproved of and found went against his spiritual principles. The teacher went on and on with more non-dual parroting and an admonition that one should never resort to anger, but see it all as a reflection of yourself.

After the disappointment of those two, I encountered a picture and article of the Dalai Lama wearing a USC baseball cap while justifying the killing of Osama Bin Laden. It occurred to me to get out of this spiritual teaching thing altogether if this was the kind of bedfellow I was to be associated with.

When I see spiritual teachers, especially those who either simply parrot what they have read or claim some special method exclusive to their teaching, I don't doubt why so many quickly build up a distrust of teachers of any sort. These teachers will tell you that you are already awareness and that you should just sit quietly every day and realize this. They will smile and act blissful, and have a big donation button on their website. Having a donation button on your website is a way of saying, "My words are so important that you are going to want to send me money to carry on my valuable work." It is sad. It is silly. And it is a slap in the face to those who live only for this.

As one who recognizes the Christ as one of the greatest non-dual teachers, I have a different view of non-dual teaching. I will not tell you to sit quietly with a blissful smile on your face, or that you are already enlightened. I will tell you to get off your spiritual backside, take up your cross and work out your enlightenment. This is the reason I have so few students as no one wants to hear there is "something to do," instead of "By golly, there is no doer, there's nothing to be done," and "You are already where you want to be."

These are the statements of parrots, not those who have struggled the roads of life with fear and trembling. Nisargadatta Maharaj said that it takes great effort to come to the conclusion that effort is not necessary. Nisargadatta emphasized earnestness. Christ demonstrated earnestness on the cross. If devotees had not looked after him, Ramana Maharshi might have died in his youthful earnestness, sitting in silence as insects ate at his living flesh.

For this is what earnestness is all about: a single-minded effort. Doing something, even if that something is to die in devotion. In the New Testament, a man described as rich came to Jesus to ask how he might find everlasting life. After telling the man to follow the commandments, which the man claimed he had, Jesus said he should sell all he had, give to the poor, and follow him. The story goes on to say that the man went away sad because he had great possessions. This is also a problem today.

Today, especially in the West, many have great possessions. We have not only material wealth, but many possess intellectual, educational wealth. We cling to our cars and our homes, and our little luxuries like flavored coffees and a nice meal out. We wear our education like a badge of who we are. We excuse our little luxuries as things that help us cope. Those who tell us we have to do something or question our indulgences are quickly discarded for the bliss bunny teachers who assure us that we are already *that*.

You are already that. You are already perfect, whatever that means. But you won't realize it until you have walked your life and carried your cross. Intellectualizing *that*, is an exercise in imagination, nothing more. If you sit before a teacher who softens the blows and tells you that you do not have to stand up to injustice or take any contrary or politically incorrect positions, then you will find yourself sitting smiling like a zombie before a liar who has more interest in your money than your soul.

"Before enlightenment, chop wood, carry water. After enlightenment, chop wood, carry water." This is a well-known Zen saying. What the hell do you think it means? It means life is living. The enlightened work. They don't live some rarified existence where they become entitled to donations simply for existing and sharing a message they don't understand outside their mind. A monk may have his begging bowl, but most teachers are not monks and live lifestyles that most in the world would consider luxury if not opulence. My situation requires me to eat beans every day and struggle during the winter to get firewood for heat. But when I think of my brothers and sisters in the third world, I thank God for the wonderful blessings of a full bowl and a twig to burn.

Gratitude becomes so much more of a blessing when it comes from simple pleasures. A beautiful tree or the warmth of the sun becomes so much more important than a movie or a concert. Yes, there may be no doer, but there is doing. If you are not doing, living on trust and love alone, you will not find enlightenment, awakening, or whatever you call it. You will just dance around the edges of life, ever trying to find an intellectual vision of bliss that won't cost you anything. You will want to make enlightenment your most prized possession.

I can't think my teaching will have many takers or followers if you will, for many will walk away sadly because they have many possessions. Nisargadatta Maharaj said that only one in ten million will get this. Only when you are ready to walk away from all you believe yourself to be, all you possess, can the door open and freedom be found. Only through effort can effort be cast aside. Fear vanishes for good when you stand naked, asking nothing, giving all.

No-Duality, the Mind, and Potato Salad

This morning, I made potato salad. The mind was very helpful in this endeavor. It measured potatoes, onions, dill pickles, and all the rest of the things that went to make the salad. It did not fight me at all. I watched as it boiled and stirred ingredients using this body, that I also watched. A great team: the mind the body and I.

In non-duality, there is a tendency to label the mind as an enemy, a usurper. Many non-dualists would rather spend time in a state of imagined silence than live with this "enemy of the one".

I say imagined silence because in the actual state of silence, nothing is experienced, nothing is remembered. If we remember being in silence, we were in imagined silence. If we remember an experience, we remember a thought we have of an experience. We do not know silence, we can only have an understanding of it.

The difference between knowing and understanding is in the realm of what I call *nebulous clarity*. Knowing is always knowledge-based, something in the mind. If we can explain it, describe it in detail to ourselves or others, it lives in the world of knowledge which is in the mind, the mistrusted enemy of the non-dualist.

Understanding is intuitive. It requires no explanation or experience. It just is. It is the unknowing talked about in the *Cloud of Unknowing*. In unknowing, we act, we love, we live, without knowledge, without memory. For unknowing happens only in the present moment. It is not only intuitive but freshly born. Brand new like a baby. It is outside the mind, outside of memory.

This is really the point. The mind is simply another concept that is built totally out of what we call memories. These memories are impressions, thoughts, and conditioning. This can happen in an instant, as time itself lives only in the mind. This is why intuition is the real deal, as it does not depend on knowledge *suspended in time* for its reality. It just is. It is outside of time, outside of memory.

As in the making of the potato salad, the mind is not an enemy. It lives in consciousness as does the body, also not an enemy, even though it can be a burden sometimes. The mind is like a monkey. Wonderful to watch it move and behave in fascinating, even hilarious ways. But a monkey in the house or anywhere it does not belong can be a disaster. The mind in spirituality is very useful for getting to the door, but it does not have the key.

The key, easily enough, is in the *sacrifice* of the mind. This is why I have written elsewhere that the understanding that the substance of the Holy Eucharist actually becomes the body and blood is based on intuition. The mind rebels, but must be sacrificed. The *oneness* of Christ, participants, and elements of the Eucharist are realized by this sacrifice of the mind. Just as in the Holy Eucharist, which is of course a ritual practice devoted to the celebration of oneness, life itself becomes one when we live in the intuitive unknowing that is always with us, fresh every moment.

When driving a car, mending a sock or fuse, or making potato salad, the mind is very useful. The mind is not unspiritual either, as it arises in consciousness like everything else. But as non-dualists, we want to live in Advaita in its truest meaning. There are not two. What we write, what we say are necessarily dual, for words are mind-stuff, thoughts are mind-stuff. Even silence as we know it, is mind-stuff. If I would teach you, I must do it by *being* only. If you sense my love, my *meaning*, it must be by unknowing and entering the acceptance of nebulous clarity.

This is a sacrifice of the mind, our useful friend, part of the team that makes us human. So it is a *real* sacrifice.

This is what acceptance and sacrifice are all about. It is not about making efforts or not making efforts. It is not about rejecting the useful mind but realizing its limits. Living with thoughts and the mind involves acceptance that we cannot kill an active mind, and must watch its antics like those of the monkey. Sacrificing the mind means seeing its limitations and being willing to go beyond them into nebulous clarity, that place of understanding without knowledge or explanation. That place where compassion becomes more important than our *selves*. That place where the other vanishes along with us.

171

Timelessness: Living in Awe

Recently I have been trying to remember when I first lost the sense of the concept of time. I know when I read Ramana Maharshi, Nisargadatta Maharaj, and other teachers of Advaita, they disregarded the concept of time. But I know my understanding in this regard goes back further than that.

I know this because when I was still in the Church at Lincoln Cathedral, I used to hope for a chance to do a sermon, and that sermon was going to be about time. It seems like I have understood that time is a concept all along, but probably not. It is very funny to me that I can't remember, as remembering and time are intimately linked in the mind.

My sermon was going to be about the absence of time as a concept, and how the crucifixion of Christ occurs outside of time and is an event in the now. I have no idea how those ideas got into my mind at that time, as this was before my Advaita days.

Perhaps the concept of time is one of the most persistent and insidious to the spiritual seeker, as we are so used to living in a linear mindset. Time is the concept by which we organize thought. The story of our lives is told by the progression from childhood to young adult, to older adult, and eventually elderly person. Words like *progression* and eventually themselves are created to expound on this concept of time.

We wake in the morning, and as soon as the sense of "I Am arises, we see a new day, but experience ourselves as a progression of the same life and we are one day older. We watch the body age, and at some point, resolve to the fact that eventually, it will die.

The concept of time is the culprit here. Not that our bodies don't change. On the relative level bodies age, get hurt, and die. These vehicles we take as our own are only a limited dream vehicle that wears out and runs out. They are held tightly in the grip of the concept of time. What is born in time, ages, and dies in time. But what we *are* is beyond time.

Past, present, and future all appear in the moment. The concept of *now* contains all three. The moment we recognize the moment, it is gone. The now is not an experience that we can recognize, for by the time it is re-cognized, it is a past event in memory. Those who say to "live in the now" are simply trading one concept (past, future) for the concept of *the now*. Everything happens at once. The concepts of past, present, and future arise simultaneously in the mind, and the mind uses the concept of time to sort them out. As you read this, you are reading it *as I write it*. We are together at this moment, reading and writing as one. My writing and your reading are one movement in awareness, not two. If we always look at life as one piece, without parts, we can see this clearly.

It's the *separation* that is an illusion, not the objects. The objects are expressions of the oneness playing with itself. There is loving, seeking, awareness, without a lover or loved, seeker and sought, or aware or unaware persons. The objects come and go, but not in time. Time is only useful in the relative, and needs to be the first concept to go.

We are timeless. The child, adult, and elderly categories are all just swimming in the concept of time. You may notice that many who we call enlightened live in that first categorization: the child. No matter how old we may be physically, living without time acknowledges that we are timeless. The vehicle we inhabit may age to our amusement, sometimes painfully. But being forever the simplicity and awe of the child is what we find. Life is awesome. When we experience nothing but awe, without words, we experience wonder. Once we grab it, conceptualize it, *bring it into time*, it is turned into a concept. Becoming as a little child, as Christ insisted was the only way into the kingdom of heaven, means to live outside of time.

Understanding that we are timeless, even as the body fades and dies is an experience of fascination and exhilaration. Life as it is unfolding, timelessly and with perfection is only available without concepts, particularly without the concept of time.

The Memory Child and the Kingdom of Heaven

I remember very distinctly when I was about twelve years old, saying to myself that I was going to be sure when I grew up to recall what it was like when I was a child. Of course, I did not.

As I approached adolescence, I felt a strong sense of nostalgia for my childhood, even though still being in it. This was the 1950s, and in those days, a child was still a child at twelve. I loved being a kid. As a big kid, I was already getting those looks from older adults who suspected I was a budding juvenile delinquent, and this made me feel creepy.

I could see that adults were lost in a world of worries and concerns that not only troubled them but created a gap between themselves and children. I could also see that this did not bother them, this separation. I could not understand this. I was aware, even then, that the bible held children in great respect. Jesus said children should be allowed to come to him, and that those who were like children were the first in the kingdom of heaven. So why did the grown ones look at us as silly?

As I grew older as a teenager, youth, young adult (all the labels we endure until the day we are officially adults), I grew more distant from the promise I had made to recall my childhood. When I was eighteen, I became a Nursery Sunday School Teacher at my local Presbyterian Church. I had a class of three-year-olds and the teaching of Christianity took on a particular importance, even though I was an agnostic at the time. I found, however, that the person who was learning the most was me. Each Sunday the three-year-olds would take me by the hand and remind me, not only who I had been, but who I was.

As I have mentioned before, I made a habit of watching Mr. Rogers' Neighborhood well into my fifties. For those who do not know that show, Mr. Rogers was a Presbyterian Minister who had a show for very young children. Every day he would talk about things that mattered to his audience, their fears, their joys, their anger, separation from parents, and all manner of things we forget as adults. The show became a quiet meditation for me. It reminded me what childhood is like, not a remembered childhood, but the childhood that lives inside me now.

When we read a biblical passage like "to such as these (children) belongs the kingdom of heaven," we are inclined to think of our own childhood. We nostalgically remember feelings and events of past days. Some of these remembrances may be painful, even tragic. We may think, "I'm glad that's over," or "I remember being so free, but of course, I had no responsibilities then."

But this is indulging in memory, nostalgia, or whatever you may call it. It is not a real experience. On a psychological level, it is colored by all that has happened since, and judged by the adult mind, so that it takes on an entirely different meaning than it did to the child that was experiencing it. On the spiritual level, a similar thing takes place. We tend to glorify the childlike state as an innocence and blissfulness that never existed outside of our imagination. The innocent child we remember is just that, a memory child. A construct of the mind.

To be born again (a Christian term I dislike for its misuse) is not to return to the memory child, but to become really childlike in a fresh way. To awaken in non-dual terms is just this, to become aware of life in its freshness, its freedom, its potential. Awakening is really no more than this. To *become like children* is not to resurrect a memory of childhood, either pleasant or unpleasant, but to begin to discover life as fresh and new every day. To see a bird, as if it were the first you had ever seen, without names for the colors, feathers, or even the word bird. Just a magical, flying wonder. To see the grass wave in the wind like the sea, only without the ideas of sea or wind or grass. This is the attitude that sees the kingdom of heaven, that lives there and has it as its inheritance.

When I look at it now, I may not have remembered what it was like to be a child, but my promise to myself has been kept. Each day in the silent sunrise. tears of joy well up, not from a remembered childhood, but in the experience of the awakened now. The child lives, not the memory child. He grew and became a man, just as he should have. The child that lives is the child I am, reawakened from the dust of memory. Resurrected from the tomb of the mind, into the kingdom of heaven.

A Non-Dual Perspective on Morality

When I was a boy, cowboy stars like Gene Autry were the ones the set the morality for us as we grew up. Gene's theme song was *Back in the Saddle Again.* One of the lines in this song was that only the law is right. In those days, we had no trouble knowing what was meant by "the only law is right."

Gene was the good guy, the guy with the white hat. The bad guys wore black hats and did wrong. Judgments of right and wrong were easy to make. Our parents told us what was right and wrong. We learned the difference in Sunday School, in the classroom, and from our heroes on television. No problem!

As I grew up, and slowly came to the realization that I was *different, gay,* I had to look at this right and wrong thing more closely. Things stopped being black and white, and informed choices had to be made. The church had taught me one thing, but I was discovering another. I was not willing to simply chuck the church but was desperately interested in seeing how I would fit in.

Today, in the understanding of non-duality, many are saying that there is no "good" or "bad", no "right" or "wrong", these being opposite poles in the mind, and judgments or preferences.

In the absolute sense, this is true. Life unfolds in a perfect way, all in one piece. But we live in a relative world, and no matter how spiritual we may be, only the truly awakened can trust their intuition to guide them in this area of right and wrong.

Most folks today believe, at least loosely, in the Ten Commandments as good guidelines. Thou shalt not kill, Thou shalt not steal, etc. are pretty universal laws, and help keep society functional. When it comes to the more politically, and socially correct mandates, the judgments become more cloudy. Where can the non-dualist look for guidance, without simply throwing the baby out with the bathwater? Sure, we can say there is no right and wrong. Judgments are dualistic and one thing is as good as the other.

These indeed, are often the excuses used by some non-dual teachers for any manner of indiscretions. Adultery, child abuse, even attempted murder are excused away by saying there is no right or wrong; the observer is projecting, seeing the shadow or any number of rationalizations. Yet, inherently, intuitively we know that cheating or taking advantage of someone weaker is not right. How do we know this? By understanding that these things run counter to oneness.

At the Last Supper of Christ, in addition to the Churches' belief that the Eucharist was established there, Christ makes some very profound and non-dual statements: *"That they all may be one; as thou, Father, art in me, and I in thee, that they also may be one in us: that the world may believe that thou hast sent me."* This was the Christ's prayer to the Father, *"that they all may be one."* Oneness is what we want for all, as it is the natural state. Christ, at that supper, also instituted the eleventh commandment, one that shows how we are all one. *"A new commandment I give unto you, That ye love one another, as I have loved you, that ye also love one another."* Oneness is prayer. Love is the method of realizing the prayer.

As I was seeking to find my kind of love in Christ's words, an acceptance of my special brand of love, these were the words I used to judge: oneness and love. Is there oneness and love in it? Being gay lost all its problems, all its sting. I have always used this criterion for right and wrong ever since. Clearly, there is no love in adultery or child abuse. No matter the rationalizations non-dualists or non-dualist gurus use for their misconduct, oneness, and love are what we seek, are, and have as our guide. Oneness and love are not two, but one. Unconditional love is The One. Unconditional Love is the right, the perfect we talk of in "*Life is perfect.*"

All that separates, divides, or distorts universal love is not one, but *self*-ishness, whether an expression of fear, desire, or envy. The One is the Universal Law: the truth itself. While ultimately, absolutely there is no division, this law of truth, this law of one love allows us to sing along with Gene Autry the only law is right.

Living Out Non-Duality: Do We Have a Choice?

I spent most of the first fifty years of my life as a Christian believer, with the exception of a dozen years or so in early adulthood as an agnostic. Even during those agnostic years, I read and searched everything from spiritualism to channeled entities. Today I live out unicity as best I can and see no separation between this body and this world.

Upon awakening to the one reality, and after a period of ten years, I attempted to write about my findings. Having been asked to write the rule for the religious community I was a part of by the Dean of Lincoln Cathedral fifteen years earlier, I decided to put my findings into the context of that rule. I would attempt to see if this understanding that came to me in an instant of awakening, could be understood in this rule that I had solemnly made vows to follow so many years earlier. The result was *Community of One – The Journey Beyond Christianity*. While, unfortunately, this book has never seen print, it was a chance to see if I had remained *true* to both the rule and this *awakened* understanding.

This was an arduous task. I was working at a HUD property for the elderly at the time and would spend my time working, thinking about the next chapter I would write on Sunday.

Sunday was the only day I had access to a computer, my employer kindly allowed me to use her office computer to write. This led me to meditate and contemplate for most of the day, every day for over a year.

One of the principal reasons that I rejoined the Church and sold my possessions to lead a life of solitude and service, was to live a life of integrity. Integration of spiritual search, the work I did, and the life I led became one piece. I had always tried to live with integrity. Indeed, I could, and cannot see any other way. If we want to understand non-duality, we must live it out every day. To say this is hard or make excuses that we must separate spiritual life from everyday life, is the reason so many who follow this path can't reach the understanding, and allow themselves to settle for an intellectual understanding. Compromise is the enemy of awakening.

Community of One – The Journey Beyond Christianity proved a success, in spite of its lack of publication, in that it showed me that the rule of life that I had established as a Christian monk could be, and indeed was being lived out now in oneness. I know that many criticize my teaching, my insistence that service and self-discovery go hand in hand. There is always the "no doer", "nothing to do" crowd that look for easy answers in the mind that they never apply to life, but keep it "special", as if life had two parts. But non-duality, life itself, is one.

In the Gospel of Matthew, the Christ says:

7²¹ "Not everyone who says to me, 'Lord, Lord,' shall enter the kingdom of heaven, but he who does the will of my father in heaven. ²² Many will say to me in that day, 'Lord, Lord, have we prophesied in your name, cast out demons in your name, and done many wonders in your name?" ²³ And then I will declare to them, 'I never knew you; depart from me, you who practice lawlessness.'"

Simply mouthing the words of the teacher, or even having an understanding that is not applied to life is not doing the will of the Father, the Absolute. Adayshanti says much the same thing in his talk about absolutism in non-duality:

"To awaken to the absolute view is profound and transformative, but to awaken from all fixed points of view is the birth of true nonduality. If emptiness cannot dance, it is not true emptiness. If moonlight does not flood the empty night sky and reflect in every drop of water, on every blade of grass, then you are only looking at your own empty dream. I say, Wake up! Then, your heart will be flooded with a Love that you cannot contain."

"A love you cannot contain" requires action; living out the teaching, not just sitting mouthing words of "no doer", "nothing to be done". If we do not share what we experience, what we have learned, then it not only dies with us, *it is dead within us.*

I have paraphrased the Apostle Paul's comment as "Work out your enlightenment with fear and trembling", meaning that living the teaching is not always easy, not always accepted. But life requires courage. Seeking is not for the weak. *Finding* requires even more courage, for here we must live it out daily. The dance of emptiness is not always an easy dance, but do we have a choice?

The Problem of God

The following is a short piece I wrote on my blog last September. I had not put it up here because it was an early writing and seemed a bit disjointed.

I thought I would post it now (with some updating) because it makes some sound points about Bhakti and Jnana that fit in with some of my recent writing. I beg your indulgence in the writing style, but hope you find something useful in it.

The reality here is more like the reverse: *Man created God in his own image*. I understand that the Hindu gods represent a variety of forms and meanings, but I know little of the gods of India, having my upbringing in Western Christianity. From an absolute standpoint, there is only *One*, both our *selves* and God being lost in the "*is-ness*".

From a relative standpoint, God is separate, yet we intellectually understand "he" is *our selves*. Advaita would say not two. From a relative standpoint, we can practice devotion. But we must always keep our hearts on the "*pearl of great price*", that oneness of the Absolute.

I recently read some advice that said that "*...householders and beginners on the spiritual path should stick with bhakti and the Gods, as non-dual, self- inquiry was not for them*." Those with true earnestness, regardless of position, station, or birth can engage both jnana and bhakti in this search for God.

When I was a boy, I lived with my family halfway up a steep hill. Every day I would walk home from school and look up at that hill and think how steep and far it was. One day when walking home with my brother, I mentioned how awful climbing that hill was and he pointed out that we only lived halfway up the hill, and that every day he imagined he had to climb to the top. This caused him to double his effort, and he came to the house before he knew it! I tried this and I found that this method worked for me too, not only on the hill but in life and the spiritual search.

The realization of the Absolute seems like quite a struggle. Devotion to God is much easier by comparison. Our minds understand a physical God. Our minds understand submission to a higher power. Yet our minds also understand the "I Am," and the concept of the *oneness of reality*. Devotion to God, if complete and self-sacrificing, will lead to the ultimate truth. But it is the *devotion* that leads to the truth, not God. For only if we recognize that there is some mystery that requires devotion because it *is* devotion, can we sustain ourselves until it is uncovered?

We must see and desire only the top of the hill, to muster sufficient effort to reach halfway.

When we lose ourselves in devotion to God, we lose our selves. And that is the point of worship: to lose the self. This applies when we lose ourselves in helping others, or in silent meditation. But somewhere along the line, we need to reconcile the separation we create in the act of worship and devotion.

We need to understand that worship has to become, not just what we do, but what we *are*. Our substance is love. We are created by it, sustained by it, and swim in a sea of it. Love, in its universal and impersonal functioning, is the Absolute. Like the perpetual opening of a perpetual rose, the manifestation, and its underlying reality, unfold into the wonder of life. Both our selves and God unfold in this wonder but only arise when consciousness is aware of itself. Separation begins with the I Am, when we mistake the "I" for the body/mind. But how do we reconcile this separation?

Bhakti, the devotion to God is the starting place. The devotional practice toward an "other" gets us to step out of our egocentric self long enough to become empty. The emptiness of this kind attracts grace, and the emptiness becomes filled with love.

This impersonal love is the soil in which true jnana grows. When the mind reaches its limit at the "I Am", the question arises: why is there devotion to a God, the Absolute, when there is only one? And what *draws* those who seek beyond, some to extreme asceticism and struggle?

And in that struggle, the mind and love itself come together and you realize that both yourself and God are flowing with and in the love, not the other way around. The love is the only reality. Love is the One. Tat Tvam Asi.

Ending in a Child's Giggle

When I was sixteen going on seventeen and was lucky enough to have squeezed into the only high school philosophy class in the district, I used to drive my best buddy nuts with it. Our periods of walking his dog or walks to school became sessions of deep philosophical discourse.

On one such spring evening stroll with Beagle in tow, my pal and I discovered a proof for the existence of God. I can't remember for the life of me, what we had come up with, but it was real tear-producing discovery at the time. I was ecstatic. The first thing I thought to do was call my philosophy teacher.

Now, this was a Saturday night, not a school night. Tomorrow was Sunday, a whole day away from school, and I couldn't wait. I had to call Mr. Curtin. He was probably my most inspiring teacher. I have written about him before. He was the teacher who inspired me to look into philosophy in the first place when I was about fifteen.

It was not so much that I wanted to show off to him that we had proven God, or that I was somehow kissing up, but in my naivety, I had a genuine belief that, now that I had proven God, he would certainly want to know!

He was, to my grateful relief, not unhappy that I called. We discussed my findings and I was a bit deflated to find that Anselm had had similar findings centuries before. He also inserted a poser: "*If indeed you boys have proven God, how would you prove he was good?*"

Recalling that incident, I am reminded that in the spiritual journey, we will be given many revelations. Some will seem new but are actually glimpses into a common consciousness. But, despite of being common revelations, they are revelations just the same and experienced through this body/mind as expressions of the movement of love, the Absolute. Old truths are being experienced and becoming *our* old truths.

I am also reminded of how the last question my philosophy teacher posed, "*How would you prove that god is good?*" A question I would ponder much of my life. Ponder, that is, until I discovered that the only answer was to delve into it so deeply that I *became* the answer. In that silence an infilling gave the answer and removed the need for the answer: one unfolding that starts with awe and ends in a child's giggle.

Time and Awakening:
Follow Up to My Internet Interview

It's one of those days where everything has pointed to what I am going to write today, so here goes.

Today a dear friend who writes frequently on Facebook wrote again on one of his favorite topics: sudden awakening. Yesterday I had an interview on internet radio, in which I talked about my awakening as being something that evolved over time and all at once. Also in that interview was a discussion of the words of Christ on the cross: *"My God, My God, why hast thou forsaken me?"*

These things all run together.

I described my awakening experience as *seeming* to have evolved throughout my life. I also pointed out that upon awakening, the seeming past is seen clearly. It is seen how *awake* one always was. This is why the awakened often point out that you are always awake, but simply take yourself as sleeping.

This *sleeping, seeking, awakened* are all part of the movement of awakening. The sleeping and seeking phases are as much a part of this unfolding as is the awakening. This unfolding is love moving as *us* within the world. The illusions are as much a part of this as what we label reality.

Awakening can and does happen in a number of ways. It can be experienced as a moment of infilling of spirit, or it can be seen as unfolding moment by moment. To say that one experience is valid and another is not is bringing in a fundamentalist notion as to *how* awakening has to happen. The important concept here is that of time. The concept of time needs to be completely eradicated from your spiritual existence. The sleeping, seeking, and awakening occur simultaneously without a nanosecond between them.

Therefore, it is of no matter if a personal awakening appears to happen in an instant or moves slowly over time. It is unfolding at its own pace.

And now the question of Christ's apparent words of despair. I can never understand why this question is not answered in a definitive way. By uttering these words, Christ is not only not falling victim to the human frailty of despair, he is affirming the *oneness* of his life and death.

"My God, My God, why hast thou forsaken me," is the opening line from the twenty-second Psalm of David. This is an amazing Psalm, as it is one that describes the crucifixion in some detail. While it is a lament and reference to the life of David, its parallels to the events happening to Christ, *at the moment of his recitation of it*, are not lost. The Christ is demonstrating his awareness of his present circumstance: the aloneness, the abandonment, and imminent death.

No. The Christ was not weakening. He is reciting a Psalm to his life and death. He is praising death as it approaches, with a kind of "I told you so" bravado that only one who is also sure of the outcome can muster. *"My God, My God ..."* becomes a rhetorical question like the one I constantly recite from the Avadhuta Gita:

"How shall I salute the formless being ..."

Just as the Avadhuta Gita's answer is in the *being* itself, so it is with the *"My God, My God ..."* The recognition that life, death, the worship of "God" or the *idea/concept* are all unfolding in this unlimited potential that is love. There is no limiting awakening to a particular kind of experience. Who would look at or choose crucifixion as a means to make a point? The point is, life moves with all the pain and sacrifice we can handle. We do not have to seek crucifixion. Our crosses will come and go, just as well as our joys and loves.

I like the idea of unlimited potential much better than the concept of destiny, which is time-bound and requires a past to arise, and a future in which to develop. Without this burdensome concept, it can be seen that life, past, present, and future all unfold as a piece, all part of the conceptual time, but having no sustained independent reality.

The Christ's pointing out that life, death, and pain are part of the submission. The life, the death, the earnestness are all interweaved.

No single point can be said to encapsulate the life and teaching of the Christ, apart from this submission to death. The teaching must be accepted. The living out the teaching must be accepted. And finally, death itself must be faced by our loved ones, and eventually in our own faces. But we can say, "The pain of life is scattered before me like the well-placed mines of an enemy, but each step that does not blow up in my face is a grace, a chance to be love one more time."

It does not matter if our awakening is not instant or even seems to be taking the rest of our lives; the seeking and the finding are all part of the same movement of love. The only answer is in total abandonment into life: your life. Opportunities open every second to live out the teaching. Live it out. Die it out. Be it.

Unfolding

I use the term unfolding a good deal in my writing. It is a term widely used by many other spiritual writers as well. I cannot explain why it is used by others, but it is easy to explain here. It is how things appear.

I don't have any vision of destiny, predestination, karmic action, heaven or hell, or any of that nonsense. I see, swirling all around, unfolding potential. I once described this unfolding potential as being like the "perpetual unfolding of a perpetual rose," always in movement, a dance of love, always fresh with dew, every morning.

The tiny hands of the child in the womb unfold like the petals of a flower or the needles of a pine. Think of the enfoldment of the forest in the seed, the world in the love of God.

Unfolding from between the soft hiding places of Father's coat, we sally forth, safe in love.

Imagining mountains and valleys in the unfolding of the sheets and blankets around our toes, life is unfolding in one sensuous, awkward, bumbling pirouette.

Non-Duality and the Facebook
One-Room Classroom

My maternal grandmother had a childhood very like that of Laura Ingalls, from the *Little House on the Prairie* series. She was raised in a small cabin in the California hills on a very small farm.

I would sit with her in the summer afternoons of the 1950s and we would shell peas, and she would tell stories of the old days. There were stories about her mother's wagon accident (she was never the same again!) and the tarantula in the cemetery on remembrance-day. But the stories I remember best were the stories about her school days in a one-room school house.

Like Laura Ingalls, my grandmother was a bit of a tomboy. She ran, threw the ball, and loved the swings. I was privileged to see the spot where she had gone to school, the school building itself having been gone for many years. She pointed out to me the tree she had used for a swing seventy years earlier. The spot remains an empty plot. Even the tree is gone now. She remembered the school with mixed feelings. On the one hand, a young girl is isolated in the woods, and on the other, a world of endless adventure with nature.

Love for the school won out over any feelings of isolation, and her dream in her early years was to be a schoolteacher in one of these little one-room schools.

Thinking about that started me thinking about the advantages and disadvantages of the one room school house we have here on Facebook. As spiritual teachers who do much of their writing and teaching on Facebook, we face a readership that spans the globe, age barriers, and educational levels. Like the one room schoolhouse, we learn and teach to all levels of awareness.

Something I wrote recently was considered unnecessarily complicated. Other times I have been criticized for being too simplistic. I may write something light and gentle today, and tomorrow something stark and to the point. But in the one-room classroom of Facebook, we write what comes to us. This moment for you, the next, who knows?

In the one-room classroom of the turn of the century, all age groups were catered to. All levels had to be addressed. This is the same in this internet classroom we find ourselves volunteering for. Today I teach the "I Am", tomorrow I insist you must go beyond the "I Am". This week silence, next month activity. The message is for all. The message is for you. Some days a bit of nostalgia about my grandmother might be just the thing. Other days, seriously looking at love as both concept and reality, is what flows out onto this keyboard.

Like the one-room classroom of the turn of the century, the older more advanced seekers can help those just starting the greatest adventure. But also the young, those fresh to the search and fresh to awakening, can bring new insights and new expressions that can benefit all.

So if you see a discrepancy in style, direction of emphasis, remember the Facebook spiritual teacher is addressing a wide readership. There is no discrepancy in the love that opens with every line written. I wish we could sit and shell peas together and discuss the old days. Then we would not have to discuss all this unnecessarily complicated stuff, but simply be.

We Are Not the Dancers, Only the Dance!

In non-duality, we tend to think of the concept of the *other* as the very heart of duality. Of course, the "I Am" thought is actually the culprit here, the concept of the other not being possible without it.

Both the "I Am" thought and the thought of the other arise in one movement of love. This unfolding movement of potential, although completely unexplainable, expresses itself in the "I Am" and the other thoughts. These expressions are innocent. By innocent, I mean that they have no independent existence of their own, being only *expressions* of the unfolding reality.

There is nothing wrong with the expressions, no matter their ultimate illusory quality. They are real in their place in the relative. Understanding or awareness is really a matter of seeing the real and the illusory mingle together in the oneness of life. The mind can seem a deceiving enemy like the snake in the garden, lying in wait to snare the innocent seeker. But this is not so.

The mind and the heart both have a place in the oneness that we are. They are not separate, but again, function as one movement. This is something we cannot emphasize too often.

Everything, past, present, and future, unfolds together in one unfolding of potential. The mind recognizes the search, and more significantly, it recognizes the importance of the search. It has no details, which it would dearly love to have. The more complicated the details the more work for the mind, and the mind is a workaholic.

Without details, or facts the mind can mull over, the mind goes either into imagination or silence. In the playland of imagination, memories of past expressions are played back as if new. Some are strung together in creative ways to form whole new fantasies, emotions, and experiences. Imagination, no matter how spiritual it is, is just a clown show that makes up new acts with every thought.

If the mind goes into silence, a real silence of both mind and heart, then both heart and mind are open to learning from that silence. This is a learning that the heart understands but the mind, while sensing the presence of the learning, is unable to express. Sensing the presence of the awesomeness of this learning, the mind assumes its natural place as a servant to the heart. This is the restoration of balance. Instead of allowing the mind to run the show, which is the typical way, the mind is seen clearly and respected for what it is.

Instead of treating the mind like it was an enemy, let the mind study, meditate, and tire itself of all extraneous thoughts. Thoughts can be amusing, entertaining, and educational! It's just a matter of seeing them for what they are. When the mind gets tired of playing in imagination and goes silent, then the real learning takes place. It is here we begin to see the other, that indispensable companion expression to our "I Am", as simply part of the same dance.

There is only one unfolding, all apparent objects being expressions of that one silent movement. We cannot separate ourselves from this movement. The other, whether something we love or something we wish we had never seen or heard of, is part of the same movement. Both the other and the "I Am" are companions, partners in this dance we call life. So take it to the floor, spin, unwind, unfold. We are not the dancers, *we are the dance*!

The Sparkling Wonder

On warm spring and summer nights when I was a boy, I used to love to lay back on the lawn and look up at the stars. Before I started attending school, the sparkling wonder spread out before me like the twinkling lights that used to appear before my eyes while drifting off to sleep.

When I was a bit older and in school, I still loved the night sky, but now it was counting shooting stars and knowing what they really were. Thinking about the race for space and all that went with that, the sparkling wonder started to become possessed by the mind. This is the problem with the mind, this tendency, this demand, to really possess.

The more powerful the mind, the more need there seems for this desire to possess. This is what makes unlearning so important to spiritual progress so difficult. When the mind sees the night sky, instead of leaving it as beautiful or profound which are already mental constructs, it goes on to, dark, brilliant, or whatever mind modifications can be applied to capture this thing. The mind constructs galaxies, nebula (one of my particular favorites!), black holes (another pretty cool one!), and so on until the sparkling wonder fits smoothly into knowledge. (Sorry to keep using the sparkling wonder analogy as I realize it too is a mental construct; but try to see it as a child would: Awe, without the word, awe.)

With knowledge, we take possession of thoughts and sets of thoughts that we gain from others or from experiences that we interpret using the thoughts of others. By the time we have left the sparkling wonder stage, we are so filled with, not only others' ideas but others' ideas about who we are, that we have long forgotten the simple awe of the night sky. But, oh, we possess the night sky now. We can tell you how it works. Kind of. We can tell you how it was created. Kind of. We have taken awe and categorized the heart, the love, the "God" out of it.

We all find that unlearning is much harder than learning. We look up at the night sky, and we remember vaguely what it was like, that sparkling wonder. This faint memory is not really a memory at all, but a calling as if through a mist of a still, small voice speaking the silence that was before night, dark, or stars. We must be careful not to construct an *actual memory* (how's that for an oxymoron?). Let's not create a story of how we saw the night sky as a child, but follow that call that beckons you home to the realization of the ever-present sparkling wonder.

My Angel

While allowing the mind to drift today, I was brought back to a time that should have been incredibly bad but has left nothing but sweet memories. It is almost incredible to me now to think back, but I actually remember none of the bad things that no doubt spun around me.

When I was about five, maybe six, my family fell on hard times and I was hit by a car. Now, these events had no relationship to each other, they were just things that happen to anyone. My folks had made some bad financial decisions (my dad drank!), and we found ourselves living in the dining room of my maternal grandparent's house.

To a young boy, this was no hardship. This was an adventure. This room was not only where we shared our family holiday dinners, but at night it had always been a spooky room that one had to run through to avoid what inevitably lurked there in the dark. It also contained the closet, a place filled with Victorian clothing and hats no one had worn since the nineteenth century, and my grandfather's secret trunk filled with treasures and ghosts of his adventures. Such a room was no problem for a boy of six. Besides, he had his brother and Mom and Dad in there with him.

Being poor was not too bad, but sometimes going without the necessities like a good collection of marbles, was rough on a six-year-old. One day, completely out of the blue, my grandfather gave me a dime. I don't know if I had done something cute, or if maybe I had just not done something bad, but I was not going to question my luck. Now, to think of what to do with a whole dime?

A little dime, so much smaller than a nickel, but worth twice as much. An important thing to remember for a six-year-old. What to get really did not take much thinking: more marbles. Even though I did not play with other kids much, I liked having a huge marble collection. After school today, I would slip down to Woolworths and get myself a new bag of marbles!

All went well, until the walk home with my new treasure of twenty-five cat's eyes. While walking across the street from the catholic school, St. Rafael's, I was stuck in the crosswalk by a speeding car. Now here comes the interesting, and spiritual part. I was thrown fifty feet across the street and landed on the hood of a parked car in front of the church. This is all part of what I learned from the newspaper story of the event. I have no actual memory of this, simply flying unconsciously through the air.

Somewhere along the line, a kind woman who was at the catholic school to pick up her children picked me off the hood of the parked car and drove me to the hospital, which was thankfully, nearby. I have no memory of this except for one image that has stayed with me. The woman's son, a boy about twice my age, was sitting at my head as I lay bleeding all over their car. He was looking down with a caring look on his face that I will never forget. It was serene and angelic, and I had, and have no doubt that love rode in the back seat of that car that day.

I remember very little of the next few hours or days. I have no memory of the pain. The only lasting memories of the event are of my first-grade teacher, Mrs. Pacheco, bringing me a little lead Hopalong Cassidy figure; and lying there, in my grandparent's dining room in the dark, with my brother and folks listing to *Ozzie and Harriet* and *Archie Andrews* on the radio. Of course, I will always remember the charming boy, smiling gently down at one shocked little puppy.

Today as I was about to write this, it occurred to me how the memories of what would seem a trying time have all become happy, even lovely memories. Although I was lucky to escape with only a few facial cuts, a lot of teeth knocked out, and a limp that stayed with me until my forties, I recovered over a period of weeks and had terrible nightmares. So I am told, for I have no memory of the headaches, the earaches, or the nightmares. All I am left with are the things that brought me love. The painful events, like the nightmares, had vanished in the love this all brought to me.

So easy it would be if we could all just live with the memories of love, discarding the pain and suffering as it arises. All memories of pain and suffering from that event are memories of those around me, telling my story. I have no memories but of a token present from a teacher who showed me not only that she cared, but that she had some idea who I was. And the memory of the late-night radio shows such as *Ozzie and Harriet* was like my story unfolding, only it seemed funnier, but no less loving. And if only, in the midst of tragedy and pain, we can realize the angel who sits with us in the worst of it all, smiling down, silently being one with us.

Pinocchio: A Story of Enlightenment

It's funny how many spiritual pointers can be found in the tales and stories from our childhood. I was thinking about *Pinocchio* today in reference to writing about the body/mind being a kind of puppet.

Pinocchio is a perfect allegory of enlightenment. The puppet, Pinocchio, is created out of the earnestness and selfless love of Geppetto. What a great allegorical depiction of creation. Geppetto prays for love, and it is fulfilled in the form of a life.

And Pinocchio himself, as all who are created from love must, has to find the balance of supposed free will and following his heart.

Pinocchio is a puppet who wants to be a real boy. This is an ideal picture of the seeker.

Everything moves well. Life is ok. School or work is ok. But there's this nagging feeling of superficiality, like playing a part, being a kind of a puppet, and longing to be real. And what is it that makes Pinocchio, and us for that matter, real? Unconditional Love.

Pinocchio learns that self-indulgence leads, quite literally, to making an ass of yourself.

Sacrifice, as in the rescue of Geppetto, brought about the *real* that Pinocchio sought.

The lesson here is clear. Life is created from love. And even though a puppet, the puppet still has the choice as to *who's* puppet it is going to be. It can mistakenly view itself as a separate *got no-strings* ego, me. But then it is a puppet only to itself, without even being aware of it. The mind sees itself as in control, the puppet now being in charge of the puppet. This, of course, is ridiculous.

Unlike with Pinocchio, in a sense, there is no getting away from being a puppet. The body/mind is a puppet, a thing that is born and dies. It is the creation of love, the residue of the movement of unfolding potential. The change we all seek, this becoming real as it were, is the handing over of the strings to the heart. It's as simple as that.

There is no need to beat down the mind or subdue the body. All that need to be done is to exchange the mind as a puppet master who calls, choreographs, and makes the puppet dance, for the heart. The heart is a puppet master who lays out potential like the well-placed props on a dance floor. In its hands, the dancing puppet is free to become the real boy it has already been.

Call it destiny or call it potential, we are puppets. These bodies, these minds are but expressions of the unfolding universe. We can live out our lives letting the puppet imagine that it is operating itself, or we can completely surrender, and let the creator of the puppet fulfill its purpose in the unfolding. Then we can all be *real boys and girls*.

"Oh, My God!"

As spiritual writers and teachers, we often use the word "God". It is a word that has a variety of meanings to a wide variety of people. But it conveys meaning beyond the specific meaning given it by any particular religion. It is the reference, the absolute authority. "God" is seen as creator, destroyer, savior, punisher, and any number of human-based images. But "God" is an illusion.

Now, by illusion, I don't mean "God" is a total figment. God, like our individual appearance, is an expression. This morning when I was planning to write this, I was thinking of using the idea of expression as in a facial expression, like a smile, wink, or smirk. I was thinking of saying that we are expressions of love (in place of "God") like a smile on love's face. But there I was personifying again.

This could be the single largest problem in really understanding. When we become familiar with non-duality, we begin to understand that the concept of "God" is mind based. Some may reject religion altogether and even change their vocabulary so pro-nouns are no longer allowed, and only oneness is recognized. Any mention of "God" in such a setting is scoffed at, at best, and could lead to rejection from the non-dual community.

This results in the kind of dry, passionless, intellectual non-duality we see in many Western Satsang situations. Some, with newly awakened expressions, believe their experience is what made them aware, so now they are devising methods, plans, and courses to help you recreate their experiences. Spirituality becomes mind games and practices, no matter what New Age names you label them with, even if you insist, they aren't practices. This becomes psychological nonsense. Push out the bad thoughts, bring in the good. Where is the passion that the love of God used to bring?

This creates, what was for me the great paradox. Reason tells us that "God" is a concept. Experience tells us that "God" is a concept. Any amount of self-inquiry should put both yourself and "God" in perspective. We find that "God" is an expression of the *all*, but the concept is an expression of us. We create "God" in our own image. The movement of love is the foundation, the space as it were, with "God" and "ourselves" being the expressions of that movement. We then extrapolate a "God" as a grand us. "God" is more loving than us, and a whole lot meaner! "God" is the original superhero.

The point is, whenever we use the term "God" we bring up images. Even in Advaita circles, "God" is mentioned repeatedly. Nisargadatta Maharaj used the term "God" often, and often in different contexts. Sometimes in a conventional way, sometimes as the Absolute. The Christ spoke of the "Father". Ramana Maharshi was/and is himself worshiped and prayed to. Even places like Arunachala, Mecca, or Jerusalem are worshiped and held as holy. What does this mean?

There is a natural desire for worship in mankind, perhaps in the universe. The Christ talked of the "stones rising up". This natural desire stems from the fact that we *are* worship, we *are* gratitude, we *are* expressions of love in movement.

My writing has been spoken of as being "from the heart". I was referred to in an interview as a "heart teacher". I hope that does not mean that I am some kind of bliss bunny. I live every day of my life immersed in love, and yet I believe in no "God". I love fairy tales, but I have no desire to live in one. On the other hand, I do not accept some scientific explanations like the big bang. "God" and the big bang are equal in relevance and intelligence if you ask me. They are both man-made answers to unanswerable questions.

I try not to use the word "God" without quotation marks. It is a word and idea deeply implanted in my brain, and I try very hard to make it understood when I do use it. I do this because the relationship we have with "God" is of vital importance to awareness. The love we feel for "God", whether in our neighbor, the natural world, or ourselves *is* what we are. "God", neighbor, world, and ourselves all arise as expressions of that love that we are.

The love is real. You could say, "the love of God" is real, but not "God". But that is confusing. If "God" is love, then to love is to be "God". To love your neighbor as yourself is also to be "God". We can only be love when we are totally immersed in our true being. When ideas of "I" are nowhere to be found, and ideas of "God" vanish along with them, we can relax into the love that remains. The only thing that was there in the first place.

Tell Us All You Dare!

When my partner and I first arrived in Lincoln, England, at Lincoln Cathedral, we quickly became aware that the clergy and congregation had made arrangements among themselves to have us over to dinner in rotation or pay us a welcoming visit at least every week.

In line with that, a wonderful elderly Canon and his wife, named Parker invited us for tea and biscuits, of course.

John and I were the talk of the Cathedral Yard, having just arrived from San Francisco, and rumored to be gay! Everyone was dying to hear whatever gossip they could, and the Parkers were no exception. But to this day, I will never forget Canon Parker's first remark, after we had all been seated with our tea and plates of biscuits, "Now boys, tell us all you dare!"

"Tell us *what* you dare" becomes the key word for me, when it comes to self-inquiry. We can look at the "I Am" or the "Who am I?" as closely as we can or want; but the seeker; that beginning adult in search of childhood needs to come to terms with that dream child only half-remembered. This can be scary stuff.

I was fortunate in a way, as I saw my first psychiatrist when I was only nine or ten. I saw him at San Francisco's sprawling (for then!)

UC Med Center. He was Dr. Shade. What a questionable name for a child psychiatrist! But I started on a run that would be an ongoing theme in my life. I was a bit nuts, but I was bright, whatever that meant. I did not want to be bright. I wanted to be happy.

But I have to admit that exposure to Rorschach Tests, personality inventories, and the simple idea of inner exploration was a foundation in personal study, behavioral scrutiny, and mask removal that has become a part of my daily life. I learned as a child to see this "Bill" as a mask. Exploring the "I Am" can lead you to the conclusion that you can experience your existence, and little more. The mind all the while, remains a storeroom of masks. The mind tells you that you are. But to get to where you are, you need to ask your *self* to "tell us all you dare".

Secrets, not little stupid secrets or big, horrible secrets, but the secrets we all tell ourselves, like, "I'm better than he is." or "I'm more advanced spiritually than they are." Or the reverse, "I'm worthless" or "I have committed great sins," are the reason we look inside. Not just for the sake of spirituality, but for the simplification of our lives. Our lives are spirituality itself, alive and unfolding before us. Integration brings spirit and the mundane together, losing the whole concept of the mundane in the process.

When we have explored as much as we can and we find we are running into resistance, it is then we must ask ourselves the Parker's inquiry, tell us all you dare. Look deeply and dangerously close. The only way to discover the angel in the castle may be to discover and deal with the demon trying to block the door.

Many so-called spiritual practices today involve psychological and therapeutic practices that may or may not work. Spiritual teachers should offer pointers that open the mind in new directions or bypass the mind altogether, and strike at the heart.

Psychologists and psychiatrists should offer guidance in the inner search of the mind. It is wonderful when both disciplines and studies are found in the same person. A psychologist well versed in Advaita or non-dualism can be a great benefit to a client or student. But this can be rather dodgy ground, this combination of therapist and guru.

Likewise, the suddenly aware guru or teacher who believes he can now offer psychological practices, no matter how rudimentary or basic without the years of training necessary to deal with unexpected complications, would be best to stick to pointing.

Until you are ready to tell what you dare in a way that hurts, a way that makes you scream "No, no, that's not me," until you drop all the masks and stand there in the strength and openness that nakedness offers, there is still an "I" hiding in the works. This "I" has to go. This is sacrifice. No, it's not some trip to the lions in the arena. It's not some idealized sacred sacrifice, or even dying for your children or friends. It's living each day, good or bad, with the most love you can express in life. You can only do this when you are open when you are free, when *you tell us all you dare*!

Swallowed Up in the Unfolding of Love

I have been on Facebook writing my little notes, and blogging on my blog account for a little over nine months now. It was a short time after that, that I posted "teacher" under "employer". As many of you know, I have mentioned in one or two notes, this teacher-calling came from a dream I had in which Nisargadatta Maharaj and I stood together, my hands on his shoulders, and I experienced a wave of love that I had only felt before in my awakening experience.

As I have also said elsewhere, I do not necessarily put much account in dreams or dreams of meetings with famous gurus. The message left by this dream, however, was clear to me. This is love. Share it. I had gone around for over twenty years with a simple open secret. I say, "You are love," and it sounds naive, cute, or at worst a little empty. I want to scream it. I long to see you face to face. I want to say, "Look, it's simple, just turn your view a bit." What I experience and what can be conveyed, are so far apart that it breaks my heart. This is why we fools who can't escape the call of love, call ourselves teachers, gurus, spiritual directors, or whatever name you tack on to one who points because we really have no choice.

The awakened, for lack of a more accurate term, discover that the unfolding that has been drawing them to the search, is actually what they are. It is the love that unfolds. When the question is asked, "Why do you feel called to teach?" the answer is simple, "There is no choice, I have been swallowed up in the unfolding of love, and as love itself, can do nothing but unfold."

Observing the Comic World

I have memories of my ninth summer. The first in our own house.

This was a fairly new house, and it had a patio. Probably the first place I heard the word patio. It was also the first time to hear of a new piece of outdoor furniture: the chaise lounge. Upon hearing the name, and seeing the thing, I was sure it must be for women. I wanted nothing to do with it until I saw my dad lying on it, reading his newspaper. A grand idea struck me.

As a small boy, I was always a big lover of comic books. Not the *Batman, Superman, Fantastic Four* kind of thing, but funny comic animals and kids. Probably most of you would not remember the ones I loved the most, *Funny Films Comics, Little Lulu, Super Duck, Smoky Stover*, and a bunch of other obscure titles. When I saw my dad in the French lazy chair, I knew that I must spend part of my upcoming summer vacation lying in that thing, re-reading my extensive comic book collection.

Comic books and my love for them were what got me started today on this note. I started thinking of how I used to look so deeply into those pictures and images that was beyond the corner of the drawing. What did the rest of that car or truck look like? A whole world was created, and as a child, it was easy to get lost in it. I remember that summer lying on the chaise lounge, a stack of comics two feet high beside me, becoming lost in the life of *Blunder Bunny* or *Lulu and Tubby*. As I remember it now, it was a complete transference into their world. This is much like the lives we create for ourselves when we get lost in the story of us.

I spent much of that and many subsequent summers, largely alone, lost in comic books or other distractions. Yes, that is what our constant concern over a me can do as well. Life swirls around us, *real life*, not some story we tell ourselves, no matter how comic or engaging. I was aware, even then, that my life was capable of switching in and out of real or imagined. As a child, I was one of the lucky ones. I knew this would not last forever. I took the lyrics from the song Toyland, "Once you leave the borders, you can never return again", very seriously. I could see how easy it was to get lost in the comics. I could also see that most adults could not see this.

We can enjoy this comic world we live in, but we must recognize the underlying substance and put things in their place. The mind runs things arbitrarily deciding what is real and unreal until we see the mind for what it is. We cannot control the mind, we can only accept it, understand its demands, and use it in service to the heart. Instead of allowing it to take over and create a world of suffering and confusion, realize that the world is already perfect and that the story swirling all around is just that, a story. It is a diversion until you're home, the *self* is realized.

The boy in the chaise lounge was lost in the stories of his comic buddies, but his hands were on the comic and he observed the embarrassments of *Super Duck* without becoming him. For us to emerge from our stories, we must realize the same thing. Stop engaging in the story. When you observe a room full of people, don't leave yourself out. See that it is *all* a story. It's this you and the others. But it can be watched, yourself being just another character. When you do this, you see that you are the watcher, the observer, both of the world and of this "you" that you take yourself for.

You are the boy in the chaise lounge. The reason you get involved with the comic stories is that you take yourself to be one of the funny animals instead of the reader, the observer of love's expression. So enjoy the stories. Participate even. But don't get lost in the exploits of one character to the point that he or she becomes the whole of the story.

Just the Beginning

Non-dualists spend a lot of time thinking, philosophising, and attending Satsang. Although I have never attended a Satsang, I am guilty of the other two. In fact, when it comes to philosophising, I have appointed myself a teacher. But it is not really philosophy I teach, as that is not where my expertise lies. It is love I share.

The particular incident that brought about the absolute conviction that there was only love here, where this "Bill" used to be, is of no real importance. What matters is how will there be *pointing* to that, which has become the unfolding found here.

I believe that one of the stumbling blocks to awakening is the fear of love itself. I don't mean a fear of the emotion of love, but the power we sense. If we have been called to seek, not just to solve a problem or seek the peace of mind, but a true calling that won't let us alone, it is love calling itself to *seek*. We are called to enter into the play of love. The call, the search, the awakening, everything, including the mind and the things are part of that play.

One of the scariest, trickiest, and ultimately rewarding things we must do is to integrate our selves, lives, and spirituality into one. We need to understand that all this talk of illusions and appearances, as opposed to the real is simple duality. The appearances and illusions stem from and are inseparable from the Absolute. In the expressions of the Absolute, I am no judge as to *real* and *unreal*. Falling into acceptance, all is One.

Accepting the realities of pain, disappointment, and grief as presented to this illusory person, are part of the real. The illusory person plays his part in this play of love. We can't separate our spiritual side from our body/mind side, as they are one integral piece.

In the beginning, we learn that the mind is in control and that it must be understood, ignored, and eventually put into its place. This is self-inquiry: the search for the "I Am". Once the "I Am" is recognized, the scary part I referred to above occurs. We now have to integrate this knowledge with life as it is. They are really one thing, but by now we have isolated the mind and it must be welcomed back into the fold.

This switch of the mind from master to servant is really the whole of the play of love. But this is what many fear. It is much easier to stay in awareness, to empty the mind. This is a safe place. Silence. Peace. Awareness. This sounds comforting to the mind, and this is where many, if not most, get stuck. Somewhere along the line, life must re-integrate.

It's no big trick, master calculation, or a philosophical conundrum. It's a gut thing, an act of grace. But it requires more than human courage. It requires a surrender of courage, a helplessness that surrenders even the thought of redemption. A trust without option. Being willing to be absorbed into all that is, losing the individual, and gaining the *all without knowing it*, just being it. And then the trick remains to bring the mind, personality, and all the illusory stuff into the understanding. This is how emptiness *dances* to paraphrase Adayashanti.

Ramana Maharshi went into a deep state of samadhi in his teens. Had he not been found and cared for by devotees, he might have died. It took Ramana time to integrate his awakening with the life around him, and he began to speak again. Isolating yourself into a corner of awareness, no matter how blissful or aware, separates what you are. Just because the wave sees that it is part and parcel of the ocean does not mean its life as a wave is over. This discovery is just the beginning.

The Loving Eyes of Poverty

I wanted to write something more about poverty. I know I wrote a previous note on poverty called *Non-Duality, Poverty, and the Cross*, but it was a bit on the cerebral side. I know that this, like much of what I write about, is not a popular topic. But it strikes me that living out non-duality must at least accept poverty, if not embrace it.

I use the word embrace a bit factitiously. In an article in the Lincolnshire newspaper, our religious community was described as embracing poverty. Again, more recently, the idea of rejoicing in poverty came up in an interview. I have never wanted to give the impression that poverty is something that I either relish or look forward to.

I wanted to tell a couple of stories that I hope will give a bit of insight into how I see poverty.

When my partner and I were forming the Community of the Living Sacrifice, we were sent to live for a time with another Anglican community. One of the things being tossed around in the community formation was whether we were going to adopt habits and what they would look like.

While we were staying with the brothers, we were all invited to the adjacent town for a church gathering. Their car having been recently in a collision, we all had to walk. It was asked by one of the monks if they were to wear their habits and the abbot insisted upon it. So we walked, maybe four or five miles, John and I being the only ones in street clothes. A whole new view of the monk's habit permanently entered my mind that day.

We were observed like the circus had come to town! As self-conscious as John and I felt, the monks seemed to relish the attention. As we walked through town, people would smile or make the sign of the cross, or back away reverently in a most embarrassing manner. These habits, these relics from the past, were once meant to be a willing acceptance of the clothes of the poor. Monks' habits are replications of medieval working-class wear. But in a modern setting, they scream out *holy man*! They serve just the opposite purpose for which they were intended.

Instead of allowing the monk to blend in, to be an unnoticed beggar, they now announce his separateness, his specialness.

Needless to say, habits were not part of the community's rule.

The second story happened during one of our periods of homelessness. We were lucky in that we were always homeless with a car. On this particular occasion, however, the car broke down on a Sunday night. We were in Monterey, California, and knew no one there. We arranged to have the car repaired on Monday, so we could make it back to the San Francisco Bay Area, but needed to sleep in it for the night.

We found a Safeway store across from a public toilet and decided to camp out in the parking lot for the night. It did not take long before we realized that we were not alone. At least another three cars came in and shut down their lights, their occupants attempting to get their heads down. And then we all saw the man with the keys.

They were shutting the toilets. A simple thing. Keeping the town clean. Keeping the homeless out. My God, that's me! This is poverty.

This is the kind of poverty that I had hoped to design into the rule for the community.

I think a monk must understand real human poverty. Not some "giving up", or wearing rough clothing, or even hard work, but the real degradation of poverty. Not having the simple dignity of a basic toilet. Being in a city and having to make do. How often do we have the grace to experience these kinds of things? Yes, I call it a grace, because this is freedom. Not the grinding poverty or the humiliation itself. That stinks. But the ability to accept, maybe even thrive in those conditions.

You might inquire, "Sure, poverty may be great in Christianity or Bhakti Yoga, but what about Advaita or non-duality?" Poverty allows you to be open. As Bobby Dylan sang you've got nothing to lose if you don't have anything. And this applies spiritually as well. With no conceptual identification, there is nothing to give up. To be willing to accept (not necessarily embrace) poverty, should it come is the willingness to flow with the movement, to relax upon a sea of trust, worrying not for tomorrow.

This means not only accepting physical, monetary poverty, but that biblical promise guaranteeing you will possess the kingdom: poverty of spirit. *"Blessed are the poor in spirit, for theirs is the Kingdom of Heaven."* When you are down to your last dime, and the world holds you in contempt. This is poverty. When you are down to your last concept (I Am), and the mind stops of its own volition in a poverty of ideas, then the holy can enter and you can possess the kingdom of heaven.

Poverty is the life of oneness. Jesus, the Christ, Ramana Maharshi, Nisargadatta Maharaj all lived in, and accepted poverty. Sometimes they accepted what was offered, other times not. You must make your decision regarding this practice for yourself. I would only say that the amount of earnestness you give to your spiritual life will be shown in that living. Poverty need not be sought but accepted with joy. The less you indulge the "I", the more readily it will take up its place as a servant to the Absolute.

The photograph of the homeless woman above always brings tears to my eyes. Not because of her poverty, but because of the determined way she eats her yogurt. I can feel the tear-filled gratitude of each spoonful. I have known those tears. Those tears are mine. Poverty has removed the separation I might feel from her. Poverty has given me the grace to see her love, in the spoon, in the *earnest* way she keeps her things. Sadness here? Perhaps. But abounding love, seen through the loving eyes of poverty.

Earnestness: Damn It! It is as Simple as That!

Questioner: *"Your words are wise, your behavior noble, your grace all-powerful."*

Nisargadatta Maharaj: *"I know nothing about it all and see no difference between you and me. My life is a succession of events, just like yours. Only I am detached and see the passing show as a passing show, while you stick to things and move along with them."*

Q: *"What made you so dispassionate?"*

M: *"Nothing in particular. It so happened that I trusted my Guru. He told me I am nothing but my self and I believed him. Trusting him, I behaved accordingly and ceased caring for what was not me, nor mine."*

Q: *"Why were you lucky to trust your teacher fully, while our trust is nominal and verbal?"*

M: *"Who can say? It happened so. Things happen without cause and reason and, after all, what does it matter, who is who? Your high opinion of me is your opinion only. Any moment you may change it. Why attach importance to opinions, even your own?"* I Am That, Nisargadatta Maharaj

"Trusting him, I behaved accordingly and ceased caring for what was not me, nor mine." As simple as that. Damn it! It is as simple as that! Nisargadatta describes his life as *"...a succession of events, just like yours,"* only with detachment. Nisargadatta trusted his Guru, behaved accordingly, and became not only detached but realized.

Whether you trust an external guru, or an internal one, behaving accordingly is *proof of the pudding* and the *practice* all rolled into one. This living accordingly, is non-duality lived out.

Living out non-duality is not simply walking around with a smile on your face telling others that they are free. To hear it told, we are all free. This is a mantra: We are all free. Do you truly understand this freedom? Is this in your experience, or did someone tell you? Could you have read it somewhere? It's easy to do! Why, you were never bound, you have always been free! But is this how you feel?

The step into the unknown seems a potentially dangerous step. We often will put up with a great deal before we will act to change anything. This is why it often takes personality breakdowns, divorce, substance abuse, mental illness, or other traumatic events to get us started on the search. Why is this? Because of the need for earnestness. When life kicks your backside once too often, an earnest desire for change begins to grow like a callous.

Of course, earnestness can come simply from a love of "God", or spirit, or the search itself. As much as many teachers will insist that there should be no search, as that only reinforces the belief in a searcher, the search itself is part of the uncovering of the truth. The earnestness is already present. It is the flow of love in action. We do not have to muster it, just catch its tail and accept the ride. Yes, it is as simple as that, but only to the truly earnest.

The strange question asked by the questioner above, "Why were you lucky to trust your teacher fully, while our trust is nominal and verbal?" tends to answer itself in the asking. *Our trust is nominal and verbal* says why the lack of earnestness, but lays it at the feet of destiny or luck. Nisargadatta's reply puts it up to grace, *"Who can say? It happened so. Things happen without cause and reason and, after all, what does it matter, who is who?"* This is his answer then:

those who are favored by grace will have the earnestness to realize the self. Is that you?

It certainly is not you if you are one of the *no effort*, *no practice* kind of seekers. It is certainly not you if you simply follow your teacher without question or discrimination. While Nisargadatta trusted his teacher, he also behaved accordingly. This means that before his complete understanding, Nisargadatta lived his life *as if* he had the understanding of his teacher, simply on love and trust for his guru. Nisargadatta did not blindly follow but lived a life that revealed both before and after realization, the truth of his teacher's wisdom.

I have written before of this living *as if*. This is not pretending. This is the earnest acceptance of the truth on trust, until realization. This is the sacrifice. This is earnestness. It's kind of like a crank starting an old Model "T." Effort is required at first, but once going it runs on its own. Without this effort, which comes from grace, there is no starting this journey let alone staying with it until completion.

Later in *I Am That*, Nisargadatta points out the ultimate earnestness he is talking about: *"We discover it (the self) by being earnest, by searching, enquiring, questioning daily and hourly, by giving one's life to this discovery."* By giving one's life to this discovery. That is really the description of earnestness: to give one's life. If this search that is not a search, is to bear fruit, it must be the most important thing. You must not let yourself be satisfied with mere intellectual knowledge but seek to be that which you seek. Does Grace offer you that opportunity? Do you have the grace of earnestness? As I said at the beginning, *"Damn it! It's as simple as that!"*

We Are All Together

In 1978, when I first encountered the *Cloud of Unknowing*, I read in
the preface that the anonymous author was most likely an English
country parson from the East Midlands. It went on to say how he had
a way of making difficult, complex ideas simple to understand.
Something I have been accused of, starting with my high school
philosophy teacher. The author of the *Cloud* also shows a very
cautious way of warning his readers not to take everything he writes
to heart without looking very closely for themselves, as his
description is in words and the *unknowing,* he is writing about is not
available to the mind. I struggle with this, with every blog and note.

When, in a matter of five years, I found myself off to do volunteer
work at Lincoln Cathedral, which I had never heard of before, I was
surprised to find myself headed to the English East Midlands! The
Cloud had changed my life. Here I was, in a strange place with my
partner, having sold all our possessions, and I felt at home. It was
like bringing the *Cloud* home, and that country parson stayed by my
side. He was like me. He was me.

In 1986 the Church proper, not liking the idea of two gay men
forming a religious community, forced its closure. During the time
the community was struggling against closure, I discovered a book
about Ramakrishna in the local library. This led to reading about
Ramana Maharshi (it was next to Ramakrishna in the library). When
the community was finally closed down, we returned to San
Francisco, but I was very keen to find more reading about Advaita
Vedanta. In searching the San Francisco Library (a real treat after the
Lincoln Library, I can tell you!) I stumbled upon *I Am That*.

When I opened *I Am That* for the first time, there in the library, and
looked at the frontispiece, the picture of Nisargadatta Maharaj
captivated me. It was like looking into my own face. I could not read
this book fast enough. It answered all the remaining questions and
doubts I had tried to answer in Christianity. It was as if Nisargadatta

was there with me, knew what I needed, and directed me to it. Advaita itself was like confirming what I already knew but had no words for. Nisargadatta, even though he had left his physical body, became my guru.

In dreams I have described elsewhere, Nisargadatta confirmed that we are one. Nisargadatta silently expressed that I should take our investment in love and share it. You are reading some of that now.

After my awakening, also described elsewhere, I became aware that both the writer of the *Cloud* and Nisargadatta were no different than me, and that the reader of both the *Cloud* and *I Am That* were no different than the writers. I have a large photograph of Nisargadatta on one of my bookcases. In my house, I have only a couple of small photos of me and my partner on horseback. When I want to see me, I look at the picture of Nisargadatta with love.

Once I realized that the English country parson and Nisargadatta were none other than the *Self*, I began to see that the developmentally disabled, the elderly and the homeless man peeing in the phone booth were also none other than the *Self*. I began to see the tree, the sky, and the snail and slug as not separate, but the *Self* also. We are One. As you read this, you are reading your own words. But not words. The *Self* is loving itself. You the reader, and I the writer are sharing love. The words can't really say it, but the love is here right now. I love you, and as John Lennon wrote in "I Am the Walrus": "*I am he as you are he as you are me and we are all together.*"

Wake Up, Wake Up

When my partner and I were at the Cathedral in Lincoln, England, we were responsible for a variety of duties, one of which was opening the Cathedral during weekdays to prepare for the early Mass.

In addition to the opening procedure (which included letting out any pigeons that had made their way in through the bell tower over night!), John served the priest at Mass and I was responsible for ringing the morning bell, calling the City of Lincoln to worship.

I cannot explain the great joy I experienced ringing that bell. The bell had to be rung a certain number of times to indicate the time and day. I am afraid, after twenty-five years, I have forgotten the formula, but when I was ringing the bell, however, I never forgot. In *The Usages of the Cistercian Monks*, it reads, *"The Abbot will confide the task of ringing the bells to a monk who is noted for punctuality, so that all may be done at the correct time."* I took this very seriously. I am a punctual person.

When ringing the bells, which was a tradition that went back hundreds of years at Lincoln Cathedral, the Cathedral being at that time over nine hundred years old, I could feel the history. I was often accompanied by a medieval ringer, who although imaginary, had left a presence that was unmistakable. To fit into a centuries-old tradition in Lincoln, being an American, was a great and humbling honor.

To call the town to Mass to worship, was a great gift. "Wake up. Wake up," the bell would ring. I sometimes thought of those who might take exception to it all. "There are those damn bells again", I could hear the unappreciative sleeper say. But the bells were for the believers, not the sleepy. "Wake up. Wake up," the bell would ring.

Today, as I write my notes and blogs, I again call "Wake up. Wake up." The bells are ringing. Know this: you and I are one. The bells ring for us to "wake up" out of this dream of you and me, and realize we are one. Hear the bells. They say OM.

The New Traditions of Non-Duality

I was going to write about this for some time, but have hesitated because I know that this will be controversial. Reading a commentary on Neo-Advaita this morning however, convinced me that this is the time.

All, or most of us in the non-dual spiritual community have heard of and respect Ramana Maharshi. He was a great teacher. He had a great smile and a great story. But he is not the where-all and be-all of non-duality. In a Hindu context, he follows the teaching of Advaita as they are laid out in the ancient texts, and by Shankara. This is traditional Advaita. But there is much more to non-duality than Advaita.

Advaita follows Hindu traditions of *samsara, maya, jiva,* and *re-birth*. These are ideas and concepts that have some, but little relevance to Western ideas and concepts. The Western traditions of *sin, redemption,* and *heaven* have little to do with Advaita, but are symbolic in Christianity and other Western traditions. To imagine one more real or better than the other is stepping onto a slippery slope.

One of the characteristics of fundamentalist Christianity is the view that Christ is the only hope of salvation, and the Bible is the only truth. When we indicate that Ramana is the arbiter of truth, and compare anyone's statement to his teaching for judgment, we are doing the exact same thing. To insist that only by understanding the concepts of samsara, maya, jiva, and all the rest of it, is the only way to liberation is simply fundamentalism. To think that non-dualism requires an understanding of Hindu philosophy or cosmology is absurd.

Christians engage in lots of missionary work, work teaching, and converting the non-Christians. This has been and continues to be, justified by the idea that only those who know Christ will be saved. I fail to see how that is different from insisting that only those who are in line with the concepts of Ramana and traditional Advaita can be realized. Now, I know that this will be denied. Just as the fundamentalist Christian will say that "God loves everyone", I am sure the fundamentalist Advaitan will be open to other teachings, as long as they do not conflict with tradition, Shankara, or Ramana Maharshi.

People go to India, particularly Arunachala, and worship the place. Ramana Maharshi has been turned into a point of worship and prayer. He has become deified like Christ. His words are spoken with the same reverence by his devotees as those of Christ by fundamentalist Christians. Christ and Ramana are stories. There are lots of stories. Some in the modern West.

We see many teachers emerging in the West. Many come from a variety of traditions. Some have contact and experience in Eastern traditions, and they bring that to their teaching. The Eastern traditions often open up our experience in the Western traditions, but that does not mean that we have to swap one for the other. After finding the teachings of Nisargadatta Maharaj, it took me ten years to integrate these concepts into my own tradition. Truth is not the exclusive property of any one tradition but can be seen in many.

I have written about how I have seen gurus among the developmentally disabled. I have seen them sleeping under cardboard in the slums and in psychiatric hospitals. Had Ramana Maharshi been in the West, this man of silence who spoke to monkeys and cows, and wore a diaper, might very well have found himself in one of these situations. The West and the East are very different in culture and outlook. It is only reasonable to expect that the teachers will be different, and the expression unique.

When we judge another's teaching or spirituality based on the placement of one or two individuals being the acme of non-duality, we miss what is before us now. This is duality and worship of personality. The article on Neo-Advaita I reference at the beginning refers to "both of the Great Self Realized Sages, Adi Shankara, and Ramana Maharshi", as if there were no other great self-realized sages, either before, in between, or after. This is absurd on its face and is no different than holding Christ or the Buddha as the arbiter of all things spiritual.

As long as we compare modern, Western teachers by the standards set by Shankara or Ramana, we are involved in fundamentalism. If one comes from a Western life, a Western tradition, it is parroting at its most absurd to use Eastern thought, concepts and words to describe something that is experiential in a Western context. If I need to add to my "knowledge" to understand spirituality it is not reality, but more concepts.

I, for one, applaud the Jeff Fosters, Bentinho Massaros and Scott Kilobys, who along with others, are bringing non-duality to the west without the parroting of Eastern teachers or using their words. These and others are finding a new tradition, one that resonates with those who find it. We in the West have our non-duality too. It may not look the same as that of the east, but it is neither inferior nor pseudo.

Expressions of Love

Like the reflection of the moon in the water, objects, including our own image are reflections or expressions of the one reality. The reflection of the moon in the water is not the moon, but is neither an illusion nor appears separate from the moon.

We, as well as the entire universe, are expressions or reflections of the one reality: love. The inadequacy of the illustration of the reflection of the moon in the water is that, in this illustration, the moon and water are separate. In love, the expressions, including ourselves, reflect the stillness of love itself.

In love unfolding, the creative power of love expresses itself through the creation of expressions. In the illustration of the moon/water, the water is either still or in motion. When there is stillness, the moon is reflected, as it is. In love, the expressions are either still or in motion. The stillness of the expression is seen in the purity of the expression, as in a tree.

A tree grows fruits, produces seeds, and dies. This is what it does. It makes no decisions as to where it grows, how it grows, or what fruit it will produce. This is all part of the potential. Not the tree's potential, but the potential itself. There is no conflict. There is not even a need for acceptance on the part of the tree, as there is never any resistance to the potential. If only that were the case with us.

To return to the moon/water metaphor, we see that wind and other disturbances to the surface of the water cause waves and ripples which distort the image of the moon reflected there. This creates the illusion of an object, like the moon, but a distortion of it in love/expression. The waves and ripples are the thoughts of fear and separateness that distort the reflection of what we are in stillness: expressions of love. When we take ourselves to be different from love itself, seeing ourselves as the waves and ripples instead of love's expression, we lose clear sight of love itself, the reflection is distorted.

The waves and ripples which we take ourselves for, begin with the thought I Am, and grow into a tsunami of ideas, worlds, and universes. With each new thought that arises that we identify with: likes, dislikes, that which we call good or bad, all form together into the false identity of us. Just as the moon's reflection is distorted by the waves and ripples on the water, our image can become distorted from a still expression of love into jealousy, greed, and even hate. The more we identify with the waves and ripples instead of the stillness itself from which they arise, the further away from our true nature we imagine ourselves.

Only by seeing the waves and ripples as expressions or reflections only, without independent existence, can we see that the whole is one seamless piece: all reality and all illusion appearing together. In the metaphor of moon/water, all we need do is look up from the reflection to see the moon as it is. As expressions of love, we must stop identifying with the waves and ripples of the expression (fear, anger, disappointment, etc.) and look up to the silent, stillness of love that we are expressions of. We are life itself. We are love itself.

God and I Are One, When God and I Are Not

There are so many words for the ultimate reality. We call it God, the Absolute, or if in action, *nirvana, moksha,* or *enlightenment* and awakening. But none of that says very much.

Many who have lived this out call it love. This is my term for the ultimate reality, as that is how it presents itself here. But love can be just another object if we see only the word, and not the reality itself. We all know love as an emotion or as a feeling. Some have felt it toward others, and some have felt it toward themselves. And sadly, some have sought it without finding it. But here, we are talking about *being* it.

Many of us have felt love of a personal kind. Familial love, parental love, romantic love are all kinds of personal love. We may look at love of "God" or love of spirit as a higher kind of love, but when all is said and done, this too is personal love. We see love as something we give or something we receive, but this too, is not the same as being it.

I was drawn back to Christianity because of the love of Christ, not so much mine for him, as his for me. How selfish is that? "God is love," we are told by the Apostle. What can that mean? God *is* love. If this is the case, then the opposite is also true: love *is* God. This may be a better understanding, as it removes an unknown, unseen "God", and replaces it with what appears to be a known quantity: love. But this is not the same as being it.

The love about which we speak and the love, you are being encouraged to become is not personal love. This "God" is not the "God "we have imagined either, no matter how spiritual we envision him or her to be. When we examine carefully the image of "God", it, like the image of ourselves, vanishes. The love however remains. No real me, no real God, just the expression of love, expressing itself through the "me" and the "God" expressions.

When we personalize either "God" or ourselves, we reduce love back to an emotion or a feeling. Sure, it's a great feeling to love and be loved by "God", but in this case, the "love" stands between "God" and "I", as it is something we are giving and receiving between two separate entities. I once wrote, "God and I are One, when God and I are not." This is the key to non-duality. When "God" and "I" are no longer believed in as separate entities, only the love remains. When we see this clearly, then we realize that we *are* love.

There is no yoking with "God", as the Christian monk strives for. We do not become "God". We "become " what we have always been: the yoke! That yoke, this love, is creating and unfolding as the universe. Our appearance in this universe is an expression of this love unfolding. All we see as life is simply this unfolding of expressions. We do not so much experience a tree, as love expresses as both observer and tree in order for love to express as experiencing. In the state of pure experiencing (awareness), there are no objects observing or observed. This is non-duality. This is being love. This is the impersonal love, the universal love, we hear about.

"I" do not love a "tree". "I" do not love "God". There is no "I", "tree" or "God" separate from the love that creates them, expresses through them. When we love another, spouse, lover, or friend, we are only one when we are love itself. As was said of "God" above, "You and I are One when you and I are not!" There is only love in expression. We call it Life.

The Little Man at the Foot of the Bed

I certainly cannot speak for everyone in the non-dual community, but to me, any kind of supernatural experiences before, during, or after an awakening are highly questionable. That said, I would like to write briefly about my personal experiences and the appearance of the guru.

I have already written elsewhere about my vision of Christ on the cross and the two dreams of Nisargadatta Maharaj. But here, I want to talk about a more subtle experience and a phenomenal discovery I just made yesterday.

I mentioned in a note just a few days ago, that when I read *The Cloud of Unknowing*, I was struck by the fact that I was able to identify very closely with the anonymous country priest that wrote that work. And again, when I saw Nisargadatta Maharaj's photo for the first time, it was like looking into my own face.

Yesterday, after hearing so much about Robert Adams on Facebook, I decided to look him up and see what he was all about. I was rewarded by the discovery of a wonderful story of a very gentle and wise soul whose picture, like that of Nisargadatta, pierced deep into my heart. Robert Adams, like the English country priest who penned the *Cloud*, and Nisargadatta, was a known quantity.

Like the others, Robert Adams seemed to have wandered through my life from the first, a familiar face of comfort and stability. This, of course, could all be a trick of the mind. As I get older, I often find that faces start repeating as if there are only so many combinations, and as you age, they start repeating themselves. But there is more than mind and imagination here. It is a gut feeling, but I am not sure I would call it supernatural.

As I read as much as I could absorb about Robert Adams, I came upon some of his words about the teacher, the guru: "The teacher is really yourself. You have created a teacher to wake you up." I have heard this before of course, from other teachers, and have discovered it myself. But it really struck me this time, as I knew him instantly, the moment I looked into his eyes. The part that involves the supernatural came in the short bio, where Robert tells of an early memory that later made his hair stand on end. It did the same to me!

Robert relates the story of his earliest memory. He tells of a little man who would appear at the foot of his crib, and lecture him in gibberish. This went on from his earliest recollection until he was seven, about the time his father died. When he was fourteen, while looking through books at the public library, he came upon a book about Ramana Maharshi. When he looked at the picture of Ramana, he relates that his hair stood on end, as the man in the picture was the little man he had seen as a babe who had lectured him.

When I read this, my heart nearly stopped. I read it again and again. One of the memories of my early years that I have never forgotten was a little man who would appear at the foot of my bed. Unlike Robert, who seemed to think this was a natural occurrence, I was scared to death of this little man. My little man would poke at me. He was always animated and clearly wanted something. I did not think then, nor do I think now, that it was a dream. I was awake, I would call my folks, but no one could see him but me. Like Robert's little man, mine went away by the time I was eight or nine. Ever since, and to this day, the appearance has been so real, I sleep with my hands on my stomach to keep the little man from pestering me. I have never mentioned this before except to my partner, but reading about Robert's experience really shook me up.

I wish I could say I remember he was Ramana, or some other teacher, but my memory does not contain an image of his face. Robert's description of him, however, as being about two feet tall and always at the foot of the bed matches my experience exactly.

The universe is so full of wonders that none can really be discounted. Robert tells, *"You have created a teacher to wake you up."* I found that it is love that creates the objects, myself, and the teacher too. This message is written by these hands but comes from the heart, you and I are created by this same heart. I am as close to Robert as if we were both together seeing the little man in the same crib. I am as close to you as the love we share here. We *are* love together.

We Have No Secrets, Only Love

When I was about seventeen years old, I went to the theater to see a film called *David and Lisa*. This was an independent film about David, a teenage boy who has an aversion to being touched. David feels that the touch of another human being will kill him. Placed in a mental institution by his parents, David strikes up an unlikely friendship with Lisa, an immature-acting teen, who only speaks in rhyme, and will only communicate if she is spoken to in rhyme.

One of my favorite scenes from the film has the patients on a field trip from the institution, waiting for a bus at the bus station. An unfriendly family, also waiting for the bus, becomes disturbed by their presence and the father tells one of his children, "Those people aren't normal." Offended and hurt, some of the patients begin to cry and become upset. David comes forward and says to the father, "If you're normal, who wants to be normal?"

As I was seeing a psychiatrist weekly at that time, this became a kind of slogan for me: "If you're normal, who wants to be normal?" I was struggling with an identity crisis at the time, my homosexuality coming to the surface. I had never been normal. I did not want to be normal. I had already had more than a year of psychiatry in my early childhood, and I did not like seeing this psychiatrist. At seventeen I already knew more about myself, my motivations, and inner life than anyone I knew, including most of the adults in my life. The shallowness, the emptiness of their pathetic lives was frightening. It was like living among robotic aliens.

Psychiatry to me, was like confession. I had told all my secrets. For a while, it was as if there was no "me" left. All those little things we keep hidden in ourselves, that go to make up what we think we are, were gone. I was naked, scared, but very free. No one had anything on me, for it was all there on the table. I was my own. Naked, I was now free to dress myself as I chose. It was then that I chose to live for love alone. Looking back, I can see that there really was no choice, as there was never any choice. Love was the call I could not resist. All I knew was that life had to be experienced here, now, in its own terms.

Now, as an aging human being, I can't say I feel any different. For many years I read and studied. I delved deeply into Christianity and Christian Mysticism, and then Nisargadatta Maharaj. I continue to have sixty or so books on the shelf that have inspired me, and I occasionally read bits here and there, but I don't read many new books or articles any longer. There are so many teachers, gurus, and people that others have labeled as clear, holy, inspired, and all the rest of it. But I have found that adapting the spiritual discoveries of others is only useful in gathering an intellectual understanding. The teachings must become alive in us. They must be lived.

When I was in school, I found that I could learn something much more thoroughly, if I took the reading and turned it into my own words, making it *my own*, so to speak. If you read any of my notes or blogs, you will see that I try to explain my experiences and understandings in my own way. I will often use terms that are understandable to those who I feel will read my writing, but try not to use too much jargon or too many quotes. As a largely uneducated person, I try not to go beyond what I have found for myself. I know I am not normal. My secrets are gone. There remains nothing to protect. Life wakes in the morning, and I open my eyes to the mystery.

In all honesty, apart from my partner, I have no friends. Yet every stranger is loved. You, my readers, are my life. I wish we could talk face to face. It would be so much clearer if we could share, and I could simply *be* with you. I was reading this morning that Robert Adams felt that self-inquiry and being in his presence were two ways to self-discovery. I never really felt that *presence* would make a difference, but as the mystery of life unfolds through me, there is a greater sense that I would love to see deeply into your eyes and speak directly to the love that is both speaking and hearing. But in a very real way, my writing is sharing a presence that lives both in it and in you.

Without secrets, we can be One. Without fear of who we are, we can see that stripped bare of masks we have the same face. Non-dual meetings or Satsangs are more than student-teacher get-togethers. They are the Self meeting the Self. They are the celebration of the unfolding of love. This is not normal. We are not normal. Who wants to be normal? There is no teacher. There is no student. We have no secrets, only love.

Nothing But Love

On a hot day, as we look along the road from the car window, we see reflections in the road ahead of water shimmering on the pavement. As we approach, we see that it was a mirage. If we accept the vision we see as water, we are fooled. It is an illusion of water only. But if we see the shimmering, and we understand that it is heat moving the air that creates the effect, then we understand that it is hot outside the car. We are not fooled, as the heat waves are a true indicator of heat, not an illusion.

It has always seemed strange to me that in spirituality, the mind is cast into the role of villain, or at the very least into the character of a charlatan. Concepts of maya, or the dream are created to dismiss the workings of the mind, and thoughts are seen as illusory.

The mind is not an independent entity. The mind is simply a bag of thoughts. The thoughts themselves make up the mind. When there are no thoughts, where is there a mind? The thoughts too, are looked at as misleading charlatans. But can they not be pointers beyond themselves to a vision of the truth?

In Non-duality, we understand that there is only one substance. Call it the Absolute, "God", love, truth, or the space in which all appear; but we can all agree that there is only one substance. This being the conclusion, it becomes obvious that the thoughts are within that space. Thoughts passing through; expressions of the unfolding, are either allowed to go on their way or are held together in time, forming the bag of thoughts that appears as the mind.

Both the thoughts, and the bag that holds them, are not unlike the mirage we observe on the road; illusions if we take them for what they appear to be, but indicators of truth if we see them as they truly are. The thoughts, the mind, are not villains or charlatans, they are simply misinterpreted as objects, movements, and feelings suspended in time. The mind, being really nothing but this collection of thoughts, is not the creator of the thoughts, but simply interprets them suspended in time. The thoughts themselves are part of the unfolding of the Absolute, of life.

Those of you who know my teaching, know that I use the term love in place of the Absolute. I do this for two reasons. The first is because this is how love presents itself here. The second is because love's understanding is in the heart. While the mind is not a villain or charlatan, it does tend to see the shimmering in the road as water. The collection of thoughts suspended in time is seen by the mind as objects, movements, and feelings, while the heart understands that there is only love unfolding.

While many non-duality teachers advise us to stay in the I Am until it is recognized, that the only thing in the bag of thoughts we can know is that we are. This only brings us to the door of understanding. To open the door, the key is in the Absolute (love) itself. Just as we intellectually (bag of thoughts) understand that the I Am is as far as the mind can go, we must exhaust ourselves in the search before this is real (realized). So it is with the key: the Absolute (love). In order to realize love as the space in which all unfolds, we need to see that we are Love. We do this by *being* it.

If we understand intellectually (bag of thoughts again), that love is what we *are*, we need to make love a *practice*. This is done through service. To a seeker, especially one who is called to solitude or silence, this is sacrifice. To serve without reward, even praise or gratitude, opens the heart in a way that may even be missed by the dedicated server. But ultimately it opens the heart to the love that is the space in which everything unfolds.

This service, this living for love alone, is the key to getting beyond the selfishness of the I Am. Trying to escape the mind that clings to the I Am, is only to strengthen it. To live for love alone is to seek the pearl of great price. Just as we continue to see the mirage as water, we understand and have the conviction that it is heat waves expressed as an illusion of water. So it is with the appearances of objects, movements, and feelings. The mind (bag of thoughts suspended in time) sees objects, movements and feelings, but the heart, opened by living in love (service) gains the conviction that this is all the unfolding of love.

In this conviction, the mind is seen, not as a villain or charlatan, but as a mirror in which the light of love shines on the mystery unfolding before us. The tree equals love. The sky equals love. The pain equals love. The I am equals love. When all is observed as love, with conviction, no matter the form it takes in the mind, we understand that we, the mind, and all else we observe are nothing but love.

Is It Possible to Love Too Much?

Can we be "too nice "? Is it possible to love too much? Not in my experience. When I was a small boy, I was taught to love my neighbor as myself. The old Golden Rule, *do unto others as you would have them do unto you*, was the credo of my family. My father would bring home the homeless and hungry. My grandparents, who ran an apartment building, would have the whole building in for Thanksgiving and Christmas. They had even done this during the Depression, and believe me, they were poor! Love was a visceral feeling in my home and in my life.

Today, psychology and some philosophy would want you to believe that you need to *love yourself first*. There are those psychologists who believe that we "hate" ourselves, and therefore seek outside of ourselves for love. And of course, the teachers of non-duality want us to concentrate on the I Am and love ourselves so we see through the false self to the inclusion of the other. These often simply become excuses for abiding in our selfishness.

This idea that if I love myself, I am loving others, because we are all one, is a snow job. It's selfish. If we are all one, then loving others is loving yourself. This is also much more to the point and is a safer position. It is much more difficult to love others as yourself than to love others through yourself. We all start from a position of I Am. This is the seed of selfishness. To lose your *self* in the love and service of others is to find the *Self* that lives in us all.

My mother used to tell me a saying my great-grandmother used to tell her, "*Brighten the corner where you are.*" An old-fashioned saying for sure, but well remembered all the same.

Bringing light, living as love, is what we are called to do. This does not mean using our minds to make judgments of who is pure or loving, but always being loving, even in the face of what appears to be evil.

The story is told of a robbery at Ramana Maharshi's Ashram. While many panicked, the Maharshi, even though mishandled by the intruders told others to let the robbers have what they wanted. This was not out of fear, but out of loving kindness. The Maharshi was loving-kindness itself. He had no choice but to follow his nature.

When I was a boy, and in my teens, others would often tell me that so and so was taking advantage of me in some way. I would simply answer that I was aware of what was happening and that no one could take advantage of me, as there was nothing that was *mine* that could be taken away. If you know who you are, you do not fear being taken advantage of, you have nothing to lose.

We cannot stand as the self and make demands for space, property, or even personal peace. If life ("God", love) sends others into our lives, then, if we are true to love itself, we accept what is sent, no matter how flawed. Jesus, bleeding and dying on the cross, after suffering brutal humiliation and apparent human failure said. *"Father forgive them, for they know not what they do."* Those who hurt us or ill use us are only engaging in love in a perverted" sense: self-love, self-protection. Our casting them aside, putting our own purposes and self-protection before our love for them is no different.

The Christ's prayer at the Last Supper asks that the disciples love one another as he had loved them. How was that? How did he show his love for them? He hung on a cross and died.

Ramana allowed his meager possessions to be stolen. Submission to life's situations is flowing with love. To hate another, to cast away another is selfishness, no matter what pretty philosophical or psychological bows you wrap it in.

An Open Invitation

I was asked in an interview about my impression of Nisargadatta Maharaj's tossing people out of his little mezzanine room, and whether that showed love, or something else. My response was that maybe on some days Nisargadatta was a bit cranky. He was quite elderly by the late seventies and eighties, and I can understand that.

There is also the likelihood that he often felt that those who came only to test him, or find an intellectual answer or argument were not earnest enough to waste everyone's time on. In his later years, Nisargadatta wanted to stick to the basics, the very heart of the matter, not engage in verbal rhetoric.

As I put up my little notes, I often get among the loving responses, these same kinds of people seeking to test, argue and quibble. Many of these are educated people who are out to prove their own vision is clearer or that they can use words more skillfully or succinctly. This is of no matter here. I am a simple man, with no high school or college degree. I do not have the words of the academic. I am not a scholar. What I understand has been placed in my heart, and from there, I write and speak.

I am love. I speak only as love. I will not say I am enlightened, as I have always been as I am. I lived in the big picture from the time I was born. I have always lived with the understanding that I am not of this world. I have described my awakening experience elsewhere, and other events that are of little importance. All these things, the reading, the prayer, and the contemplation have only confirmed what has always been present: I am love.

I am no different than you. I appear to you out of your dream to tell you to look, see, that you are love only. The persons, teacher, and seeker are only expressions of love. I speak of love unfolding. This is not something I have heard and repeated but what is seen here. That wonder, that blessing is what is being conveyed. I have nothing more to say or teach, and nothing to argue about. So far, I have not tossed anyone out (unfriended) for simply arguing, though it is tedious when I am only sharing love which can be accepted or not. It is only entertainment or a desire to show off your knowledge to argue with one who offers only love. I will not argue with you.

I am mostly silent. All my life, I have been described as a quiet person. I have always lived for the "not of this world" truth. This has been costly in human terms. Psychological breakdowns, forced institutionalizations, not being social enough to stay in school, have been my reward for living by the "not of this world" truth. I often wonder what would have happened to Nisargadatta, Ramana, St. Teresa, or Ramakrishna, had they been forced to live in modern, Western society.

But this is it, isn't it? Many of us do live in modern society, and we attempt to find the truth while still being part of it. We get education. Can you believe, that some PhDs actually argue with me, and become sarcastic? I simply tell them what is seen here, and I am drowned in sarcastic intellect. It is so funny. Nisargadatta, Ramana, St. Teresa, and Ramakrishna are my brothers and sister. We smile at each other, and understand. I don't agree with some, or in some cases, many of their words, but their hearts and mine beat in unison and love.

As long as we hold that a place in society is important, are unwilling to give without reward or assurances of tomorrow, and feel the need to argue instead of being silent in the face of love, we are simply spinning our wheels and playing at "seeking" or "enlightenment", which are, after all, only words we have heard.

Many of you may say, "He is just an uneducated buffoon playing at being a teacher," and will unfriend and run away before anyone sees you associating with the likes of me. And this is fine. I know nothing. I can tell you nothing. I can only say, you are love unfolding. Explore it for yourself. I am love only, calling you out of your dream. After all the pain, I can only reach out to you and say, I am the little boy who always trusted. I am trust itself. I am love. Remove the superfluous, stand naked in life, and join me. It's an open invitation.

Surrender Everything

In relative terms, the human being is made up of spirit, mind, and body. Absolutely, there is just spirit: love. In what we refer to as spirituality, there is the seeking and investigating into the realm of spirit. In the West, when the intellect and psychology (mind) become dissatisfied with organized religion, there is often a search for a more meaningful spirituality.

In this search for meaning, many turn to Eastern philosophies, many of which also contain an element of religion. Some seekers will swap a religion that has lost its meaning for a new religion that seems to answer questions that were left hanging in the old belief system. But many in the West want to jettison all belief systems for a logic-based, "scientific" view, a spirituality without spirit.

At the other extreme, we find those who put great value in spiritual experiences. We hear of blue light experiences, mysterious figures, or rising up to heaven in a kind of self-styled transfiguration. Some of these also like to use the name "God" as if such a sky captain were a reality. Where is a simple seeker after truth to go in this spiritual marketplace?

Those who advocate the logical, scientific view teach a kind of biological/psychological spirituality, or as I said above, a spirituality without spirit. These are the ones who see love as a biological process inherent in the brain. They also are the ones who engage in psychological games and tricks like "watching the mind", "shadow work" or simply asking us to stop our minds in order to experience "awareness" without thought (as if that were possible to do with the mind!). These are all wonderful psychological practices and are helpful in quieting the mind and finding psychological blockages. But they are not spiritual. They are in the mind.

And again, the spiritual experience junkie, with his visions of "God", explosive awakenings, or blue light experiences is also living in the mind, as this is where these experiences happen. These are the teachers who tell you to look for a particular experience, particularly one like they have had that can be defined in a particular way. They see no problem with being able to say you must have this kind of experience or it's not authentic. Again, this is obviously in the mind. If your experience is definable or describable, it is in the mind. Again, where is the simple seeker after truth to go in this spiritual circus?

We have been given examples of spiritual masters, gurus, and teachers for centuries. There have been examples in every major belief system from Buddhist, Advaita, Christian, Islam, and to those of no fixed or specific system. They are all different, have different approaches, and have formulated, or not, methods and practices. Although they vary widely in their behaviors, they have some things in common. The first being that they lived out their teaching in lives that were unique and set apart. Lives of humility, unconcerned for the conventions of the world. Buddha, Christ, Ramana Maharshi, Nisargadatta Maharaj, all lived lives that were not only different from ours but different from the time and people they lived among. Of those, Nisargadatta lived the most ordinary life, but his earnestness, love and generosity were anything but ordinary.

To say that there is nothing special about these teachers or spiritual masters is foolish on its face. How many Christians live as Christ? How many Buddhists, outside the monastery, live as Buddha? How many live as Ramana Maharshi or Nisargadatta Maharaj? This is really the key.

The spiritual life is a life apart, a life unique. It is a *"being in the world, but not of it."* It is a life worked out by oneself, following the call life gives you.

To think that you can engage the world in an ordinary manner, with ordinary meaning in this context, living for ordinary worldly values and aspirations is foolish. But this is what many of the teachers of *spirituality without spirit* will tell you. On the other hand, the teachers of spiritual experience with their rarified awakenings, visions of "God" and all the rest of it, are separating those with "The Experience" from those who have not had "The Experience". They will tell you of course, that you too can have this wonderful experience as well, but are sure to tell you that you have not had it yet unless you are like them and see it in their way. The intellectual, *"spirituality without spirit"* teachers are living in and teaching from the mind; and the "spiritual experience" teachers are living in and teaching from the world of ego (also mind).

To be *"in this world, but not of it"* is clear in a Buddha, a Christ, or a Ramana Maharshi. Why fool yourself by being a Sunday Christian or a Satsang participant who forgets all the inconvenient truths while living your daily life? When Christ told the rich young fellow to sell his possessions and follow him, the fellow went away sad. What makes you think you can follow and hang on to anything? You need to leave all behind, be it mind games of psychological discovery or dream visions of "The Experience", and follow the call that calls you to *be yourself.*

Nisargadatta's famous quote, "When I see that I am nothing, that is wisdom. When I see that I am everything, that is love, between the two, my life continually flows," is the beginning. To live that out, without psychological self-indulgence, or experiential spiritual pride is the beginning. To do this is to *step off the cliff* into the unknown, the unsure, and the potentially unsafe. But to the true seeker, the one who is called by something other than a desire for peace of mind or to relieve personal suffering, there is no choice. Love is calling, calling from within. You will either follow or remain in the safe world of the mind.

Which Came First?

I want to toss around a few things here and see if and how they land. This morning I read somewhere the idea that love, among other things, like wisdom and joy are simply byproducts of clear seeing, seeing through separation. This would seem to be in line with Nisargadatta Maharaj's famous quote, which I use all the time:

"When I see that I am nothing, I call that wisdom. When I see that I am everything, I call that love. Between the two, my life continually flows."

That statement would seem to confirm that love and wisdom are indeed byproducts or at least the results of seeing through separation. But is this really true? Let's have a look.

I think that we can at least assume that love, joy, and divine wisdom are beyond the mind, not describable in words. If we can box in love, joy, or divine wisdom in our words, concepts, or thoughts, they are not the genuine article; the genuine article is indefinable.

"When I see that I am nothing" "When I see that I am everything." That certainly sounds like clear seeing, seeing through separation. And it is. But does the seeing come before the love, joy and divine wisdom, or is the clear seeing a byproduct of love, joy, and divine wisdom?

I would propose that the love, joy, and divine wisdom must come first. Clear seeing is not available to the mind. Clear seeing lives only in love, joy, and divine wisdom, the byproducts of love only, all being beyond mind. The mind, of course, wants to come first. It will try to usurp the love, joy, and divine wisdom, and try to present them as its byproducts, its discovery.

This false belief that the mind is seeing through separation is one of the pitfalls of "spirituality without spirit", that I have referred to in previous writings. As soon as the heart opens to love, joy, or divine wisdom, and the truth is revealed, the mind, like a hidden snake, sneaks in and grabs the awakening. Love, being our very nature, the "very form of God", as Ramana Maharshi put it, is the only place where no separation exists, all else being dualist. This is not available to the mind, but the mind tries to claim it.

The late, and loving American jnani, Robert Adams took this idea even further, in that he felt it was valuable to worship the Absolute as "God" *in form*. He expressed that worshiping (loving) a formless "God" would not produce sufficient energy:

"If you worship God without form, the energy is not as strong. For what kind of a God are you worshipping? An invisible God that has no form, no shape. Therefore, you have doubts. You are not too sure. And, the energy you send out is not that strong. But when you worship God as form, you can give that God all of your energy, or totally surrender (to that particular deity). That is the purpose of worship. Finally, totally, surrender your ego, your pride, your body, your affairs, your life, to that deity. And then, You (as divine Self rather than human person) become that deity, itself."

This energy that Robert is talking about is love itself. Only through loving can we *be* love. Only through practicing love (silence, devotion, service) can we step into the unseen realm of love itself. We can practice all the mind games and awareness techniques that we like, but to allow that the mind is quieting itself, illuminating itself, is to follow a road that leads only back to the mind and not beyond it.

Here, in this teaching that has been given me by grace, there is difficulty in this idea of "God" in form. Robert Adams believed that "the importance of loyalty to one teacher in personal reverence and practice" results in "powerful practical results in life". He went so far as to say that:

"Worshiping God in the form of Sat Guru or in the form of a Buddha or a Christ, whichever, is even better."

To many, the personal "God" in form, becomes a stumbling block. The guru as "God" also leads many astray. This is why seeing love only is the start of understanding. You can look at it as "God's love" if that helps, but to see something personal in the universal, unconditional love is an error. We, the world, and the whole of the universe are not nouns, but a verb. We are not a thing, but life itself.

But this argument with Robert is a small one. We both see that love, devotion, and worship are vital to any awakening. To simply say that love, joy, and divine wisdom are byproducts of clear seeing is to believe the deception that the mind *saw it first.*

We open our hearts by loving, as that is what the heart does. No matter how clear we can explain the mind's discovery, it will not open the heart, love being the only key. Love in silence (contemplation), and love in action (service) are the shortest route to awakening. The mind with all its clever words, concepts, and ideas will try to tell you that with it you can, and indeed you have discovered "truth"; but it is simply deceiving you by swapping a vision it couldn't understand, for one it makes up.

Make no mistake, the mind exists in love, not love in the mind. Clear seeing results from love. Everything is a byproduct of love, including this *clear seeing.*

Enlightenment and Depression

What? What's that you say? Depression and enlightenment in the same sentence? How can that be? Isn't enlightenment supposed to be a cure for depression? No, it's not, but the two work together in a very mysterious and wonderful way.

I am not talking here about the blues, some momentary setback or disappointment, but genuine clinical depression, the kind that leads to despair and suicide. And I don't want to forget anxiety, depression's companion, and playmate. What do these have to do with enlightenment?

They seem the opposite of enlightenment, the very kind of thing that many seek enlightenment to save them from.

This is one of the reasons that I so dislike the "once enlightenment takes place there is peace of mind" crowd. Sure, if you are one of the "normal" people with regular neurology, NTs, or neurotypicals as we Asperger's folks call the rest of you, some kind of enlightenment may bring peace of mind. But to us, who suffer clinical depression, neurological depression, enlightenment brings understanding. In fact, I have found that the neurological kind of depression may indeed bring about the shift that is so necessary for enlightenment to take place. We are special people, and our differences, including our depression, are our special gift; a grace waiting to be discovered.

How can I call neurological depression and anxiety a gift? Once it is discovered that depression, neurological depression and anxiety is present, it is discovered that it is a chemical process and part of the body. The body/mind we appear to be born with is a complete system of functions, mostly unconscious. We can dismiss it as an illusion, but its reality is part of the functioning of the whole. If you prick it, does it not bleed? Among the functions of this complex mechanism are both the personality and the way it perceives the world. Enlightenment does not necessarily change the personality, only the perception.

This is why we have so many different kinds of gurus. The personality is part of the body/mind complex. It lives until the body dies and ceases functioning. It's something we have to put up with in our acceptance. It will be gone soon enough.

But to get back to the gift of depression and anxiety. Many people are treated for neurological depression with drugs. This works for a certain number of cases, but not all. The drugs work because they trigger endorphins, those little happy-making hormones in the chemical body. This process makes clear to the mind that depression or anxiety is simply a functioning of the body.

When one looks at this kind of depression, it becomes apparent that there is depression and anxiety without external causes. But until this is discovered, the mind thinks it feels depressed and anxious, when it is really only a bodily function. The mind usurps the feeling and desperately starts to seek a cause. "It's my horrible wife or husband." "It's my boss or job." "I'm a terrible person, and deserve no better." Any number of possibilities arise in the mind.

The gift comes in seeing that the depression is simply a happening, and has no relationship to you. Sure, it still feels bad. It still hurts. But now you are actually able to stand to the side of it and watch it. "There is the depression again, but it's not me." "These thoughts of anger and personal judgment are all in the mind." "I am not my thoughts." It's that body, that guy in the dream that hurts, and not me." The "me" being the reality you are, the "I Am". Right understanding of depression and anxiety can take you beyond the "I Am". This is its *gift*, it's a wonder.

For the last few decades, I have lived as love alone. In the last twenty years, it has been an unshakable conviction. The depression still continues but is seen for what it is. I am able to live without medication because I understand who and what I am. I am that unshakable love and awareness that is neither born nor dies. I have described my anticipation of death as being like a child anticipating Christmas. Now you know why.

Somewhere I read the idea of the body as being like a wheel that is rolling downhill. It keeps going based on momentum. It keeps going until it either hits something or loses its momentum.

Our body/mind contains the vital force, the personality, and the thoughts. When it stops functioning, it is simply gross matter. To escape the body is to be totally free, provided there is awareness of the Self; that unfolding wholeness that we are.

This is the purpose of life, if we are to accept there is any purpose at all, this discovery of the Self. So many seekers who are looking for peace of mind, find that they get so far and then find depression, anxiety, and other distractions that they consider backsliding. They say, "Oh, I can't have found the answer. I'm not enlightened, because I'm depressed or anxious." But this isn't so. Perhaps among the neurotypicals, there is constant bliss in enlightenment. I could not tell you.

But what I can tell you is that it is possible to constantly behold the face of "God", even through the physical and mental depths of depression and anxiety, when it is seen clearly that you are not the depression, but the observer of it. The depression and anxiety can itself become the guru, the awakening to that shift of consciousness that takes you to love. I have no doubt that I am love, and I wait with great joy for Christmas.

Offering False Hope

On Sunday I put up a Note called *Enlightenment and Depression*. It was about those who suffer from clinical/chemical depression, and how by seeing through the body/mind, it is still possible to live as love. It was well received, and many resonated with its message.

The following day, another Facebook friend, put up a note saying that enlightenment or awakening could turn that around and even suggested that the DNA could be changed. I must admit that this note made me rather angry. Regardless of the language, which basically called those with depression, people with a victim mentality, it was the offering of false hope that upset me.

It was my intention to let people with depression (myself included) know that awakening is happening right now in the present moment, even in the face of apparent depression. I wanted to say that love is what you are, even if sadness, even if despair, is present in your mind. In my note of response, I questioned why someone who claims awakening could make such a hollow promise of hope.

The first response I received from the writer, was "An ugly distortion by a depressed mind".

Not a very kind remark, but it made me laugh, coming from one who makes a point of touting his love and compassion. The personal remarks aside, he later wrote that "my writing is meant to offer hope". And therein lies the rub! Hope is holding out a carrot of some future event that will make everything blissful and pristine. Not going to happen!

There is only the present; the past and future are only in the mind. To offer hope is to make a false promise of change, even a change in DNA, in some imaginary future. Hope lives only in the future! Even the Christ had his agony in the Garden of Gethsemane and turned it into acceptance. He asked the Father to remove it from him, but he knew it must be endured and accepted. His suffering in the face of being an actual victim did not give him a victim mentality. It gave him the opportunity to accept and surrender. Depression gives us such an opportunity.

To offer false hope, when acceptance of what is, is the only answer, is cruel. and misguided. Like hope, depression lives only in the mind. Living in the heart accepts the externals, pleasant, or not. Pleasant or unpleasant are only judgments of the mind, and have no power over the understanding that Love is what you are.

The Shadow as a Weapon

As I have stated before, I was seeing a psychiatrist when I was nine. I could not face any kind of social life, so I refused to go to school. I either spent my days hiding out on top of my grandparent's shed or in the wonderful hills and rocks above my home.

I have never been social, always disliked parties, and avoided large groups. When I decided to start writing and sharing my spiritual musings on Facebook, it was a big step. I really shouldn't say I decided, because the pull of love has deemed it so, and I really have no choice but to share.

I knew when I came to Facebook that I would be challenged. As I have said repeatedly, I do not hold any degree or even a high school diploma. True, I do have a year of college, having past the entrance exams, but remain undereducated in contrast to many of my Facebook friends. My college studies were mostly based around psychology courses, as I had hopes of becoming a teacher, but the social side made college trying and I soon left the academic world.

My years of psychiatric inquiry started at nine and the courses I took added to a good understanding of what makes people, particularly me, tick. By the time I was twelve, I had a good handle on the concepts of repression, regression, denial, and projection. I was alarmingly open.

I have found that in the spiritual community, the non-dual community in particular, projection has become a facet of self-inquiry. The concept of each of us projecting the other has become an article of faith in non-duality. This projection as conceived by Freud was later named the shadow by Carl Jung and adapted by Ken Wilber in a kind of spiritual psychology. It is a wonderful way of self-examination and has great benefits when used properly for self-inquiry. It has, unfortunately, been turned around and become a kind of spiritual weapon.

In the last couple of days, this weapon has been turned on me twice, by those who are unwilling to look at themselves and their actions.

This is of course, ok, as no one needs to look at themselves if they don't want to. I will admit to being frank. I am Asperger's, and I will tell you things others won't. Honesty and integrity are very important to me. I pull no punches with myself or others. I have seen and continue to see, the ugliness in my life, my actions, and my thoughts. Sometimes it isn't pretty, but I could not live without full discovery.

The weapon aspect of projection (the shadow), comes in when someone is told an observation that they don't like or want to deny. The first reaction is to throw the shadow at the observer and dismiss the observation as a projection of the others' own faults. This has become very common and is often used by the self-proclaimed enlightened. If it is pointed out that what is seen is not indicative of an awakening or enlightenment, the shadow is thrown. This was demonstrated by Ramesh Balsekar in his infamous sex scandal, and in the subsequent defense of his actions by Wayne Liquorman, Ramesh's protégé. This is not what the shadow is for.

The shadow projection is a method of self-inquiry. It is not for making judgments of others' observations. First, there really are no "others", so any observations are only appearing out of the one. Looking deeply into ourselves, and seeing our fears and doubts cast upon others is deep work, and is a lifetime ongoing process. It is useful and can bring about understanding. But the use of it as a weapon has just the opposite effect. It says, "I do not have to take advice or criticism seriously, as I am enlightened; so it is just their inadequacies being projected onto me. I did not have sex with a student, behave unprofessionally, or resort to name calling. It's your shadow that sees this."

This throwing of the shadow is not only a weapon against criticism, it is a weapon against our self and our spiritual development. If we are honest, we need to look at our motives, question our thoughts, and see deeply inward. Even if we see ourselves as enlightened (which is often, if not always, a stumbling block in itself), we must be vigilant. Awakening itself brings this about. The awakened becomes the observer. Inner details become obvious. Flaws are seen and accepted, not thrown at others. The proclamation of no faults, all bliss, should be a red flag to any coming in contact with such an enlightened.

Many of the self-proclaimed enlightened remind me of the lyrics from the Steely Dan song, *Reelin' in the Years*. If you question one of these enlightened about their enlightenment, you had better duck, the shadow will be thrown. Question your own shadow, by all means, but if you throw it, you need to really question that. With openness, you need no weapons, just love.

Living Skinless

When I left the religious community to return to the real world, I felt skinless. I had always, since childhood, felt a bit skinless. The adult world seemed crazy. People said things they didn't mean. They lied, cheated, and covered up the truth while telling me not to do the same. They spoke of "God" and spirituality as being of the greatest importance, but constantly figured out ways to get around things that were inconvenient. It was confusing, and it hurt.

We often refer to *becoming like children* as if we really understood what that means. In spirituality, it is highly prized but rarely practiced. Oh, we try to act innocent, non-judgmental, and accepting, but we avoid the vulnerability that is required to actually rediscover those things in our lives. We need to become skinless. We wear masks that hide our true selves. We read about a Ramana Maharshi, a Christ, or a Buddha, and we may attempt to live our lives based on their words and actions. But those are just more masks.

If I put on a Ramana mask, and base my life on his words, his actions, what happens to the true face I hide? If I follow the ways of a Christ or Buddha, live in their skin, try to think with their thoughts, where is the expression of the one that lives in this wave? We hold up particular characters in this play as examples: Ramana, Nisargadatta, Christ, Buddha, and a number of others. Do we need to do what these men did, or do we need to do as these men did? When I refer to what "these men did," I am referring to being themselves, being open to being themselves.

Being yourself seems to be very hard within any system, be it fundamentalist Christianity or non-dualism. The fundamentalist Christian makes all manner of rules to follow, to be like Christ. So we put on a "humility mask", a "righteous indignation" mask, a "caring mask", and all the rest of them. In non-duality, we put on a "oneness mask", a "no doer mask", a "no judgment mask", and all the other masks that define our thinking and who we fancy we are. But to really discover our expression, our potential, we need to become skinless.

Becoming skinless involves more than just removing the masks. It requires the removal of skin, an open vulnerability. To look closely at this skinlessness as a metaphor, we have to see that the openness of skinlessness, not only makes us available to what is, it makes us sensitive to the salt that gets thrown our way. We may wince and cry sometimes in this vulnerability. Salt hurts the skinless. This of course, is frowned upon in non-duality circles. If you are enlightened, free, one with the all, you are told you live in bliss. No tears, no pain, no salt.

I recently was forced to unfriend one Facebook friend and was unfriended by another. This disappointed me, as I was a fan, an enjoyer, a friend in every sense of the word. I attempted, as a child might, to be open and point out the need for skinlessness, vulnerability by being vulnerable. I pointed out that I suffer from time to time from depression, but keep it under control by seeing it for what it is. They took exception by putting on the mask of enlightenment. From behind this mask of enlightenment, I was told that I "had not made it yet", or I would be happy and blissful like some kind of cartoon chipmunk. When I took exception to this, they threw salt. It hurt, and once they knew it hurt, they threw more.

To get away from metaphors for a moment, I felt hurt. Now, I know in the rarified world of Advaita or non-duality, one is not supposed to feel hurt, only bliss or nothingness. But I was hurt.

If you take a child who offers his best openly, no matter how innocent, non-judgmental, or accepting children may be, and slap him in the face, he will cry. And I did. I sat in front of the computer screen and cried the bitter tears of a child. I recovered, as the footing of my life is on solid ground, but there was momentary hurt. I do not pretend to be in some blissful state all the time, although that is my experience. I offer what I offer skinless. I do not give two pins if it fits with Ramana, Nisargadatta, Christ, or anyone else. I offer myself, as it says in the Bible and as we named our religious community, as a living sacrifice, skinless.

To be open, as a little child, to oneness and bliss, I must be open to pain. I must not trade all the masks I so valiantly tore from my flesh, for the mask of enlightenment, a false enlightenment that promises a false bliss. I must not care if anyone, even myself, thinks I am enlightened. I must live only skinless now. It hurts sometimes, but I will not wear another's spirituality, mask, or skin. When life throws salt, as life will, it will burn. I might cry. But the skinlessness that allows the salt to burn also allows the balm of awareness and love to sooth.

Love without Reward: The Dance Itself!

I just read the statement, "At some point, all spiritual effort is rewarded," again, that carrot is being dangled out there. I suppose in a pay-off-oriented society, that is what is sought: a reward. This is just simply not good enough.

Love is all there is. To use an old clichéd phrase: Love is its own reward. And this is it, isn't it? The search is not for something. There is no treasure to find which is not already present. Wisdom, peace of mind, happiness, or whatever is sought as a reward, is not good enough.

What is sought is what calls. It is also the journey itself. Until it is realized (the real manifest) that the call, the seeker, and the path followed are all the same love playing out its game with itself, the journey continues. After it is realized that this is simply a play of love, the journey continues, until all is absorbed back into love itself.

Love is calling, calling to itself. This is expressed in a wonderful manifestation, or a silent stillness depending on the angle of view. If love itself is not leading back to itself, it is simply wandering, and it isn't love. It's the mind's idea of love, a mistaken identity. When a reward is sought, no matter how lofty, a possession is sought, a pay-off for imagined efforts. This is self-seeking, selfishness, and has nothing to do with love.

Any spiritual journey, that is a true one, starts with a calling. It doesn't start with a desire to fix anything. Searches for happiness, peace of mind, wisdom, or even understanding are all reward oriented. Seeking understanding or relief of these things may be found in psychology, or even possibly religion, but that is not the purpose of spirituality. Spirituality has no purpose. It just is, and there is either a calling or not.

Spirituality is the circle of love unfolding and loving itself. The call is an invitation to join the dance, the dance itself being the call, and the called. If love is offering its invitation, it does not matter if happiness, peace of mind, wisdom, or understanding are present or not. In fact, the call can, and often does, come in the midst of unhappiness, a troubled mind, ignorance or lack of understanding. The invitation comes in spite of those things.

The invitation to the dance is not declinable. It may be resisted, resulting in much of the unhappiness, etc. mentioned above, but it cannot be ignored. Seeking a reward leads to an attempt to crash the dance. In fact, seeking a reward prevents the invitation from being sent in the first place. Perhaps a better way to put it, is that the attempt to crash the dance, causes the invitation to become overlooked.

All are invited to the dance. Overlooking the invitation by seeking a reward, we miss the dance itself.

The Trouble with "God" Revisited

I find it both amusing and strange that referencing the concept of "God" comes up in non-dual discussions so frequently. This concept seems to be so persistent that it takes on a life of its own, even in supposed non-dual expression. The concept of an individual self seems easier to lose than this troublesome concept of "God".

A friend and I, while in high school, had independently come upon the thinking behind Anselm's ontological argument, which we considered a proof for the existence of "God", as did Anselm. This concept, as Anselm framed it, is that "God" is that, of which nothing greater can be conceived. I remember excitedly calling my philosophy teacher on a Saturday night to tell him the good news. After he explained that Anselm had already beaten us to the punch, I simply accepted this argument for decades.

I come from a Christian background, and one would think that this concept would be one that would persist, and it did, in my period of intellectual understanding. Initially, in the Christian sense, there developed the concept that "God" was *in* things, or everything was *part* of "God". As more understanding took place, "God" was seen as everything. The sky is "God", the forest is "God", and so on.

After reading Ramakrishna, and then Ramana Maharshi and Nisargadatta Maharaj, there developed an intellectual understanding of non-dual expression. But the concept of "God", finally seen as only a concept, was missed. My development from childhood had always seen that love was the most important aspect of "God", and that aspect remained, both in my mind and in my heart. How could there be love in non-duality, without subject and object: "God and myself"?

As I have said before, after a heavy rain, in the beauty of the clouds, I was struck with the realization of the answer to that question. The only way I can explain that using the inadequacy of words, is to say I vanished. And along with me, the concept of "God" vanished. What was left was love. Not my love, not "God's" love, but love only. All personal identification ceased. While the body, mind, and personality appear to remain, the constant, abiding, reality is love only.

This realization of love, without the concept of "God" opened the door. "God" was no longer necessary, just as "I" was no longer necessary. After "stabilizing" in this for a decade, I was able to see that both "God" and myself are simply expressions of love; the appearance of the body/mind and personality persisting as before, but now servants to love only. I have tried ever since to proclaim that love is your true nature.

This is why I find it so important not to look at "God" as anything but a concept. That is why I always try to put the term "God" in quotations. I don't believe it. It is an expression only of the one love. As to our "selves", we can, at least reach the "I Am". The mind can go that far. But the concept of "God" is not even demonstrable to that degree, unless we wish to stop at Anselm's argument, which by it very words, is a concept. Only the heart can understand love, as the heart speaks only in silence.

Robert Adams, the great American jnani, felt that one was helped in the spiritual journey by seeing "God" in form, even though his understanding was similar to my own. He even felt that one could worship "God" in the guru. He felt that one could not build up a strong enough love for a formless ideal. Both Ramana Maharshi, and Nisargadatta Maharaj used the term "God" frequently. They used it in reference to the Absolute sometimes, and in reference to the relative at other times, which I feel is very confusing, if not misleading, as were Adams's views. Not wanting to pick a fight with some of the non-dualities most revered teachers, I would still say that the understanding of love, loving itself, without the unnecessary baggage of an "I" or a "God" is vital to the understanding of truth.

The Call from Nothingness to Life

I was recently unfriended by someone who couldn't stop arguing over "nothingness". It is astonishing how far some in the spiritual community will argue over "nothing". This seems to be caused by a fear of becoming involved with life itself. "Nothingness" becomes a safe place to hide.

How does this come about? The concept of neti, neti, not this, not this, is a beginning. The mind, not being able to land on anything solid after settling in the I Am, starts thinking in negative terms. It tells us that the only way to describe *what is*, in thought and word, is by describing *what it is not*. This leaves a blank, a hole in thought that becomes described as nothingness.

Again, meditation looked at as mental activity rather than an emptying, leads to negative thoughts. When one works at meditation, and achieves success, it is referred to as *stillness, silence, nothingness*. The self, the world all vanish into this silent stillness. The mind stabilizes in this silent stillness and believes itself to be aware, or awakened. This is a point where many stop the search. In this state, which is completely in the mind, the mind enjoys a stillness and silence that it creates out of its view of those thoughts and words.

I was lucky to be introduced to contemplation before I ever got too far into meditation. In contemplation, the emphasis is on emptying. All words, thoughts and activities are rejected. Not to enter into some negative state, but to allow for an *infilling*. In contemplation, one is, in Christian terms, "waiting on the Lord". You are offering everything to the *unknown* in contemplation. You are not seeking. You are not imagining anything will happen. You are simply saying, "Here I am, take me." You are giving up your life for the unknown. This takes incredible courage and demands an incredible *call*.

While everyone eventually hears and follows this *call*, most spiritual seekers remain in the imagined silent stillness. When someone, like the one who unfriended me, argues for this silent stillness, you know that they are stuck there, and no amount of reaching out in the dream will reach them, as they think they have made it. They take the nothingness, presented to and by the mind as enlightenment.

Nisargadatta Maharaj said that he saw he was nothing, and that was wisdom. Of course, that is wisdom, this nothingness we see is the end of the mind's usefulness. "I am nothing", is the mind's wisdom. But this is only the start. Nisargadatta also said that when he saw he was everything, this was love. This seeing that we are everything, is what takes one beyond the mind. When the empty heart is filled with love, there is no vision, no thought, no words. It just is.

Giving up the search; emptying out the mind of thoughts of *still silence*, as conceived by the mind, even giving up the thought of love itself for the reality beyond words and mind is what is required. But fear of actually letting go is what keeps most stuck in the apparent, comfortable still silence. If you suggest, as life itself does, that there is more than this background of still silence, this neti, neti, this incomplete enlightenment that is seen by these fearful seekers, they will reject you, unfriend you, and say that you are the one who is deluded. They will only accept a total rejection of everything as their reality.

To be love, this seeing oneself as everything, opens the world, others, and yourself to what is. Not some negative screen upon which the illusions appear, but seeing the illusions themselves as part and parcel of the screen. Sure, you can say that the illusions are all in the mind. But the mind is also both an illusion and part and parcel of the screen. Non-duality cannot admit an illusion and a separate screen and still remain non-dual. There is both movement and stillness. One can't be separated from the other, or one held to be higher or more perfect or real than the other.

It is time to call seekers, especially those who have had an incomplete awakening to nothingness or silent stillness, back into life. Just as the Christ is described as being both fully human and fully divine. Life is both illusory and real. We cannot separate temporarily from eternal and remain outside of time, the great illusion. We have to dive deeply into paradox and dare to live there. Not taking positions, choosing real (eternal) over illusion (temporary), but accepting all that is, as it unfolds in love.

An Exquisite Frustration

Emotions are at least as much distrusted in non-dual conversation, as are thoughts. But these emotions that we can define, explain, and illustrate are also just more thoughts, only now attached to a feeling for further separation.

I think that emotions are one of the often misunderstood, but key elements in the spiritual search. Unfortunately, the emotions become something to watch out for, rather than something to experience. This is a grave mistake.

As one who experienced a good deal of psychiatric confusion as a kid, I learned to look closely at emotions and feelings as they arose, and arise. This had a strange double effect. While on the one hand, it separated me from my peers, I was able to understand why they acted as they did and also why they reacted to me, in the way they did. Learning early on how your behavior seems to affect others and how it all stems from one source is a valuable lesson.

Emotions, like thoughts, are not separate from their source. The source of all emotion, spirit, and feeling is in love itself. Before I go on any further, let me express what I am calling love here.

Love is not a feeling, but it is also. Love is not an emotion, but the emotion is in it. Love is all there is. Call it the Absolute, enlightened awareness, the one, but try not to call it "God". For "God" is another image, concept, or idea complete! While love is also a concept, it is a nebulous one.

This is why I am defining my concept of love. Love is that which unfolds into life, an ever-present stillness onto which life is projected and observed. Emotions, like thoughts, arise from that stillness. These thoughts, stored as memory, will repeatedly play back if we allow them to. Otherwise, there are only fresh thoughts, floating through, leaving no trace but the pleasure of observation. The same is true for emotion.

Memory thoughts can trigger *memory emotion*, a reliving of a past experience. These remembered emotions are as strong as the original emotions and are played back as the same feelings as the original. These are the emotions we need to expose, understand, and watch vanish.

As I have explained elsewhere in my notes, all emotions, from the most sublime to the most base, arise in love only, and are simply distorted and perverted by the desire to make the universal into the personal. Love is only what it is when it is not attached to a person, even "God". Love as *spirit* is what we are. The body/mind is simply love's expression. The unfolding of love itself not only creates both the body/mind to express love but the objects of its affection as well. There are no objects, no things, just the love expressed through them.

Just as medieval man observed light to be a physical manifestation of spirit, it is that love is that same spirit, abiding as everything. Emotions, just like thoughts, arise from the core of the source. They are there, and they are real. While the ripples on the surface of the water, are a temporary manifestation, they are real while they have an appearance. We would be indeed foolish to ignore a temporary hurricane. To ignore a temporary emotion, may also be a rejection of what is.

Even in a realized person, there will arise feelings of bodily dis-ease. Emotions, even expressed strongly, are no less a part of the sage than any other body/mind. A sage is living in the heart, we can expect some emotion. Love will flow freely, but any blockages encountered will be met with equal determination. You can't stop a sage who comes at you with love. He will steal your heart and brake it simultaneously.

Just as we learn to navigate shallow waters by understanding the hidden rocks that make the waves appear in the first place, emotions guide us in a world of pure feeling, an understanding without knowledge. You can't explain love to me. Either my concept or your concept loses their meaning, as well as they should. But we can *feel* love. I can look at you and laugh. I can see the love and joy in your eyes, but I can't explain it. It is an exquisite frustration.

Phantoms

I have always liked the word phantom. The dictionary defines a phantom as something apparent to sense, but with no substantial existence. That's really fabulous, something of the senses, but no substance. I appear as a phantom in a phantom world. Again, amazing, but what about it?

The senses themselves, by this definition, have no substance either, being only sensors of that which is without substance. That seems to give them some kind of value if not substance. *Value without substance*, is an interesting combination of words, that upon examination run through the mind like water through the fingers.

We have taken these senses, these channels of feeling that by this definition give birth to appearance which has no substantial existence, and concentrated all our attention on them.

We center the feelings, the senses themselves in what we falsely perceive as the "I Am". This is what we come to accept as the limited little "I". Senses become *my feelings*, thoughts become *my thoughts*, and the projection of *others* is sensed along with the projected *me*. Phantoms.

We are all phantoms here, *apparent to sense, but with no substantial existence*. You can touch me. I can touch you. That, in itself, is wonderful. Fabulous, even, but there's more! The phantoms rise up out of the substantial! Clearly the substantial cannot rise up from the insubstantial! The insubstantial, the illusion, the phantom, arises from the substantial.

It is part of the great paradox that, that which is substantial is also not definable. This nebulous stillness upon which all this plays out is life itself, nothing else. The child's smile, the elder's cry, all play out against this stillness I call love. Call it what you will, the Absolute, "God", pure awareness. It does not matter what brings you to the understanding of our wonderful phantomness.

As phantoms we have little or no input into the play of life, save maybe a little style or panache. We can either surrender or resist.

Resistance is futile, surrender is imminent. But there is nothing wrong in reveling in our phantomness. I guess that's the *"what about it?"* You can touch me. I can touch you. That, in itself, is wonderful!

A Lovely Bear

This hot weather in New Mexico, I am remembering a cool Winter spent in London, and the reactions of a small boy in Harrods's department Store.

Visiting Harrods's for the first time, being me, I wanted to see the toy department. It was the holiday season, and the store was fully decorated especially the toy department. While I was getting lost in the fascinating displays, a boy, about eight to ten years old was coming along with his father. We were in the stuffed animal section, and all at once the boy exclaimed, "Oh Daddy, what a lovely bear!"

Having been in London for only a few days, the accent grabbed at me of course. But the sincerity and absolute love in that voice was startling. First, no boy in America, even back in the 1970s, would have called anything *lovely*, and in particular, a stuffed bear. While I accepted this difference, I was unable to let it go without examination. An American boy in that age group exclaiming, "Oh daddy, what a lovely bear", would attract all kinds of the wrong attention. A psychiatrist may be summoned. But that gets us off the point: freedom.

That boy was not thinking about what others (me) were analyzing about the situation. At eight to ten he was able to be free enough to exclaim, to his dad no less, *a lovely bear*. This may seem a small thing, but it's the biggest thing there is!

This is what is meant by becoming like a child. Although, in this case, it was simply giving in to a recognized but diminishing force. Opening up, being free and open is so much more comforting than hiding. There were times in my life when a lovely bear would have been much more comfort than a baseball. But boys in my time hid their old bears and monkeys from one another, just as we often keep secrets apart from loved ones. To finally open up our tender hearts, not only showing the lovely bear, but our love for it, willingly accepting what may come next is to open that door, closed for so long.

"Oh Daddy, what a lovely bear! Oh Daddy, what a lovely world!" To openly, not only say this, but proclaim it, is the very essence of freedom. Shout it like a three-year-old, or an eight to ten-year-old who is sure of who he is!

Teaching, Life, and the Potential of Love

My approach to teaching is founded on living life as an example and sharing life as it is lived, day to day. This no doubt has arisen, in part, from my having written the rule for the religious community my partner and I founded.

Writing a religious community rule is very much different than composing spiritual prose or doctrine. It has to be more than words because these are words that need to be *lived out*. While I followed loosely the Rule of St. Benedict and a style suggested by *Rule for a New Brother* (Rogel voor een nieuwe broder) of the Brackkenstine Community of Blessed Sacrament Fathers, Holland, much of the Rule was based on my life together with my partner.

Our life together had involved middle-class beginnings, but quickly found us living in less than modest surroundings. Our downtown Tenderloin experiences, however, became a classroom of acceptance and sacrifice. Prior to that, both my partner and I had experienced youthful years of psychiatric treatment and torment. By the time it came to writing the rule, much life had passed this way.

I was not so much concerned with the rule in shaping another's spirituality, but to shape a life around which the spirit could shape its own way. Meetings and meals were set aside as places to communicate. Meetings based on a little bit of group therapy in a "family meeting" kind of setting. Quite sharing during meals. These all need to be part of a community where Brothers and Sisters can not only get along in joy but grow in spirit.

Spirituality is a very personal thing. It is the great recognition of oneness. There is nothing more personal or universal than that. But earnestness, devotion, and love call for a life, not just for some space to be made in it. This is why I teach. Not that I possess a great secret, though I might. Not that I am realized, though I might be. But because I call you to a life. Not an idea, a philosophy, or a religion, but a life. It involves eating sandwiches and talking on the phone. It involves sitting up with sick parents and children and cleaning up puke and urine. It involves becoming lost in a child's laugh and the best sunset of your life. It is life, and it giggles through the tears.

That's what I teach. After 44 years with one partner, years of psychiatric inquiry, bubbles of magic happenings enchanting my life on a regular basis, I feel called to teach. That life is what there is, in all its wonders and sadness. I was reminded by a cloud, like a thoughtfully silly child, that I am love. My whole purpose is to tell you that. I cannot explain this to you, as it is beyond words, and you know all this stuff anyway.

All I can do is live my life before you. Knowing I am watched, I must accept the pains and joys and fail again and again. For I am no example if I only win. Our life may not seem like a Satsang or spiritual gathering on the surface, *but it is*. Every smile, gesture, sigh, or tear is an expression of the one, the love that we live in. When our lives become a continual gesture of worship, devotion, and silence, the ground is prepared for the growth of potential, the potential of love.

Peace of Heart

I have written about this point again and again, but find that it can't be mentioned enough: the call. I'm not talking about some call from "God" or a pull toward something, but a constant drive that leads you, often in spite of yourself.

So often we hear about gaining peace of mind through spirituality. Visions of bliss and silence fill the mind, but this is where this idea of peace of mind belongs, in the mind. The nagging we feel, if we are truly called, is a tugging at the heart. In this case, only *peace of heart* will do.

It is the heart that is the observer of love. The mind tries in vain to organize love, but the heart watches it unfold in complete trust. No judgment, that's the mind's job. No matter how peaceful, the mind will continue to try to *organize*, for that is the dualistic nature of the mind, and thought itself.

If the call is from love, calling to itself, then it is a call to the heart. This does not bring peace of mind. In fact, it recognizes that peace of mind is a desire of the mind, and one that can only be satisfied by its elimination. It is only when we live for the whole of love itself, seek it for itself, that we follow our call. Try to use spirituality or the search for personal gain, even peace of mind, and you will bury yourself in the search.

There must be more than a desire to make things better or improve life. We must seek more than our idea of truth, or yoking with "God". The pull to love toward itself is the only power that can make it cross the line and bring you home. Your own desires, no matter how desperate, or sincere will not do it. Peace of mind and any ideas of it, must be abandoned, and replaced with acceptance. There may be peace of mind, or not. With peace of heart, peace of mind becomes irrelevant.

Reinventing the Wheel

The old adage about not reinventing the wheel is useful in most of life's endeavors. In spirituality, however, it may not always fit. The spiritual texts, books, and literature are filled with sage advice and sound descriptions of the journeys of others. Making these things real for us requires our *own* experiential contact, not simply listening to the words of others.

Any advice given to us or made by us must live in experience, all the while realizing that experience itself becomes a story, after the fact. I can only engage this moment. If I try to avoid reinventing the wheel in spirituality, I find myself accepting the concepts of others, even repeating their words. The truly scary thing is that we all sit on the perch, beg for crackers and parrot the words from time to time, and we don't even realize it!

It is very easy, over time, to fill the mind with so many non-dual concepts and words that you don't even realize it's happening. There have been so many studies of the wheel from before Shankara to ongoing Facebook notes, including this one! I quote him or her, you quote me or someone else. We paraphrase, we clarify, we may even argue, but we are just a breeze against the cheek. To quote Bob Dylan: "But something is happening here and you don't know what it is, do you, Mr. Jones?"

Unlike Mr. Jones, we do know what it is, we just can't squeeze it into the limited world of words. Not unlike the clown, we can silently point to the big smile, even in the face and awful reality of pain, and mime a follow-me gesture. But I can't think that you will perform my pratfalls, accept my pies in the face, or be asked to squeeze into tiny cars designed for me. No, your embarrassments, show stoppers and vehicles are waiting in today's script. You will find them as you go. No rehearsals here. Everything is live.

There is no wheel until *you* rediscover it, and it makes you its own. Once rediscovered, this pearl of great price is understood to have been there all along. Yes, I remember, it's all one.

Nothing was ever lost, it just looked that way. So I run out and say, "Look, nothing was ever lost! Stop seeking. Identification as the seeker will just keep you bound," as if I expect you will understand my words. Here, you must reinvent the wheel. You will only understand that there is no seeker until he vanishes before your very eyes.

As I have said, as we repeat the biblical or traditional verses or memorize ancient texts, they become *part* of us. Some of us, like myself, scatter biblical references around like salt and pepper. I, for one, have to say that I try not to. I try to describe my experiences in my own way, but we live in a world of words and memory, and it all becomes a muddy stream, a piece down the line!

Your rediscovery will not be like Ramana Maharshi's or mine. The wheel exists. It does not need so much reinvention as rediscovery: your rediscovery. Maybe not so much about death experiences or clouds at all, but *your* rediscovery. It may come from the appearance of a person, guru, lover, or the sudden overwhelming feelings over finding a dead butterfly in the gutter. It may come from finding the love in a child's eyes or seeing for the first time the wickedness in your own.

Yes, dare to reinvent the wheel. Look for your own experience. Not an experience that will live in memory or anticipation, but *this experience, this life*!

Enjoy the Show!

If I told you that the universe was unfolding right in front of you, and *past, present,* and *future* are being played out *right here, right now,* completely outside of time; how would you react?

Perhaps with understanding, but more likely, confusion.

This, of course, is what is happening. The appearances continue, even to the enlightened. Only the enlightened see them for what they are. The thoughts, impressions, and manifestations are all just the play of the Absolute loving. Not loving, as in making love, but being in a state of loving.

All of this loving, thinking, manifesting, and leaving impressions creates a lot to absorb for a linear mind. It all happens at once: the past and future are projected out of the present. The mind cannot think that way. In fact, it is just the opposite of how the mind thinks. The mind wants linear order and time is created to give the appearance of duration. Past, present, and future become the way to explain anything; what was, what is, and if all else fails, what will be.

The mind, bless it, performs these wonderful feats of creation in an instant. An instant object in an instant present needs the creation of an instant past to explain its existence in the first place. And then an instant future must be created for the duration and potential improvement of the object. All very confusing, and funny as hell, by the way.

This play, the creation of this story with past, present, and future happens so quickly, and seems so natural almost from the beginning, that we get into the program so quickly that we may not recognize it for years. As we awaken to new truths and experiences, it may seem a bit, perhaps a lot, confusing. To awaken one day and see it all unfolding, as it is, not just the appearances, maybe a bit overwhelming for some if not all.

I suffered for years during my early adulthood with panic attacks. Almost always occurring when around crowds, these embarrassing attacks would take form in anything from the inability to breathe to simple but sometimes spectacular fainting. Too many times I found myself coming on to the sidewalk or on a department store carpet surrounded by my partner and way too many curious strangers.

Finding these were caused by stress and extreme anxiety, a psychiatrist recommended watching for danger signals. These danger signals are triggers: little thoughts that start a cycle of memories and newly minted thoughts that fit into the pattern already established. It's a kind of setup that sets off the panic attack, even before there is a reason. To short circuit, the panic attack requires catching it at that trigger.

This can apply to spirituality as well. If we learn to catch the little triggers that set the mind to creating appearances, we can see through the appearances, and eventually learn to simply enjoy the show. This requires understanding that the past and future are part and parcel of the *present*. A step outside of time, even for an instant, allows for freedom from the tyranny of time. The mind will always *try to make sense* of the appearances it believes it sees, just like an idle mind will try to make an object out of the abstract pattern in the wallpaper.

Life is really about simply enjoying the show. The show follows a basic plot, but may not be understood by the mind. Free will is only an appearance. Love, in an unfolding flow, creates the objects that appear to "do" the actions. The "objects" then take it upon themselves, (cheeky little devils!) to think they are the "doer", and that the "actions" come from them. Again, this is funny as hell!

When I was a boy, the British Cinema, particularly its comedies, had a reputation for being enigmatic, and something needing close scrutiny. Don't try to get all the jokes, get into the flow of the damn thing. Life is like that. We don't need to get all the jokes. We probably wouldn't like many of them anyway. Getting *into the flow* shouldn't be that hard either. Lie gently on your back and float. Down woodside stream or ghetto gutter, the flow goes on, and we are more than carried with it. We come to realize that we are it. Grab a bag of Popcorn, lie gently on your back, and float. Get into the flow and most of all enjoy the show!

The Illusion of Evil

A Facebook friend put up a status questioning evil in a universe, presumably created out of love. He did not expect a definitive answer and received many interesting ideas regarding the subject. I don't expect that my view is either superior or a better answer, but simply a view from experience.

Love unfolding brings into potential an unknowable number of possibilities. The perfection we live with every day becomes distorted, perverted, and potentially evil when seen as having a personal center, *you*! Only clear seeing will give you a clear view of love in action.

As a photographer, I like to use optical illustrations, optical illusions in this case. Early spear fishermen learned thousands of years ago to adjust for the water's little trick of distorting the target (fish) and making it appear a few inches from where it really was. In modern camera lenses, all manner of adjustments has been made over the last decades to eliminate distortion and other optical aberrations. Aberrations is a perfect word here, as this is what happens in other areas of life as well.

Evil is an aberration. An aberration of love. When love is taken as personal, something I need, something I want, and I can dispense, love becomes distorted through its expression (you, me, whatever) into selfishness. I need, I want, I can dispense. How far from selfish to evil is really only a matter of degree. Just as in the complicated workings of light inside and outside camera lenses, phenomena have endless possibilities even more subtle in the spiritual or psychological worlds than in the physical world.

Pure love projected or held as a possession is like Superman hugging a ball of kryptonite. Love, like in a perpetual game of Hot Potato, needs to be continually shared. As a boy, I had a huge marble collection. My grandmother had made me a huge marble bag, and I set about filling it. Of course, I need to explain that I did not play marbles, just collected them. I couldn't take a chance that someone might win some of my marbles, so I simply bought more and more. I had a huge collection. It was meaningless.

Without sharing my marble collection, basically using it for that which it was intended, I was losing the whole point of marbles, *of life*. Life calls us to make an investment, be it marbles or an investment in courage and earnestness. Love calls us to play the game, all the while recognizing it as a game but playing our little lives out with all our hearts. This means simply sharing love. Evil sneaks in when we fail to examine even the tiniest of aberrations.

Everything we see and experience is perfect. This is one of the non-dual community's mantras. The unfolding of love is so complicated that it is conceded that it is not explainable.

Mother Nature may cleanse herself with drought or fire, but the persons experiencing this may have a less benevolent explanation. We know not what comes. All we can do is share what is given. To experience evil, to participate in evil, to look in the mirror and see the face of evil is one of life's truly terrifying moments. But we know that this is its home, this mirror creature, this ego.

Only a complete eradication of the ego will allow you to see this evil that lives in you. Once the "you" is gone, recognized for what it is, the evil in others is seen for what it is, a distortion of love. The friend who wrote the status mentioned that this came up after reading of the young Orthodox Jewish boy from Brooklyn who was murdered, dismembered, and thrown into a dumpster, his feet preserved in the refrigerator. Pretty awful. Pretty evil.

The torture of the perpetrator, the story that got him there, and the story he now faces, I feel these here too. The sadness of the boy, his family and neighborhood are matched by the twisted life of the perpetrator, his family, and his neighborhood. It all unfolds before us, and we shout, grieve, and ask why? Why? But the answer is withheld. We must live with the love that comes our way, and live beside (sometimes within) these distortions that we label "evil". We must live for love alone. Not a personal love, but one that is shared constantly without fear.

Fred Rogers of *Mr. Rogers Neighborhood* told the story of his mother advising him in times of emergency or terrible events, to *"look for the helpers,"* those who emerge in the midst of the events as agents for good. Sure, there is evil in the world of the dualistic mind, but it is always surrounded by love. We are swimming in love. Enjoy the swim or drown, it makes no difference!

The Tingle itself

If you write notes on Facebook very often and if you write about non-dual spirituality, you will, without question, begin repeating yourself. There is only so much to be said, and much of that shouldn't be. Yet, one of life's little paradoxes is that the pull to offer, console, and even attempt to explain remains like the pull of gravity, even when there are no objects to be pulled.

I don't think that you can point to love as our true nature, or becoming like a little child too often, or emphasize them enough. We are one with "God" through love. We do not become "God". We do not dissolve into "God". Love connects us, to each other as well as "God". "God" and we are only expressions of love, our existence coming out of the need of love for expression.

If I reach out my hand to you like a child looking for that magic of touch, the magic lies in that connection, the second of touch itself. Love, the tingling in your friend's hand. It's palpable, it's in the air. Even as adults the tingling remains: a visible spark, a recognition of connection.

Your hand is in mine and for that moment "you" and "I" are gone, only the tingle, the connection. Love is present.

Of course, if you remember way back, not in faulty or enhanced memory, but remember back to the heart of the dancing open-hearted child that lives in you still, your encounter with the sunrise, the sunset, the hawk on the wing, or the grief of a friend, will bring that tingle, that connection, that love.

Opening the heart exposes it to pain. As soon as this is discovered in childhood (childhood is also a very scary time!), masks go on and defenses go up. Love is cast out or at least filtered in such a way that we feel in control. To cast out pain, often life itself, we reject real connections.

We replace them with power and sex. These are tangible control and connection. The spirit that flows from love is distorted and perverted into lust and desire. Control and possession stand in for true connection which comes only from surrender.

So becoming as little children and therefore recognizing love as our true nature, is a constant rejection of masks, a fearless living in the connection. When we hold hands, I don't ask you to vanish, nor do you seek my absence. We seek, are indeed pulled to be what we are created for, to be expressions of love, the tingle itself.

The Call to Exit, Stage Right

When I was in my middle years of High School, during classes, I would occasionally feel the need to just get up and walk out. And I did. This did not go down well with many teachers, as you waved their questions aside and left the room without so much as a glance. Daring move? They thought I was nuts!

In my day they had a Dean for every class from Freshman through Senior. I was lucky to have Charles Fesler as my Dean during this time. Fesler was a fat man. I don't mean that in a derogatory way, in any way. It was simply a characteristic that was unavoidable enough to be part of his whole persona. He was also brilliant and sarcastically funny. As a fifteen-year-old, I worshiped the ground the man waddled upon.

Mr. Fesler took me aside after my second incident of walking out of some class and explained that he too had had a difficult time staying in some classes he had in college. He told me that I already knew everything they were likely to teach me in the next couple of years and that missing the classes was not so important as changing my manner of exit. "I was prone to nosebleeds in college", he said, "it proved to be the best excuse. I used to carry a handkerchief around that was covered in blood from previous nosebleeds, and whenever I felt that need to exit stage right, I would wave the bloody handkerchief in the professor's face and head to the door. Worked every time."

He advised me to simply hold my hand over my mouth, point desperately to the door, and exit on the assumption that no one was going to ask questions. I never used that advice.

The simple *I understand* attitude, the implied permission to be myself, to "freak out" once and a while removed so much pressure, I never felt the need to run again, at least in that way!

This brings me to the point of this note. Facing the fact that a call to the spiritual search is as life-altering and dangerous as the awakening that inevitably follows a real call. The *call*, the *search*, and the *awakening* are all part of one unfolding. They appear in succession due to time, but the awakening is present at the first call, that call to awaken. The average fellow in the street does not think of this unless there is the call.

Simply looking for answers or peace of mind are reasons, which a number of seekers use for entering the path. While this kind of self-improvement can be commendable, the spiritual search that brings you home comes only from love calling to itself. This requires walking out sometimes. Life on your own terms. Trusting instinct.

I have always marched to my own drummer. Lots of trouble. Lots of trouble! But the march has brought me home.

Home is calling. If you don't hear the call, pretending to answer it will only create more problems than it will solve. An intellectual understanding will not open the door. The call is to the heart, don't let the mind hack it. If it calls you to exit class or a business meeting, so be it. When life seems confusion, simplify it by walking out. You are not of this world. Live your life in service to the call.

If you are quiet and lucky enough to receive this grace, this awareness of the call, you will find the goal. The process is already underway. Follow the call. Don't waste your time looking for self-improvement or peace of mind. Both are noble goals, but only love seeking itself, perhaps even despite of you, will take you home because it *is* home. So remember, when life starts to get you down or confused, simply remember the freedom outside the room. Hand over the mouth without needless or wanted explanation, exit stage right, into the real. Mr. Fesler will cover for ya!

Limitless

Only a Monarch Butterfly caterpillar will turn into a Monarch butterfly. There are over twenty thousand species of butterfly on the planet, but only the Monarch caterpillar will turn into a Monarch butterfly. To think of all the varieties of personality and character that each of us is imprinted with or has created, the varieties of expression in enlightenment are truly limitless.

Limitless is a good way to look at this, as limitless is what we are dealing with here. Is it silent? Oh yes, but dynamically so. Is it stillness? Yes, among the unfolding, within the unfolding, there is stillness. Darkness? But with infinite light. Limitless. As soon as it's one thing, it's another. It's a shape-changer like the butterfly.

Shape-changers. We are this. I went to sleep as a boy and dreamed I was a man. I awoke to find I am a man, and the dream appears as a nightmare. But shape changers don't need to accept this illusory reality. Oh, the "rules" have to be "accepted" (the quotations are a kind of fingers crossed behind my back), but only the limitless reality needs to be actually accepted.

I can, by "God" I must awaken that boy, that sleeping fool dreaming of being a man. But this is it, isn't it? We dream of manhood or womanhood and liberation from imagined oppression we have piled on ourselves since we forgot the joy we traded for security. Along comes a guru, a teacher. He or she tells you that they have experienced an awakening, a new view, a new life. They have books, CDs, DVDs, a newsletter (social networking!), and a website to die for.

On their Facebook page and in their notes, they let you know what a real enlightenment experience looks like as opposed to, I guess, everyone else's. Yours. I have had people write me and tell me how saddened they feel when their experiences are held up as being inauthentic and judged by someone else's measure. The Monarch caterpillar is born, eats, and has its life experience on one type of plant. If it takes advice from a Swallowtail, eats what it eats, tries to imitate the life of the Swallowtail, it will die. Why? Butterflies all, seekers all?

The innumerable unfoldings that occur within the great unfolding of love that each of us, sentient and non-sentient alike are created in, result in a kind of temporary uniqueness. There is but one unique awakening for us, built in from the beginning. You are not a Monarch caterpillar, no Monarch Butterfly in your future! The Swallowtail can't convince you either, as you are not a Swallowtail youngster with a Swallowtail dream. You are a unique illusory character, a puppet seeking desperately to see where your strings go as they vanish into the darkness above.

When you come to realize that the puppet you have taken yourself to be, is manipulated by none other than the observer of the show, you can open your uniquely marked wings and fly. Not as some other butterfly. Not in their colors. Not on their plant. Not parroting another's words or behaviors, but a spreading of wings (awakening) that is yours alone and with you since birth. Limitless.

Spiritual Surrender

What about this surrender thing? Wikipedia defines surrender as "Surrender is willful acceptance and yielding to a dominating force and their will." The surrender we talk about in non-duality has no one's will to surrender, but a surrender to life itself.

Surrender is nothing. Surrender is everything. Nothing, in that it is a passive action. It is simply the cessation of an action or resistance. What can be more easy and simple than that? What could be more easy than lying passively in a bear attack? Oh yes, courage is needed in the extreme! Surrender is everything because the courage needed to carry it out is the sadhana, the *practice*, the life necessary to *achieve* the thing.

One musters the courage to passively and silently remain motionless as a growling, salivating beast is poking, sniffing, and terrifying one; based not so much on the faith that this works, but on the understanding that all else is completely futile. So it is with spiritual surrender.

The mind doesn't like surrender. It's a *take-charge guy*. It has been telling you *to run from the bear* for all your life. Run from the pain. Hide behind a mask, get lost in concepts (a great way to run!) No, the mind doesn't like surrender. Make up a story. Life as an excuse! The spiritual search then, becomes the search for the end of excuses.

It is really as simple as that. You want to love? You want peace? Stop the excuses and have them. They are right here. Amongst the terror and death that this world is subject to is the peace, the love you seek, constantly abiding. Take it by the hand. Its hand is ever-reaching. Surrender? Yes. In the face of fear, surrender. You know running is futile.

Like Dorothy, off to Oz by surrendering to the tornado and returning by realizing that there is no place like home. Clicking her heels together, surrendering to trust, Dorothy found her way home. The way is through surrender.

Love's Other Expression

We can wax philosophical, and say that there is no *other*. It is all just the one manifesting as objects and persons. We can take the psychological view and think in terms of the shadow and projection. Both approaches have the basic problem of requiring us to have a center where the projection or manifestation comes from. Such a center is no more existent than the *others or projections* that arise.

Are we going to spend our lives looking at others, even our loved ones as others and projections? How incomplete and selfish, this seeing others only as expressions of ourselves. Of course, we are expressions, but expressions of love, not each other. Do you ever wonder in an encounter, "Am I projecting them, or are they projecting me?" For these others, if not simple projections of mine, have a projection quality of their own. It's like the old idea, "Am I a man dreaming I am a butterfly, or a butterfly dreaming I am a man?"

If I find myself angry or depressed, what I am finding is that there is anger and depression, and I, jumping to the center, assume it's mine. I may project it onto others and blame them, or being a wise non-dualist, blame it on the projection of the shadow. But there is still this *I, that projects*. It is the capital "S" Self that projects. Yes, love itself, the Absolute. The small "s" self via the mind tries to usurp this position. The mind perverts the "I" that is the love itself into a false center it calls the "I Am". There is no center.

Love is. Nothing more needs be said. Love has no center. Love has no edges. No beginning and no end. Love is still and yet unfolds into a universe of the other. We are all the other to the other. Nothing special here. I'm just your projection, as you are mine. But as expressions of love, projections with a potential within potential, we are special indeed. We are love itself. Love is. Nothing more needs be said.

Loping

When I was fifty-five years old, I decided to take horseback riding lessons. From around the time of my fiftieth birthday, I had found myself being drawn back to the old cowboy days of my youth in the 1950s.

I had started collecting some old videos of Gene Autry and Roy Rogers which sprang into road trips to where the films and TV shows were made and eventually, across the Southwest. I was dressing in Western clothes, photographing the West, and doing much reminiscing of my cowboy heroes and their effect on my life. But I was haunted by the fact that I was afraid of horses. That fear became secondary when I actually decided to take lessons.

The only riding stable I could afford was an old stable on the very edge of the coast, just off San Francisco, hanging over the sea. It was owned by a curmudgeonly old cowboy and was a hang-out for wranglers in the area. I could always count on an audience of old cowboys, as I gingerly set upon my mount, waiting to be jettisoned into the mud.

My teacher was a young college girl, one who admittedly taught mostly adolescent girls, so we had a good deal of fun with that. She was raised on a horse ranch, was a rodeo barrel racer, and was an excellent teacher. But I'll bet you're wondering where is the spiritual hook in this rambling old guys story. Here goes:

I am not bragging, but this whole adventure took courage. It was something that I wanted so much, there would have been no rest if it had not been tried. It taught me to trust myself in one incident, and in another, it simply taught me to trust.

In the first incident, I was riding late, almost dark. My teacher had been held up, and when I arrived at the stables it was the horses' feeding time. My horse was in no mood for practice turns, not with its food within nose range, but I was stubbornly pushing it along. All at once, the horse bolted for the stable and its eats. I was going along for the ride, slightly scared past the laughing cowboys, as good ol' Silver headed to dinner.

I could not let this happen I told myself, and grabbed the reins with both hands and gave the pull of my life. To my amazement, Silver stopped, and I was able to turn him and bring him back to the practice area. It was a personal triumph. But I was still scared.

The breakthrough moment came in learning to lope. I had read that learning to lope was something that should come later in riding, after the novice has learned to trust the situation. My teacher, being a teenager, was very keen to get on with it and we had lessons in loping almost from the beginning. We would ride out on the beach dunes, and she would get her horse into a lope and my horse of course would follow.

I became like the seeker who reaches the point where surrender is what is needed and it is known that surrender is needed, but there is conflict, hesitancy. I would let my horse follow with great willingness, but at the same time grip the reins almost unconsciously, for safety. "Yes horsey, go fast, I want you to!" And all the while pulling back on the reins. The horse hated me.

Mixed signals. Surrender has no pulling back.

The last time I rode with my teacher came the breakthrough. I had watched Yakama Cannut, John Wayne's stunt double and former rodeo champ, ride flat out in a movie just a few days earlier and had watched how he held out his hand on the reins, giving all power and freedom to the horse. As the horses ran this time, I tried this. I let go of everything. She rode ahead and my horse was freedom itself. It was a feeling akin to the spiritual freedom I had felt some years earlier. This is all it takes. Surrender.

Freedom is right here in front of you. In fact, it is all around you. It *is* you. Light grip on the reins, trust your seat, and lope. That's all it takes: surrender.

The Absolute and the Relative: Separation?

Awakening is not a choice or position. It is not about choosing the right path among others or landing on a better concept. Awakening is awakening from all those things, not awakening to them.

One of the self-declared awakened teachers on Facebook continually talks about the mixture of absolute and relative language as being at the heart of all understanding between seekers and teachers of non-duality. This is also used to point to the "neo", that somehow not quite legitimate teacher, who mises his absolute and relative like cocktails.

The Absolute contains the relative within it. They are not separate. The relative is not some bastard stepchild of the Absolute, but an expression of it. You are an expression of the Absolute: love itself. Separating the expression of love from love itself is in the mind. The expression is the love itself in expression. Your *form* is the expression of love. Temporary, from dust, but the substance is love.

It may be difficult to mix Absolute with relative, but this is the choice of the universe in its expressions. This is what acceptance is all about. Our self-declared awakened teacher mentioned above seems to have difficulty in accepting the nebulous quality of *clear* understanding (see Nebulous Clarity, Chapter 3). Yes, the awakened see clearly that there is no clear seeing. As I once wrote in my blog, "When you completely understand that there is no complete understanding, your understanding is complete."

This need to separate absolute from relative may be present in the early seeker, but once awakening takes place, the two blend into the understanding. The relative including the "I Am", and the persona, are seen for what they are. The "I Am" and the body/mind are still there but seen as useful tools necessary for their own survival only, but not at all necessary for understanding.

Initially in the search, we may need to discriminate, viveka. But once all this separation in the name of non-duality is seen through, we need to accept it. Accept the paradoxes, the nebulous clarity. Embrace the relative in the name of the Absolute, the expresser of the expressed. Life opens before you. Every moment is a miracle. Don't separate the miracle into absolute and relative, but embrace both as one, Tat Tvam Asi.

There Is Only the Present,
Where Else Should I Meet Ramana?

What is the relevance of the scriptures? What is the degree of reference we should show for a Buddha, a Christ, or a Ramana Maharshi?

I was reading some comments to a thread a friend had put up on Neo-Advaita. It had deteriorated into a discussion of the need for following past sages, such as Ramana Maharshi. Ramana is dead, it was said. Ideas about him are only imaginations and a need for heroes. Is that all they are? More stories?

Ramana's story entered mine back in physical time, in 1986. Now, they are both stories with a time-bound history. But at that nano-second of what was then the now, Ramana and I met. Described out of another's memory (David Godman's), Ramana became a part of my mental and visual experience. Not a dead Ramana wrapped in history, suffering from poor translations, but a Ramana that lives for me right here, right now. There is only the present, where else should I meet Ramana?

We are all expressions of love, unfolding continually. When the folds of love's potential reveal both the expressions of *me* and *Ramana*, the expression of love for Ramana, and Ramana for me is complete. This is not the loving or worshiping of a past or dead being, but a new presence of my expression and the expression which is Ramana. If Ramana enters my life in the form of a dream, a book, or even a reference on Facebook, this is a new experience, a now experience.

This is why it is so important to have your own experience with Ramana, Christ, or Buddha. Regardless of translation, reference, or concordance, ask yourself, "What does this say to me?" Even if someone else recommended it or compels you to read it, it is you that it speaks to, you alone. There is but one voice to hear, and one voice to speak.

What is the relevance of the scriptures? When they present themselves, their voice meets your ear, their heart meets your heart.

No time intervention, the voice speaks, the ear/heart hears, an unfolding. New with itself, not "past", but always lively in the now.

And the saints? The sages, the Buddha, the Christ, Ramana, or Nisargadatta? Do we owe them reverence or respect? They asked nothing, but our attention. But they, and we, are expressions of love itself. We are created to love each other, our guides, as well as those entrusted to us. There is only the present, where else should I meet you? There is only the present, where else should I meet Ramana?

Follow the Resonant Drummer

When I was called upon to write the rule for the Community of the Living Sacrifice, I largely followed traditions in terms of types and kinds of rules. Poverty, sacrifice, chastity, and all the rest of it. The Rule of St. Benedict was my guide, along with some, more modern guides to community life. But I am no Benedict, and likewise, he never walked a step in my shoes.

So, even after sixteen years of life together at that time, chastity in its traditional meaning was cast into the rule. After the first vows were said to the rule, it was set. My partner and I quickly came to the understanding that it was the nature of our relationship, its intimacy, *its love in action* quality that gave life to our lives and to this community that now has written it out. The first vows were for a year and one day. We would wait it out, but we would change the rule.

Integrity, and everything the community stood for, required rewriting that section of the rule and submitting it to the Bishop and the Archdeacon who would oversee the taking of our vows to this new, revised rule. We figured getting approval for a change that traded traditional *chastity*, usually interpreted as *celibacy*, for a view of purity, whether with a partner in a committed relationship or as a single person was not going to be easy, and probably, not going to happen.

The revision of the rule started me thinking, not only about celibacy but even more about how important it is to follow our own calling. I was called to a life of service and sacrifice. Something in the depths of San Francisco's Tenderloin, sometimes counseling people in trouble, but it is my calling: a unique expression. I am not Benedict. He had his road and followed it. My partner and I, after sixteen years, had looked into who I am, who he is, and who we are together. This was an old, but ongoing business.

To follow Benedict, Ramana, or Christ at the expense of our own given life and circumstances is not spirituality, but an exchange of our identity for another. All those who appear before us in books or in person should be looked at, examined, but the life experience given to you is the learning ground, the testing ground out of which you have to *get it*. Good or bad, the only way to earn from experiences is to have them fully. Again, acceptance is the key. Spirituality is what you are, an expression of love. Be your own expression. Ramana and Benedict have already been expressed.

Oh, by the way, the Bishop and Archdeacon did approve the revisions with the Bishop of Lincoln becoming our official Visitor, an important step in forming a community. The Community of the Living Sacrifice became the first Anglican religious community to allow committed couples, both gay and straight, as well as celibate and non-celibate singles. After twenty-five years and still ahead of its time, follow the resonant drummer!

The Same Dragonfly

After nearly a year without rain, we have had a few hours of rain during August. Not much rain in the course of things, but changes have taken place in the desert. The Spade Foot toad has emerged, and dragonflies are everywhere. I saw a memorial one this morning.

While typical, the dragonfly I saw this morning transported me back, maybe to infancy. My heart said, "It's the same dragonfly." My mind immediately wanted to intervene on that, with all the reasons it could not possibly be the same dragonfly, but the heart was insistent.

Yes, said the heart. The same feeling, the same expression of love, expressed as a dragonfly. The unfolding of love, the expressions, me and dragonfly. The dance of love; the hovering dragonfly, in relationship with the observer. The expressions created by the dance itself.

We have often heard the saying, "They were made for each other." In true love, the kind born of and called by love itself, it is this exactly: made for each other. The persons and manifestations that we love were made for that purpose, as are we, to expressing love. If you say to your life partner, "We are made for each other," that is exactly it. We are love expression in action, in us, as us.

Love expresses as "God" while there is a need for one. It is the dynamic of the stillness of love to express itself in the flow that manifests into these things we so easily want to dismiss as illusions. I am an illusion, I am an expression of the Absolute, "God", love itself. It's a grand illusion. The same dragonfly, the same love.

Hidden Love and Human Fruit:
Expressions of Love

Mushrooms and toadstools are some of nature's most fun, and in some cases, useful and delicious creations. The mushroom is also a super metaphor and pointer toward the moon.

The mushrooms we see are the fruits of the plant. While looking like a little plant in its own right with its stem and crown, this fruit we see on the forest floor is the creation, the fruition, the expression if you will, of the mushroom plant which lies hidden in the dark soil.

Many mushrooms are delicious, some are very poisonous, but all are fascinating. Some have psychoactive properties as any consumer of "shrooms" will attest to. The biblical and language scholar, John M. Allegro, published *The Sacred Mushroom and the Cross* with too much controversy in 1970, alleging that Jesus was, in fact, a reference to the Fly Agaric, a very psychoactive and poisonous mushroom indeed. It was this mushroom, Allegro contends, that brought about awakenings, new insight, and opening of the heart. Pretty far out man!

But all the controversy aside, the mushroom itself in its simplicity, is a great metaphor for the *creative power of love*. The body of the mushroom plant is the mycelium, that complex network complex, with one single plant spreading over miles underground. This is the mushroom at its heart.

Love, like the mushroom plant, largely unseen but permeating everywhere, has complex fibers that continually unfold into objects, love's fruits. Love fulfilling its pursuit of itself, *realizing* itself in Itself. The mycelium lives and fruits as what we call the mushroom. Of course, the mushroom is the entire plant, not just the fruit. The fruit is the reproductive part of the plant, and as soon as the purpose is fulfilled, the mushroom deliquesces. It melts.

Deliquesce is another of those wonderful French words that describe, not unlike the Wicked Witch of the West's melting upon being doused with water, the absorption of water to the point of decomposition. The fruits of the mushroom simply dissolve, leaving the ever-present mycelium to grow and unfold.

The mycelium, like love, lives unseen, hidden from ordinary view, known only by the expressions, the fruit. Love lies unseen, hidden in the unfolding of the manifestation. The manifestation, including us, are the fruits, the expressions of its presence. We have our moment to express our expression, a unique mushroom, a unique manifestation, a unique person.

The person, like the mushroom, is real as an expression. It is limited in duration. We all "deliquesce". We appear, we vanish. But that, of what we are expressions, lives forever. The mushroom tells us that we are part, the *expressive* part, of love itself. Both we and the mushroom are momentary expressions of the hidden network of life and love. Hidden love and human fruit, expressions of love.

The Gospel According to Bugs Bunny

I have always loved cartoons. I watched them as a boy and continue to do so to this day.

Cartoons take a very easy and carefree view of life, bending reality to fit in a humorous way. The Warner Brothers cartoons were always my favorites, especially Bugs Bunny, particularly the ones from the 1930s and 1940s. I longed as a boy to be like my hero, Mel Blanc, and dreamed of doing voices as an adult. I never did, but over the years have come to see a number of spiritual lessons in my beloved cartoons.

The continual "resurrection" of characters after some disaster was always appealing. Of course, there was always the character that would be blown up and then be seen floating up, wings on back with harp in hand, to cartoon heaven. But the usual procedure for any Elmer Fudd or Sylvester the cat was to be shot in the face and have dynamite thrust down their trousers only to be shown disheveled and blackened after the explosion. The next scene would show them back to normal as if nothing had occurred.

This kind of resurrection is not unlike the re-creation of our lives and the manifestation that we experience upon waking every day, the illusion of time given is all continuity, even though it is recreated every second. A new life, every second, always fresh, no matter the explosions of the previous day.

Then there is the view of problems existing only when we are concentrating on them. In the wonderful cartoon masterpiece, 1946's *The Bit Snooze*, Elmer and Bugs are racing through a hollow log. Bugs keeps turning the log so Elmer keeps repeatedly running off a cliff in space. Elmer, with no visible means of support, keeps running after Bugs in mid-air until he stops, looks at his situation, feels around to find no substance under him, and either falls or runs like mad for the cliff edge!

Like Elmer, we often find things going well until we *examine* our situation and see the troubles the mind churns up. Then we see a dangerous situation, not realizing that ignorance is bliss. Instead of realizing that we are always safe in the flow of love, we want to use the rational, linear mind, to judge a situation instead of simply letting it be.

One of my favorite gags used frequently by Bugs Bunny is the freestanding door, put up between Bugs and his nemesis. This is a closed door and frame that keeps the nemesis at bay, pounding on the door for entrance or exit, all the while ignoring the fact that he could simply walk around it. Well, this is us, isn't it?

How often do we find an imaginary door or block to our understanding? The mind constantly whips out a door and sets it between us and the simple truths we intuitively understand. When we let intuition guide us, we can simply walk around the mind blockage, seeing it for the illusion it is.

Cartoons are for children and the comic truths taught by them are also the province of a child-like being. I live in that stage. Bugs, Elmer, and all the rest of them have been with me since the beginning. Truth is found in reality, unreality, and illusion. Being open to all, we can resurrect, run in space, and overcome obstacles by simply realizing that we, like cartoon characters, are not limited by the mind, but free in the heart. "Do ya get it Doc?"

Pain, Depression and Awakening

As many of you know, I have been recovering from a dislocated shoulder. After going to the doctors and having a cat scan, it has been decided to give me some pain pills and simply leave it to heal itself. The pain has been debilitating at times, and it has been hard to sit at the computer for long enough to write anything much, but I have missed it and there have been some posts worth responding to.

This pain thing is a great way to look through the troubles we often feel we experience. Prior to knowing what is wrong, we tend to speculate as to the origin of the pain. This, of course, is the mind seeking information it can use to understand what is happening. This gives doctors and patients alike the opportunity to find, hopefully, the best course of action for healing. However, it does not stop the pain.

Even with the pills the doctor gave me, there remains underlying pain. This pain, now understood, is less painful than it was when it was mystery pain. Now I know what hurts, why it hurts, and that the pain will diminish over time. It is very much this way with psychological problems as well.

Finding the cause of our depression or pain gives us understanding. This understanding does not remove the pain or depression, but it places it in the background. The pain or depression is still available to us, just as the ego is still available to us in enlightenment. But ego, left in the background, is not in control unless I let it assume control. If I think about the pain, concentrate on it, I can make it worse. In the same way, if I concentrate on the ego or the things of the ego (memory, separation, personhood, self, etc.) I lose touch with that which is beyond ego.

Awakening, realization, or whatever you choose to name it, pushes ego to the background, its proper functional place, but it does not eradicate it. Ego, like pain or depression, continues, but seen for what it is, goes to the background. Just as I can concentrate on the pain, thereby increasing it, I can *grow* the ego.

This is a sad truth. Even the enlightened, awakened person can fall into growing the ego. Perhaps, the enlightened, the awakened are even more vulnerable, as the ego often seizes the enlightenment and calls it its own. This is sad because such an enlightened one begins to believe that their enlightenment is the model of all enlightenment. Just as some people have to live with pain and depression, that does not mean that enlightenment and awareness are not present.

All things, all dualities, live and have their being in non-dual love: the unfolded. The illusions all have their substance in the real. There is no separation. When we stop separating the Advaitins from the Neo-Advaitins, the truth from the illusion, and accept all, pain, depression, freedom, and joy, we are truly free. Acceptance leads us to the door of freedom. Trust is the key to the door.

Love is Calling You to Die

What does love ask of you? It asks you to die. When I was in the Church, we learned that to follow Christ is to follow him to the cross, whatever our cross may be. Non-Duality asks no less. All you think you are, all your dreams, all your past, must be given up for the love of the moment. This is why we see so few authentic teachers and seekers.

Most teachers and seekers fear this death of *persona*. Many teachers have a "style" or an approach that gives off the feeling of peace and understanding, and only certain words and ideas can be used to *describe the indescribable*. I, personally (what an incredible statement for a non-dualist!) think that (Oh, my "God", now personally thinking!) gurus, teachers, and others built around them a protective persona with rules and values that would put the Abrahamic religions to shame.

Seekers are obviously seeking, and label themselves as such. It's a great feeling to be a seeker. We can say, "We are on the path." Those who know, understand that the seeking is the finding. That which is sought is calling itself back to itself. Love calls you to seek, fully understanding that you are already home. The journey is your life.

A life is spread out before you. This is life's gift. All love/life asks of you, is to give it up. We are born to sacrifice, born to the cross. Death, imagined as some specter in a dark robe, waits to catch us out. Born for death. It's a puzzle, but not one to be figured out, but lived. If we are seeking the reward of bliss or even peace of mind, we are caught up in seeking a "me" protector or a "me" enhancer. These are not to be found in the Absolute. The "me" itself must be eradicated. Peace of mind does not mean no more pain and suffering, but an acceptance of pain and suffering as part of the unfolding of life.

We can play with the dream life for a while, but we know, if only vaguely, that we are being called. We are left in this imaginary, but intriguing life so we can vanish back into the flow. Like a wave on the ocean, we build up into magnificent proportions. We are taller, swifter, or more powerful than all the other waves. Or on the other hand, we may see ourselves as smaller, slower, and less powerful than the other waves. But when we vanish back into the sea, none of that matters. We realize that the powerful wave and ourselves are one.

In our lives, a short span of a few decades, we can enjoy being the wave, and if we are a seeker wave, we want to live that life of understanding that we are the ocean. If we remember that the *calling*, the *seeking,* and the *finding* (awakening) are all one piece without seam, we will understand that we are both *being and becoming*. This is why I have, and continue to say that *living as if* there is a full understanding, puts you in the groove.

The groove I speak of is love and sacrifice. Love and sacrifice will take you on a wonderful adventure that ends in death. But death is here, right now, alongside life. Giving up this false identity through sacrifice, truly puts you out of yourself and into another place. You are the world, but not of it. You are the ocean, not falsely identifying as a single wave, but seeing the other waves as all one ocean.

Living as if is not pretending. It is living out your understanding as far as it goes. This is why I have stopped criticizing Neo-Advaitins, or any other seekers, as we are all *working out our salvation with fear and trembling*.

Living as if, creates trust. We, who call ourselves gurus or teachers, must have a silent understanding that is not conveyable with word but rock solid. Our means of expressing what we understand and the actual expression vary widely from teacher to teacher, some may resonate, others not. But just because one teacher has a totally different expression is no call to criticize. As I have said before, "When we judge another's spirituality, we often say little about theirs and much about our own."

We all are marching in procession toward death. This is our calling: to live the life given to us, no matter how insubstantial or how great. Loving others, sacrificing our lives, kills the ego and frees the heart to hear and respond. Death awaits surely, but death is as nonexistent as life. Awakening is a sign of complete death. The awakened is no more. What is left is that which was there all the time, love. You are love.

"Living As If..." Revisited

Because of some of the comments I received on my last note, I wanted to write a bit more about "Living as if..." as a concept.

Living as if... is not *pretending* or faking it. It is living on trust or faith, if you are so inclined. Like Nisargadatta Maharaj, who trusted the words of his teacher until the words became *real*, as in realization. This was not simply blind faith, but an intellectual understanding waiting for that touch of grace that causes you to say, "Of course!"

When I was a younger man, I was interested in acting. I attended classes at the American Conservatory Theater in San Francisco and studied the Stanislavsky System. Constantin Stanislavsky developed a system of acting based on the development of emotions through actions and movement.

In Stanislavsky's system, an actor would prepare for a role by studying the emotions of the character, and then bring up bits of the actor's life that aroused those emotions in him or her.

Once these feelings and emotions are aroused, then the actor can observe the actions involved with these emotions. Actions like a clenched fist, a lowering of the head in desperation, or tears, become the movement of the character, but this is not faking.

Just as a phonograph (my age showing!) reproduces the sound of repeating vibrations that were recorded on it, the actor when on stage, reverses the process he has learned. Now the clenched fist, the lowering of the head, not only reproduces the action of the emotion, but they arouse them. The actor experiences the emotion in a very real manner. This is an example of "Living as if..."

In spirituality, non-duality included, we are the actors playing out our assigned roles. If we find ourselves cast in the role of seeker, then we seek. We read about the great sages, we may even meet a teacher we like, but only through *experience* can we go beyond the flawed teachings of all the masters. This is where "Living as if..." comes into play.

You want to recognize *Oneness*, then base your life on that. Self-inquiry will not only lead you to the "I Am", it will show you that you are not only part of it, you are *all* of it. It's your life, a gift of love to you in moments of gratitude, who do you thank? The *Oneness* is the gratitude, and you are that. This is what is meant by self-love: understanding that it is all working out. You are grateful for the unfolding, and the "you" vanishes into gratitude.

In "Living as if..." you are living on trust. You have an intellectual understanding of "Oneness", the concepts are understood, but the *realization* is not there yet. Nisargadatta and his teacher before him talked about "living accordingly". Nisargadatta's teacher told him that he (Nisargadatta) was the infinite and that he should live accordingly. Living accordingly is no different than "living as if...".

"Living as if..." is actually very simple, but it requires trust. You want to be more compassionate? Then be compassionate. You want to be more loving? Then love. I am one of the few teachers who actually suggest you *do* something. Non-Duality, Advaita, or whatever you choose to call it, is not just an intellectual game but must be integrated into your whole life, your whole being.

Once realization takes place, love, and compassion flow freely, and no fear remains. Until then "living as if..." takes great courage. It is a life-changing experience and a singular one.

You may not be crucified or forced to drink hemlock, but you are required to live a life that follows the truth, whatever that truth may be to you. For "living as if..." requires you to be your *self*.

In a world of conformity, it becomes harder for each generation to be themselves. But following life in its strange twists and turns is what it is all about. This is it, enjoy. It's a gift. You are already free, understand this and *live accordingly. Live as if...*

The Teacher-Student Relationship: The Invitation Is Clear

Gurus and teachers of spirituality are always a topic of conversation, both for seekers and teachers alike. The guru/devotee relationship is much different than the teacher/student relationship. These have become a bit muddied when brought to the West.

The traditional guru/devotee relationship is a matter of not only learning from the guru but of seeing him as God and worthy of worship. Now, of course, this alarms many Western seekers, as they fear cults and being dominated by a powerful person. Certainly, this happens, both in the West and in the East, and it is a tragedy because it demeans a practice that has much merit.

Nisargadatta Maharaj said that he continuously flowed between wisdom and love, based on whether he felt he was nothing or everything. Everything meant love, nothing meant wisdom. Every morning, Nisargadatta would decorate a picture of his guru and pay homage to him. This was love. The wisdom he gained from his guru was simple. And Nisargadatta quickly learned the wisdom of nothingness. But also devotion was stirred in Maharaj. This was the lesson of love and wisdom, the two that are one.

In the early days of psychiatry, it was a common practice to have the patient transfer emotions to the therapist. The therapist, after weeks or months of opening the patient up, would assume in the mind of the patient a kind of familial love relationship. Yes, love. Relationships are always about love in some form. If you have read any of my notes or blogs, you know that I see love as the Absolute unfolding. In this unfolding arises the manifestation, and the body/Mind that interacts. There is a patient in need, and a psychiatrist or psychologist enters the dream to allow relationship. Relationship is one of the paradoxes of the non-dual universe.

Relationship is how love expresses itself. The Christian story tells us of a need for "saving" (realization) that is so great that a man was created to explain the relationship of man to the Father (Absolute).

The relationship is "*I and the Father are One.*" One, in relationship. A paradox for sure, but easy to feel.

The Western guru often wants to emulate the Eastern guru/devotee relationship. This often involves the chair, the flowers, and often a picture of one's teacher displayed in a frame near the teacher. This is all very nice, but to my taste, Western people sitting around casually talking, with the teacher simply part of the group, is less contrived. We must have no pretense in our spiritual search. A truthful guru will tell you he needs no special chair or flowers. He is sharing, not lecturing. But perhaps it is the worship thing in disguise.

It is difficult to bring love into a group of intellectuals bent on discussing the great mysteries. And, let's face it, much of non-dual words and concepts can be very dry and appear empty. It's the "I am nothing = wisdom" thing. Great! This needs learning and experience, but without the love, the relationship is not there. The relationship is "*I and the Father are One,*" that sweet, inexpressible understanding of *no separation*. It applies to the trees and the sky, and the entire manifestation. This is life. As we unfold as the petals of a rose, life unfolds into all the expressions of love. Our life is an expression of love for us to enjoy and love in turn. At its end, we return to love.

The guru or teacher is love. They are aware that their being is constructed by nothing other than love. They are no different than anyone else, with the exception that they understand that they are love only. When the guru or teacher enters your dream, be it through reading or in person, this is the beginning of that which is actually already there. The guru can give you pointers but cannot lead you to the end of the journey, as it is your journey, the guru being only a character in your story. The time will come when the seeker will stop being a seeker and the guru leaves the room, leaving only love behind.

It is often asked whether one needs a flesh and blood guru, and I would say yes and no. If sufficient love is related via videos or written works, then a simple encounter with a written guru may be enough for some. It is because the love that is transmitted is more important than the words themselves. I first discovered *I Am That* in the San Francisco Public Library. When I opened the boo, the frontispiece had a picture of Nisargadatta, and the love that was transmitted to me by those eyes was transforming in itself. I ran home clutching the book as if it were a lover. Nisargadatta and I were expressions of love, unfolding together.

A flesh and blood guru can give you two things, pointers and love. The pointers can be good or bad, but the love must be genuine. When we say to someone that our words resonate, this does not mean that they are understood, or that some new knowledge has been conveyed, but that it touched the heart. Minds don't resonate, they create separation. Hearts resonate. A guru invites you to love. Whether his words are in person or from a book or article, the invitation is clear.

Knowledge and Understanding

I often use the words knowledge and understanding to differentiate between intellectual information and intuition. I know the dictionary makes little distinction between the two, placing them both in the mind. I see them in the realm of spirituality as quite different.

To me, knowledge is the accumulation of other people's experiences and thoughts. We grow up indoctrinated almost from day one. We learn quickly that at times we smell bad and people are disgusted with us, and at other times we are a delight to the formerly offended. Choosing to be a delight rather than offensive becomes a goal of sorts. This is the beginning of knowledge.

Prior to this discovery, we lived on intuition alone, free spirits for but a few months, and then the appearance of separation formed. Now, as a separate entity, I do not smell and am loved in turn. The ego, this little thought collector, now knows what to do: don't smell and be loved! From there it's don't yell and be loved, learn math and be loved, get a degree and a good job and be loved. All these thoughts are filed away in little categories and put in order in a little file drawer in the mind. We know how to be loved, but something is missing.

That intuition, that call from love itself, is silently seeking to fill us again. The knowing has so completely filled all the drawers which the mind searches over and over, looking for this missing thing. The problem is, that missing something is not in those files at all. In fact, it is not in the mind at all. It resides in the heart. In the heart is *understanding*.

Understanding is placed in the heart by grace. The mind can't reach it. When the mind tries to get a grip on this understanding, it gets frustrated and tells you things like the search is stupid or all you will find is emptiness. Or worse still, the mind will usurp the whole thing, claiming to have a method, an exercise, a step-by-step path to enlightenment. The understanding, however, can't be categorized. Unlike the pieces of information, thoughts, and experiences, the understanding has no drawer to fill it in, as it has no name, no initial even. I won't fit in the mind, as the mind is its byproduct.

Just as the tooth fairy used to place a reward under your pillow, the understanding is placed in your heart by grace. It can't be broken down and placed in linear order like a thought or a concept. As you vaguely remember the freedom that was and has been yours right along, you close the doors to the files of the mind (the knowing) and begin the unknowing. Once all the clutter of the known is cleared away, the understanding is clearly seen.

But Where Can I Go? I Am Always Here

In a couple of interviews, I did over the last year, I referenced my thought while in the monastery about looking at death is to me like anticipating Christmas. Death, the final mystery, the duality of life. Birth, death, and life, are all illusions, but part of the flow of love.

If you are wondering why I decided to write a note about death, it's because on Friday last, I learned that I have cancer. And not just a "little" cancer, but apparently there are multiple major organs involved, including my lungs and bones. I said to the doctor, "This is pretty bad, isn't it?" The doctor said, "Do want me to tell you the truth?" I said "Of course", and he said, "It's bad!" He let me know that there was little to be done. And I thought to myself, "Christmas is coming!"

And then I thought of my partner of forty-four years. No Christmas for him. The only sadness I feel is for him. I have an inexplicable sense of fascination and joy. I took a walk in the desert today, which was hard, as I am in a good deal of pain due to a tumor on my spine. But as we drove into the desert area we love, I was overwhelmed with joy. We will work this out as we have done for forty-four years. My partner is a saint, unbeknown to himself. I told him the quote from Ramana Maharshi, "You say I am going away, but where can I go? I am always here. You give too much importance to the body."

I gave an invitation to those who would like to meet and talk to me, to come here to see me. This is even more important now. Now that I am awaiting transportation, I want to speak frankly. I can offer you something personally that is not transmittable in my humble writings. I can show you a life that has been lived for the Absolute. I can arrange for a group meeting, or individuals. Just message me. Also, depending on my condition, I can come to see you, but I would need transportation costs and a place to stay. No charge for the teaching, but you might bring goodies for everyone to share.

When my partner and I heard the doctor's grim news, I said to him, "Now I will have plenty to write about on Facebook," and I will. I will follow the journey, as long as it takes, and share my joy with my loving friends. I feel like a vapor. The body is failing, but the love that I am is well and eternal. I am only that: love. So I repeat, "...but where can I go, I am always here."

Nothingness or Unlimited Potential?[4]

Nothingness or unlimited potential? There doesn't seem to be a problem of choice here. But nothingness is chosen by the majority of spiritual people, most of the time. Why would you do that?

This phenomenon has been going on for thousands of years. The ancient texts use only negative terms to describe the Absolute. Neti-neti, not this, not this. This has been the mantra.

The nothingness described is not empty, but fullness itself. The neti-neti stands only for the no thing, nirguna, without attributes. The mind cannot imagine a thing without attributes, as the attributes are part and parcel of the thing. They *are* the thing to the mind.

But just as the mind creates and desires things, it also creates and desires nothing. To move away from this concept of nothing, this desire for an empty or frozen mind, we need to understand the dynamic quality of the Absolute.

From my standpoint, the Absolute is unlimited, energetic, potential. For convenience, I simply call it love, as that is how it came to me, but whatever you call it, it is the direct opposite of nothing. It is correct in that it is no thing, but it is not the mind's view of nothing.

It is hard to have an understanding and be unable to communicate it clearly. I want so to point out the swirling, dynamic that is what you are. Let me use the reflection analogy. If you take a large mirror into the woods, you can get a reasonable reflection of the look of the wood. Of course, it will, like a photograph, lack the sounds, the smells, the feel of the breeze on the cheek, and all the things that go to make an experience real. Such it is with the Absolute. The world is a reflection. An illusion? Yes. Real? Of course, it is the reflection of reality. It is not what it seems. It is not describable (only neti-neti), but it is real, as part of the functioning of the Absolute.

---

[4] The following is not included in the 1st edition.

The mind does not understand unlimited potential, because the mind is limited, and potential is too vast. An understanding of unlimited potential is available only to that which is unlimited potential.

Once established in the "I", and meditation and practice have calmed the senses and mind, find a connection of earnestness and devotion to God, or the Absolute, or however you wish to call it, and then remove the images of yourself, "God", the Absolute, or whatever your object of devotion, and become the devotion, the earnestness, the love, the unlimited potential.

Adyashanti on being stuck in emptiness

I came upon this quote from Adyashanti on another spiritual site. It is so similar to my teaching and some of my recent posts, that I wanted to include it here:

"Many spiritual seekers get 'stuck' in emptiness, in the absolute, in transcendence. They cling to bliss, or peace, or indifference. When the self-centered motivation for living disappears, many seekers become indifferent. They see the perfection of all existence and find no reason for doing anything, including caring for themselves or others. I call this 'taking a false refuge.' It is a very subtle egoic trap; it's a fixation in the absolute and all unconscious form of attachment that masquerades as liberation. It can be very difficult to wake someone up from this deceptive fixation because they literally have no motivation to let go of it. Stuck in a form of divine indifference, such people believe they have reached the top of the mountain when actually they are hiding out halfway up its slope. Enlightenment does not mean one should disappear into the realm of transcendence. To be fixated in the absolute is simply the polar opposite of being fixated in the relative. With the dawning of true enlightenment, there is a tremendous birthing of impersonal Love and wisdom that never fixates in any realm of experience. To awaken to the absolute view is profound and transformative, but to awaken from all fixed points of view is the birth of true nonduality. If emptiness cannot dance, it is not true Emptiness. If moonlight does not flood the empty night sky and reflect in every drop of water, on every blade of grass, then you are only looking at your own empty dream. I say, Wake up! Then, your heart will be flooded with a Love that you cannot contain."[5]

Adyashanti

---

[5] http://www.stat.wmich.edu/naranjo/zennotes/adyariver.html (21.4.2023)

The Simplicity of the Little Child

Studies of spiritual or religious beliefs, doctrines, and practices can become very complicated.

But the masters have taught very simple truths, very simple practices. Ramana Maharshi asks us to inquire "Who am I?" Nisargadatta Maharaj tells us to stay in the "I Am". Jesus, the Christ, said, "Except ye be converted, and become as little children, ye shall not enter into the kingdom of heaven."

Becoming as little children is a humbling experience that allows love, the reality of what we are, to flow. There is nothing complicated about it.

Once we have resolved the fact of our "I Amness" and can abide in it, it is a simple step to awareness. Perhaps it will take much study of complicated beliefs, doctrines, and practices for us to realize that our minds cannot reach the truth. Because we do not listen to the masters, we feel we need to *reinvent the wheel* and fill our minds with spiritual dross. But those who trust like little children, will listen and follow the simple teachings. Some need *to exhaust the mind* to come to the realization that the mind cannot grasp, or even approach awareness, while the simple child-like ones come upon awareness naturally.

Many masters from all spiritualities have spoken of simplicity: Lao Tzu said, "I have just three things to teach: simplicity, patience, compassion. These three are your greatest treasures." The medieval monk and author of *The Imitation of Christ* Thomas a Kempis wrote: "Purity and simplicity are the two wings with which man soars above the earth and all temporary nature." The Indian sage of the late 19th and early 20th centuries, Papa Ramdas says, "Simplicity is the nature of great souls." It is not hard to see and understand that simplicity is the road to truth.

We are no less than God's Love. The creative flow of love is all there is. "God", the "I Am" and the world all vanish in that simple flowing love.

I am telling you, become like a little child, forget all your "wisdom" and concentrate on this passage from Dattatreya's Avadhuta Gita: "How shall I salute the formless being, indivisible, auspicious, and immutable, who fills all this with His Self and also fills the self with His Self?" Dwell on this question. It is beyond the mind. Your heart will answer.

Karma, Bhakti and Jnana in Service to Others

Matthew 25:

[34] Then shall the King say unto them on his right hand, Come, ye blessed of my Father, inherit the kingdom prepared for you from the foundation of the world:

[35] For I was an hungered, and ye gave me meat: I was thirsty, and ye gave me drink: I was a stranger, and ye took me in:

[36] Naked, and ye clothed me: I was sick, and ye visited me: I was in prison, and ye came unto me.

[37] Then shall the righteous answer him, saying, Lord, when saw we thee an hungered, and fed thee? or thirsty, and gave thee drink?

[38] When saw we thee a stranger, and took thee in? or naked, and clothed thee?

[39] Or when saw we thee sick, or in prison, and came unto thee?

[40] And the King shall answer and say unto them, Verily I say unto you, Inasmuch as ye have done it unto one of the least of these my brethren, ye have done it unto me.

[41] Then shall he say also unto them on the left hand, depart from me, ye cursed, into everlasting fire, prepared for the devil and his angels:

[42] For I was an hungered, and ye gave me no meat: I was thirsty, and ye gave me no drink:

[43] I was a stranger, and ye took me not in: naked, and ye clothed me not: sick, and in prison, and ye visited me not.

[44] Then shall they also answer him, saying, Lord, when saw we thee an hungered, or athirst, or a stranger, or naked, or sick, or in prison, and did not minister unto thee?

[45] Then shall he answer them, saying, Verily I say unto you, Inasmuch as ye did it not to one of the least of these, ye did it not to me.

[46] And these shall go away into everlasting punishment: but the righteous into life eternal.

This passage from the King James version of the New Testament speaks of Karma Yoga. It talks not just about helping others, but how the helping is actually the worship of the Lord (Christ Consciousness). It also gives us some idea of who we are to help: the hungry, the thirsty, the naked, the stranger, and the prisoner.

The hungry, thirsty, and naked are needy, and arouse a degree of sympathy even in the hard-hearted, who may give a small token to relieve their own sense of guilt. The stranger and prisoner are less sympathetic to all but the most devoted, who will be able to see them as the Lord, or the one. This does not happen by accident or chance.

This is where bhakti, or devotion, and jnana, or knowledge come into play. Only through love and contemplation can one be able to see the Lord in the poor, the outcast, and the troubled. Jnana brings the understanding that the world is all one. Bhakti draws on the Lord's own reserves to give us strength to carry on in our work.

Jnana, while giving us the understanding of no-separation, will not give us the understanding of what is needed to actually help others. This is the province of bhakti. Through worship, we draw the Lord's strength by *being* it. We become the love of God when we worship without subject or object, resting only in the love that we are. This not only gives us the ability to carry on, but takes the "I" out of the equation, making us closer to both the needy and the Lord, who are, after all, the same.

Without this worship, this bhakti, this abandonment of our *selves*, we will look for thanks, praise, or the "good feeling" we get from helping others. My barber has a little sign on his mirror that says: "Every day do something for someone who can never pay you back." This is it. Worship becomes helping. Helping becomes worship. Not for reward, or a better conscience, but to simply be loving the Lord in the form of the needy, or even the despised.

Give love without thought of reward, and you become love, your true nature!

Self, self and Love: Being a Verb!

Some words in spiritual practice, concepts, and ideas are so familiar we tend to stop thinking critically about them and fall into accepted meanings and traditional views. This can be dangerous, as it engages sloppy thinking and produces blockage to discriminating effectively.

One such word, or "words" actually, is self and Self. The personal self and the concept of the Self are concepts, albeit different concepts in Hinduism, Christianity, and Buddhism.

The individual self, the "self" with a small "s" is the "I" we uncover when we stay in the "I Am". This is also the personal self of Christianity, only with an added sense of sin, and a need for redemption.

Then, there is the "Self", with a Capital "S". This is the ultimate Self. This is the Atman. This is the Self that holds all small "s"-selves. This is what we are. The Atman is the same as Brahman we are told. Our small "s"-self is within the capital "S"-Self, which is the same as Brahman.

Fine concepts, but confusing words, maybe dangerous words.

The idea of an individual self is, of course, misleading, the individual being only a collection of gunas, or attributes. The individual self is also the first place of identification. Even in the "I Am" state, the "I" remains. Even without identification with the body/mind, the "I" remains.

Through meditation on the "I Am", there is a movement toward the Self. This is where the possible confusion and entrapment take place. Self, with a capital "S" is the same word as self with a small "s". The mind understands the small "s"-self very well. The mind has had control of the small "s"-self for a long, long time. It knows the territory, and it knows how to rest and hide there. This familiarity with the known small "s"-self makes assumptions about the nature of the capital "S"-Self. This leads to ego expansion and blockage of further discovery/uncovery.

This is why I have found it so important not to get lost in this Self. Let me further explain:

The average person feels safe in his personal self. He will go to a lot of effort to maintain that sense of self. His view, even with a degree of understanding, is that he is the self, and it is he who seeks enlightenment, awareness, or whatever. He develops a sense that "he" as an individual, must absent himself, for more progress to be made, but comes up with a concept of the "higher" Self so that "he", or "he transformed", can still be present to witness it all. This leads the mind to commandeer the uncovery of the Self, and make it in its own image.

Both the words self and Self are nouns. The words Atman and Brahman are also nouns. This is part of the problem. These nouns are all things. We see the self as a thing, just as we also see the Self as a thing! We also tend to see the Atman and Brahman as things. This is very misleading.

Instead of Self, I use the word love. Not love as a noun, but the action, being, verb: love. Our nature is love in action, the stillness of every movement. This love in action is not easy for the mind to conceive of as our nature, as the mind tends to think of itself as a thing, not a movement, not a potential. This quiets the mind, and opens the heart.

Self is where so many get trapped. We do not become the Self. We do not become Brahman. We do not become any "thing". We uncover as love. We realize love.

When the lover and loved are absorbed in the loving, only the loving remains.

The Unfolding of Love

Recently I had the opportunity to observe the blooming of a century plant. Very interesting growth pattern. And the term *pattern* is a good one here, as this is exactly what I observed. First, a *pattern* is *imprinted* on the stalk. Almost like a line drawing. Slowly, over days, the lines become real as the stalk slowly turns, and the lines become separations, and slowly unfold into leaves, stems, and future unfolding flowers.

Pictures I have seen of human babies developing in the womb offer a similar *pattern*. Fingers appear as little flower-like buds that unfold into delicate little hands, beginning as nothing but lines and *patterns*.

So it is too with the *patterns* we observe in our minds. First just ideas, the *patterns*. Then the separation, and on to the unfolding reality of the "I Am". Once the "I Am" unfolds, the entire manifestation unfolds with it.

This unfolding is the constant movement of the love that creates. Thoughts are created, and taken as one's own. A body is created, and taken as one's own. A tree is observed and seen as separate from the observer. All there is *creation* and *observation*. No *need* for an observer here. No *need* for a body. Not even a *need* for a thought. Just the creation and observing happen, spontaneously, and the objects appear with the creation and observation.

This unfolding love is what we are. Not the objects, just the love. We unfold like the century plant, like the fetus, but not as objects created from a line drawing, slowly unfolding as real, but as the unfolding reality, ever unfolding, ever creating love.

Who is the Teacher?

There is no question that learning experiences, *spiritual or otherwise*, can come from anywhere. I have been often asked if a person needs an education or high intelligence to find awareness, freedom.

When I am asked this, I think about Jimmy.

Jimmy was a forty-something developmentally disabled man who lived in a home where I worked with the mentally challenged in a home setting. Jimmy was perhaps special, as he stood out to me in a particular way. He was dual diagnoses, being both Down's and autistic. His communication was narrow. He had lived with an over-protective mother until she died. She had never let him attend school, or learn handicapped skills. He was nearly blind from her neurotically washing his eyes with peroxide since his birth. He would spend his days, when left on his own, slowly rocking in a chair (it need not be a rocker!), and tearing up small bits of paper.

This may paint a sad picture, but it was not like that. Jimmy would rock and smile. Not just a contented smile, but a smile of joy. He would hum to himself in a chant-like manner, and it was not hard to see what was happening; Jimmy was almost constantly in samadhi.

This is something I have often found among autistic people in particular. They live in a different place. Their attention is drawn inside themselves. Of course, much is done to help autistic people, as it was for Jimmy. But does it help? And more importantly, is there understanding?

Jimmy went to school every day. This was a place where he was *looked after*, and an attempt was made to teach him a trade. Jimmy, being low functioning, was being taught to sort beads by color and size. This was something Jimmy found boring, and if the opportunity arose, he would soon be tearing up any small scraps of paper he could find. This troubled his psychologist to no end. Jimmy was to be kept away from the paper of any kind. If Jimmy would not leave a particular chair he was rocking in, he was to be pulled out forcibly.

My partner and I did not agree with this philosophy and continued to observe Jimmy and become friends with him.

Jimmy was very affectionate, and when given the opportunity, he would hug as many people as he could. He would also kiss on the cheek a few select people who he particularly cherished. Jimmy was full of love. It was interesting because when you gave Jimmy a picture of something he liked, like flowers or small animals, he would hold onto them for a short while, tearing only the outer edges. Slowly he would work his way inward until the picture was gone.

It was like watching the guru sitting, rocking, and chanting in silent meditation, slowly letting thoughts pass by, enjoying them momentarily, and then dismissing them in the tear of a sheet of paper. His smile would let you know he knew what he was doing, and it was obviously *for you*.

This, doing things for others' benefit, is such an important work, but is often missed by people trying to "help", or simply not willing to see what is before them. People often ask, *"Why did this parent's innocent baby die in its sleep?"* Or *"Why has my child, or my husband been afflicted or passed away?"* or any number of similar *why* questions. The answer, while not relieving the pain of loss, offers an explanation. They are lessons. It is said, *"Touch the wing of a butterfly, and move a star."* All things are connected. All happens as part of the unfolding of the one. Jimmy was there to *teach*. Not in a conventional way, but by *being a demonstration*.

Maybe someday they will teach Jimmy to sort beads. Maybe they will be proud of themselves, that they tore him away from *his world* long enough to do something "useful". But they are unlikely to learn from what they see, as their minds are clouded by what they *think they want*, to see what *already exists*.

The whole scenario is a lesson; awareness, peace, sit quietly, and dismiss the *paper* ideas and images, while the *world* tries to get our attention and *pull* us away by distraction after distraction.

Sit quietly. Rock if it feels right. Let the ideas pass through, *tearing* them as useless, as they pass by.

329

This is the teaching of guru Jimmy.

Note: Since my days working with the developmentally disabled, a number of studies have been done looking into the spirituality of the autistic in particular. There seems to be a fascinating link. It is so very wonderful to know that all of us, no matter how constructed, have a divine purpose.

Time and the Now

Time is a difficult, but fascinating concept. I have often used it in my writing about past spiritual events; to point out the way everything kind of *happens at once.*

This was an idea that occurred to me many years ago when I became aware that time has no reality apart from what we endow it with. I became aware that the Eucharist I was attending was commemorating, participating in an event that was happening *right now.* This was a stunning revelation.

In non-dual spirituality, we spend much time thinking about time. These days of New Age spirituality, or so-called Neo-Advaita, we hear much about *living in the now.* This is an interesting concept that I often think is not really carried to its ultimate conclusion. We dismiss the past as living only in memory. We dismiss the future as living only in imagination. But we love the now. Let's examine this.

Past, now, and future exist in the mind only. We cherish the now because we recognize that *we* are in it. The "I Am" exists in the now only. The now is the quiet place. The safe place. The lasting place. But what of the past and future?

The past lives in memory, the future in imagination. Most of us agree on this. But does this not mean that the past and future are illusions? And if only the now is real, and past and future appear in the now as illusions, what substance do they have, if any? The now, in this context, becomes part of time.

Most of us read scriptures that are hundreds, even thousands of years old. They are old, written in the past, the world of memory. We do not dismiss these books for being from the past but cherish them. Why? Are they not from memory? If memory is of the mind, how can books, no matter how noble or holy, possibly be of any value? The concept of time here becomes the all-important factor. Without the concept of time, reality is uncovered; everything unfolds at once. The scripture is written now, you read the scripture now, the scripture is absorbed into the life that created it now. There is no need for time.

The writing, reading, absorbing is a single act that appears in time only because the mind needs to understand the progress.

The future is made of imagination. We are intuitively aware of the unfolding potential, but the mind fears the lack of definite plans and creates possibilities and structures to make those possibilities we like happen. This too happens in the now.

This understanding that the now cannot be part of time but must be something out of time, and eternal, gave me a better understanding of the real meaning of now. In my meditations, I could see that Christ is being crucified right now. Not an incident from the past, but unfolding right now. The now is the unfolding, not a part of time. When all is one, all is love, the now is the Love. The now is the unfolding life we see, feel, and are.

The sufferings of the world, as well as its joys, are all happening right now. Past happenings and future potential all happen in the ever-present now. Not a now that exists in time, as a sort of middle ground between past and future, but an unfolding of the universe. Ever opening, ever loving.

Wise Love

*"Remembering your self is virtue, forgetting your self is sin. It all boils down to the mental or psychological link between the spirit and matter. We may call the link psyche (antahkarana). When the psyche is raw, undeveloped, quite primitive, it is subject to gross illusions. As it grows in breadth and sensitivity, it becomes a perfect link between pure matter and pure spirit and gives meaning to matter and expression to spirit. There is the material world (mahadakash) and the spiritual (paramakash). Between lies the universal mind (chidakash), which is also the universal heart (premakash). It is **wise love** that makes the two one."* Nisargadatta Maharaj*,* from "I Am That", Chapter 21

While engaging in another reading of "I Am That", Nisargadatta's definitive work, I came upon the words *wise love.* This use of language is so close to what I have been stressing in my blogs and so very important, I thought I would look at it closely for a bit.

As we all realize, the mind can take us only to the door of truth. *The key to the door is Grace.* We need to look into the *heart* for grace. The mind must be clear. The mind must be empty and lost in the frustration of seeking without finding, to the point of total exhaustion. *Then grace has a chance to enter.* There is no guarantee it will; that is the nature of grace. But an open and loving heart, free of desire, smooths the path of grace; for grace and love are the same.

Wisdom brings understanding. Love attracts grace. Together they open all doors, answer all questions.

The mind is full of discoveries, memories, and all of the story that is you and your life. It also contains what you know of scripture, meditations, and any other spiritual practices and knowledge you have acquired. The heart contains the *intuitive sense that you are*, and a vague sense of *what* you are. As much as we fight it, the innate sense that we have something to do with love is hard to deny. We mistake it for *desire.* We call it an *emotion.* We contrast it with *hate.* We feel it *pull* us in the very *seeking.* But we seek with our minds, which really don't want to be left behind, so they convince us the door is *locked*. The mind tries to convince us there *is no key* it can find; so there must not be one. So it confuses and confuses itself so it won't have to face the need to step into the apparent darkness of the unknown.

The heart belongs to the unknown. The step into the unknown is all about trust. Trust is all about how much we love *what* we trust. If we trust in love itself, get lost in it, we become it. Once we realize that we are love itself, all the wisdom we have learned, indeed, all the wisdom of the ages unfolds in an instant, the key is found. The key is *wise love*.

Your Right Balance

I have written a few blogs about the need for *bhakti*, in addition to *jnana*. It is such an important concept, that I want to drive it home. As "*God*", the *one*, are *love itself* in its most impersonal sense, we must *be* love to *know* it.

As much as I have emphasized love, I want to remind you that this relationship between *love* and *wisdom* has to be in *balance*. Unlike the illustration, your balance may not be *equal* but require a bit more of one or the other.

Perhaps you tend to be on the academic side, maybe a bit dry, maybe afraid of emotion, or close to human or even animal involvement. Then you may want to work on the heart. Open up. Dwell there in devotion to *something*. If you have no *belief* in God, then *open to the universe itself*, or *that longing that has brought you to this moment*. Use your mind to ground yourself in your usual way, and then open to love. Dwell on that which arouses devotion. Once that is established, remove both the "I" thought and the object of devotion. Be still in that place of empty devotion. This is your nature. *The balance is found.*

Maybe you are just the opposite; you are *very emotional*. Maybe a bit *over the top* emotionally. Maybe always deciding what others need is without thinking about their person-hood. Then you may want to engage in self-inquiry. Find out *who* is being emotional. Step outside the *person* you take yourself to be. Find who *you* are *in the person who's needs you aim to satisfy*. Think of them as the *Supreme*. Do for them with the love and respect you would give to the Supreme. Give them, *and all you meet*, from the *depths of your mind* as well as your heart. Once the mind is established in the "I Am" thought, remove both the "I" thought and the object of your assistance. Be still in that place of an empty mind. This is your nature. The balance is found.

Each has to find their own Balance.

Wisdom, which is informed by love itself, will perform only acts in line with the Eternal. Love, informed by wisdom itself, devotes itself to only the *highest*.

Guru: Our Self as Guide

Recently I have encountered a number of posts, here and on other spiritual sights, relating to *fully enlightened* gurus. As a Westerner, not established in the guru tradition, I have looked into this for decades. What I have found is this:

The Idea of fully enlightened tells us, right at the beginning, we see *stages* of enlightenment. This needs some explanation.

Awareness, enlightenment, union with "God", whatever you call it, or however you characterize it, happens all at once. By that, I mean that there is an event or movement that brings lasting clarity. The nature of this clarity is such that it *changes everything*. There is no forgetting it, or going back. But it is an event of great magnitude, no matter how simple the actual event may seem. It will take time to become established.

Just as it takes time, practice, and earnest meditation to come to the conviction that one is not the body, it takes, maybe decades, to realize the Self once enlightenment happens. So there are degrees. Just as a child learns to crawl, then walk, then walk well, one gets used to the new reality of awareness. We see a sage like Ramana Maharshi, or Nisargadatta Maharaj, and tend to assume they are special. God must be with them constantly, they were born with only good karma, or some extraordinary event occurred to them. Ramana envisioned his own death. He meditated deeply on a subject most would like to ignore, or dismiss altogether. Through this, he saw who he truly was. This is surely going beyond what the average person will do, but not extraordinary for a devoted seeker. The degree of devotion is what made Ramana special. His ability to totally give himself to life in any situation, his ability to love unconditionally, was the fruit of his devotion as well as its practice.

Nisargadatta Maharaj was a man of limited education but had spent a long life of devotion and curiosity. When he finally found his guru, it took him only three more years of staying in the "I am", to fully realize. This was not an instant realization. The devotion was deeply rooted. The knowledge was there due to devotion. Devotion opens the mind, and more importantly, the soul. When the mind and soul are open and empty of any "I" thought, the real is uncovered.

I do not perceive the guru as a magic person. Special surely, in the sense that the enlightened are free. Free in their thinking. Free in their behavior. But always loving and true.

The guru/student relationship has to take on the character of a love relationship. The guru realizes from the start that the relationship is already established and that it is a one-sided love affair. The student is there for a purpose. The guru is there out of compassion. The student wants something. The guru needs nothing and wants nothing but the good of the student. The guru sees no difference between student/guru. Only the natural flow of compassion. The relationship culminates in the student's realization that the student/guru is one and the same, and then the guru is no longer needed.

In the Western church, one turns oneself over to God, or God in the person of Christ. This is the surrender, the giving up of one's life. This is symbolically done in ritual, and perhaps in some way of service. It is meant to get us away from ourselves and build our trust in the other. The guru relationship fulfills this place in the East.

The guru relationship, *if it is to be a real one*, requires, at some point, the identification of the guru with God, the Self, or consciousness itself. The guru wants to bring you to the realization that he is not necessary, that you and he are one, engaging in conversation with himself. The student, at some point, needs to surrender to the guru. Again, the giving up of one's life, not for the guru, or in service to the guru, but simply for the giving up.

The guru simply tells you how to *pull the cord* on the shutters of your world. You have to pull the cord yourself, and experience and interpret what is uncovered by means of your own lights. The guru enters your dream with words to wake you up. Listen for him.

The deer in the forest, the beggar in the street, the simple teacher, all can be a guru. Open your heart to love. Let it be open to all. An open heart is an invitation to an enlightened guru. Enlightened ones love to converse upon the Absolute. It is their greatest joy. They love you with their words and worship the Absolute simultaneously. This is the joy of their life.

Open your life. Let everyone in. Learn to love the unlovable. Give yourself away. The guru will arise, and with him, enlightenment. *Don't expect. Enjoy surprise.*

What is Love?

I suppose an easy way to describe *love* would be to describe what it is not. This is how the *Absolute* is described, and I see love and the Absolute as the same, *our true nature*.

Love is not an *emotion*, although there is the emotion of love that hints vaguely toward it. This emotion of love is an *attachment*. It can also be a *desire*, but desire and love are not the same. Desire occupies and often *controls* the mind. Love needs constant freedom, the mind wants to *channel* it, limit it. This is especially true when the mind is in the grip of desire. One can desire *good* things, for *good* reasons, but desire is still not conducive to spirituality.

Being content with what we have is a lack of desire. *Love is contented in itself.* Loving another person, or loving to learn is part of the whole that is love, but must be placed in the perspective of the greater meaning of love. Desiring to find truth or enlightenment are noble desires, but until you develop trust that you will find them, even if the *"you"* must not be present at the meeting, it will not be found. Trust is from the heart. Trust is of love.

Above I described the emotion of love as an *attachment*. We love ourselves. Our greatest attachment is our body/mind. When we love others, in a true manner, we see them as the same. We see them as God, or the Absolute. Just as we must see the body/mind as different, illusory from our true reality, we will come to see the other beloved, as illusory from the true reality as well. The only reality is love. This is how we overcome attachment, by being the love, not the lover.

Love of family is strong. It grows to love of home, town, country, culture, religion, and if not tempered by wisdom, often leads to war!

It is the nature of love to look after itself. Nowhere is this more apparent than in the parent/child relationship. A parent will sacrifice, both *financially* and in *bodily protection*, for their child, as if *protecting himself.* This is natural. When a stranger reacts *naturally* and risks their life for another, we hail them as a hero. But parents do these things as a matter of living. The stranger, *for that moment of danger*, sees *no separation* and reacts *as if his own life is in danger*. The parent seeing no separation gives all to the child. This is the natural flow of love in action.

This love, which *involves sacrifice*, is called *agape*. This is a love that *becomes*. By that, I mean that love, as the Absolute, unfolds so that each part, each instant becomes what is called for. Not predestination, but a wise love that knows what is needed, and brings it about.

A former Bishop of Durham in England, David Jenkins described the incarnation of Christ *as God so loving the world that the love itself became manifest as Christ.* This is an example of becoming that love is capable of. The *infilling* of love becomes manifest.

So we have described love as *becoming*, and trust as being of love. For this *infilling* to happen, there must be complete trust. This is the realm of *sacrifice*.

Sacrifice is not the *giving up* of something, but an *emptying out*. When the "I" is absent, the *infilling* has a *space to fill*. We are always as *full* of love as we *allow* ourselves to be. We can be full of love or full of *ourselves*. The choice is ours. Sacrificial love is the love that moves the love away from ourselves, concentrates it on another (God, a person, a situation that needs our help), and in so doing, discovers it is all that exists, just this flow of love.

So, to conclude, I have to say that a description of love, like any other description of the Absolute, or "God" is not possible in words. It is accessible to the heart. All we can do is uncover our true nature, and that takes sacrifice. Not just the sacrifice of the body, but of everything we have come to identify as "I". It is this *annihilation of the mind* we fear. Overcome this fear through sacrifice, and *become the love*. Then you will know what love is.

Destiny or Unlimited Potential

The Ideas of *predestination* and *unlimited potential* are often discussed, argued about, and sometimes *reasonably considered*. I hope to do the latter here.

I will grant, right from the beginning, *that we are but actors fulfilling roles*, and that we have no independent will, but I will *not accept* the concept of predestination. Predestination requires the existence of time, and time exists only in the relative, not in the Absolute. Predestination admits to a *past*, where the *"pre" destiny* took place and a *future* in which the *destiny* will take place. Time, being an *illusion of the mind* makes predestination a *mind work* as well.

With *unlimited potential*, we have just that: no restriction of time, *all happening at once*. Unlimited potential unfolds like a plant in a garden, or a child in the womb, always moving, *always loving*. It is the love that leads, which makes even the *mistakes* right and perfect. The wingless fly, the armless man, the developmentally disabled child, *all find their place in the flow of loving potential*.

The story of the seed is an apt one here. Of course, the story of the seed can be used to demonstrate predestination as well. In the seed, *tiny as it is, is the whole tree*. This seed contains *the potential for the tree*, indeed ultimately, *for the whole forest*. This would tend to prove predestination we might say. But wait! Where does the potential for the tree that is within the seed come from? *It comes from ultimate potential.*

This life force, this *love*, that is unlimited potential is the *glue* that holds everything together, holds us in love, and unfolds before us. *We see the reflection only*. Beautiful as it is, we create flaws through *separation, time, and ego*. Instead of living in the real flow of energy and love, we live in the "I", which is *separate* from everything and everybody else.

Predestination says *all is fixed*. This brings about *complacency*. Many of the great masters have said that we are evolving toward enlightenment, and everyone will reach their goal sooner or later.

This no doubt is true, but even if we are simply *role players*, we can work to be *the best role players we can.*

I am an on-and-off bird watcher, or birder as it's now called. Birds play their roles very well. They follow the seasons and wait for just the right combination of temperature and daylight to time their migrations. They know where their food sources are, and where to find just the right nesting materials. This could be predestination or in this case *instinct*. But the interesting thing is, when there is a change, *everything adapts.*

If the winter is especially long, or the summer unusually hot and dry, there are more or less insects. If there are fewer insects, the birds have fewer young. They follow the time changes and work around unseasonal weather. This is not a *pre-written script*, this is flowing love, *adjusting instantly to its own flow.*

Every day, you wake up and begin all over again, *believing yourself to be a person with a destiny* or at least a *random life*. Until you see yourself as the unlimited potential that is love, you will try to live up to your non-existent destiny as a person, *even as a seeker*. Until you realize that you are the *seeking,* not the seeker, you will keep looking. And what is this seeking? It is *love fulfilling itself.*

We are the substance of love, the *unlimited potential itself*. We can *adapt* through prayer, service, and sacrifice in a way that uncovers who we are. Not some person with a destiny, but *unlimited potential itself.*

Celibacy, Chastity, and the Spiritual Life

When I was an *Anglican monk*, one of the curious things was how many people would perceive the *idea of a monk*. Silence, living in poverty, silent prayer, and meditation was never on the top of the list when outside people perceived the monk. It was *celibacy* that immediately came into their minds.

Monks are celibate. *That was the perception*. Many were surprised, *shocked even*, to find that *The Community of the Living Sacrifice* had no vow of celibacy, and indeed allowed married couples to join, even couples with children!

This *celibacy thing* is a sticking point for many in spirituality. The Catholic Church has a vow of celibacy for its clergy and monastics. Hindu sadhus practice celibacy, as do Buddhist monks. It was a *very daring thing* to write a rule for a religious community that did not include celibacy. But I found no choice.

In Advaita, we understand that we are not the body/mind. The body/mind is a construct of the mind itself, and is, therefore, *illusion*; the mind itself, is nothing but a *bag of thoughts*. To believe that this *illusion* is either *clean* or *dirty* is to give it more attention than it needs or deserves. The thoughts in the mind are simply that, thoughts drifting through on their way to nowhere. If we do not *grab* at them, they drift on by and are of no bother to one's peace. If, on the other hand, we dwell on the thoughts, they begin to take on a life of their own and grow in importance to our *thought world*. The simple division of thoughts and actions into *clean* or *dirty* becomes an entry into *duality*.

Sexual thoughts can be very strong. If suppressed, they can become even stronger. Our body/mind is a reflection of the Absolute, as it is a part of the manifestation. Being part of the manifestation, it is the expression of God's, or love's lila, or play. It is a reflection of *love in action*. To discount *or even despise* any natural function of the body/mind is a slap in the face to the creator. Sexual function, even beyond the reproductive function, can unite two souls into one.

Sexual function can be as much of the creator's plan as any other. But this needs to be an act of love, never desire, never selfish lust.

At this point, it would be a good idea to look at the difference between *celibacy* and *chastity*. These two are often mistaken for each other and are quite different.

Chastity is the *purity of sexual expression*. A *non-married* man or woman who abstains from sexual behavior would be considered chaste. A *married couple* who only engages in sexual behavior with each other would also be considered chaste. I, personally, would consider a couple who for whatever reason, can't be *properly* married, but who are spiritually dedicated to one another, and who engage in sexual union *only with each other* to be chaste.

Celibacy *is a gift*. Just as one's personality, or one's hair color, or place of birth is a gift. This all unfolds with the play of love. If we attempt to *force celibacy* on souls who are not gifted with it, we attempt to twist God's plan for us. Those *gifted* with celibacy cannot understand the gift of sex offered to others. Even the great masters have had trouble with this. The Buddha, in order to follow the true spirit as he saw it, left his wife and child behind. Other spiritual people have done this also.

No doubt the Buddha, feeling he must follow the *proscribed life of the sannyasin*, saw celibacy as the only choice. Catholic priests and bishops, who are called upon to be celibate, often have difficulty taking on false celibacy, with drastic results we read about every day.

If the Buddha had stayed with his family, he would have discovered *another truth;* the family can be a great training ground for spirituality. God calls many, if not most of mankind, to family life. The cleaving of man and woman in marriage, the responsibility of raising and caring for children are wonderful places to learn about *love, sacrifice, and renunciation*. If God *calls you* to learn your way by raising children, and you *will fully* insist on celibacy when it is not your call, you will not only *not* reach your goal, *you have violated God's role for you.*

Blessed are those who are called to celibacy. But also blessed are those called to family. You cannot follow someone else's calling. To enter a *pretend* celibacy, against your call, because you *will* it, or some church or organization *demands it*, is to put it front and center in your mind. You will try to *will* sexual feelings away. This will *hold* that thought in your mind. If you *dualistically* regard sex as *evil* or *dirty*, you will experience guilt and shame, again destroying any mindfulness of spirit.

God has made us all different, yet one. The *play of God* loves diversity. The only way to the truth is to follow *your path*. Try to force another path, and you are lost.

As I said, even the Buddha felt compelled to follow the proscribed path that was laid down before him. He even added it to his own way, and now others, *who may not be so called*, try desperately to follow. As mentioned above, those who have the calling to celibacy cannot understand the calling of others. Many of these, entering the path of spirituality, will become teachers or gurus and insist others *be like them*. Also, psychology tells us that many people are celibate due to a sexual disorder caused by incest, rape, or other traumatic event. These people, *who fear sex*, will want to instill this fear in others, justifying their own fear.

We must remember, the most celibate fanatic, who *insists* others have to be celibate, came into this world via *the very thing they fear or despise*. Were our parents non-spiritual? Were we conceived in lust? Does the celibate monk, with his idea of renunciation, have anything on the father or mother, who sits up with a sick child, or the man or woman holding their dying spouse's hand?

So we must strive for *chastity, in all things*. Pure celibacy, as well as pure loving sexuality, are part of the functioning of the whole. *Each to his calling*. Spirituality ultimately is about *Spirit*. Chasity is important to Spirit. How we lovingly use our bodies is a temporal thing. If that use leads the person to the Spirit, we must not stand in judgment as to which is better. *It is a matter of calling.*

From God to the Absolute: Stepping Beyond the Mind

Spirituality begins for many of us as children. We learn about God or Gods. We learn about the life and adventures of Gods and the spiritual lessons associated with these adventures.

We learn the rites and rituals of our religion. We are told our place in all this. As we grow, we either accept or reject what we have learned. Maturity brings discernment, and we come to a more *realistic* view in our spiritual life. We learn that the body will pass away, but the *spirit* lives on. We call this *spirit* a *soul* or the *self.*

Our spiritual practices, *no matter what religion*, attempt to make us aware that this *soul* or *self* is the permanent aspect of our existence. We grow to have less interest in the body, realizing that it will surely pass away. But we cling to the thoughts of the *soul* and *God*.

Our learning as children may have given us thoughts of a *heaven* or a *hell*. It may have given us scientific theories regarding existence, such as physiology, cosmology, and all the rest of it. We may have accepted or rejected concepts such as *the resurrection of the body and salvation*, or *the gunas, the five elements, and karma*. But if we are on a *spiritual path*, we cling to the *soul* and *God* as the reality that stands beyond the concepts, no matter which we accept or reject.

As we grow in spirituality, we combine all this knowledge and come to the conclusion that what we see around us is passing and changing with time, including ourselves. So, eventually, we come to ask the question *Who am I?"*

Ramana Maharshi told us to ask this question *Who am I?* He told us to meditate on this. *Nisargadatta Maharaj* said much the same in his admonition to *stay in the I Am*. If we follow this advice, we become aware that *I Am*, or awareness of our consciousness is the only true thing our minds can observe. We come to see that, as the *observer* we not only *observe the world, but ourselves in it*. So we come to the conclusion that the "*I*" must not be this *person* we observe. When we see the *person* we have taken ourselves to be as simply another part of the manifestation, no more important than any other, we begin to stabilize in the *I Am*. We now experience consciousness. This *I Am consciousness* Nisargadatta Maharaj expressed as *Brahman*, or "*God*".

This experience of God as consciousness, or the *I Am* allows us to go beyond the body, but the mind still clings to the thoughts of both the "*I*" concept, and the "*God*" concept. We see that both are the same; this "*I*" and "*God*". However, both the "*I*" and "*God*" are still in the mind. This is where many get lost, or mistakenly take *themselves to be God*. This is nothing but *ego*.

The *ego*, being a *thing*, wants to remain a *thing*. It cannot imagine itself as *nothing* or even *everything*.

This is where *experience* comes. Once you realize you are not the body, you now must let go of the concepts of both the "*I*" and "*God*", and uncover the *love* that makes the two one. *Love* is not a *thing*, it is an action of unfolding.

Love, the ever-unfolding, unchanging reality is *Parabrahman, that which you are.*

This is why we are told that we must renounce *everything*. *All concepts must go*. All dualities must be resolved in themselves. *Good-bad, right-wrong, guna-nirguna.* All dissolve in this understanding. No one can tell you this, it must be found for yourself. As Nisargadatta Maharaj used to say, one must come to this conclusion on your own, *and live accordingly.*

Living accordingly is the most important part, as the mind cannot conceive it, and words cannot express it, you can only *be* it.

"Sometimes I feel I am everything, I call that love. Sometimes I feel I am nothing, I call that wisdom. Between love and wisdom, my life continuously flows." Nisargadatta Maharaj

The Dream Guru

The dream guru is the guru we have been waiting for all our lives. They are the ultimate; where a touch or even a single glance can bring transformation!

Too bad if our *enlightenment* is to come from the guy in the *form* of the trash man.

Seriously though, a guru or a *guru experience* can come from anywhere or anyone. Recently, on a popular social networking site, among *non-duality* circles, there has been more criticism of gurus and New Age or Neo-Advaita teachers. While much can be said on this subject, and some criticism is warranted, it is not particularly wise or spiritual to spend much time or concern over what others are doing. If you don't like a particular spiritual teacher, don't go see them, don't read their books, don't go on their retreats. But don't spread negative opinions, *without being asked,* because someone turns out *not* to be your *dream guru.*

One such critic was insisting that all *real* gurus must be able to perform shaktipat. Some gurus claim to do shaktipat. Others do not. This critic claimed that many teachers and gurus claim to be *aware,* but do not, *indeed cannot* do shaktipat, so they are charlatans. This is nonsense. It is the stuff of the dream guru. One is only a charlatan if one claims to do shaktipat and is *unable to.* Claiming to be a teacher or even a guru does not make one a charlatan. It does not make one a teacher either!

Part of the search is learning discrimination. But *we* must learn it. Another's opinion, *if asked for,* is welcome in the search, but we must make the final decision based on knowledge and intuition. We too have our dream guru hidden inside our minds. He has to meet several expectations, all gathered from the search and past disappointments. When I left the Christian Church, the need for the dream guru arose.

Apart from disappointments with the structural church, which were many, I came to have difficulty with the creed. The part that called *Jesus Christ Our only mediator and advocate,* gave me pause to the point that honesty compelled me to leave the church. I lost no respect for the being of Christ, but the *search* began again with even new fervor.

First, I came upon Ramakrishna. What a dream guru is Ramakrishna! Coming from a Christian setting, Ramakrishna, even with his affinity for Christ, was a big leap. I was however very impressed by some of his followers. Vivekananda, while writing some wonderful works and introducing Vedanta to a wider audience, seemed to me to be the predecessor of many of the *money-making gurus* so prevalent today. Because Ramakrishna and Ramana were next to each other on the library shelves, the next part of my search for the dream guru had begun.

Ramana was very refreshing. Very Indian, but dynamic and peaceful at the same time. Closer to what I was used to, but *mysterious* enough to keep up my interest. Perhaps a *dream guru?* Many today see Ramana as the ultimate Guru. Silent. Spoke only when necessary to compassionately teach. Many today teach in his lineage, even though he specifically did not establish one. Why? Because he is *a dream guru.*

None of this makes any of the successors of Ramana invalid in their teaching. Some may be good, and some may be just in it for the money, but we can only judge for ourselves. None is Ramana. He would not want them to be. We should not demand them to be the dream guru. They are simply the teachers they are. Some may be our dream gurus, and if that's the case, fine. If we learn, become independent and grow away from them, we gain. No guru is for *life.* We all must go into the *One* alone and naked.

I discovered my guru with the works of Nisargadatta Maharaj. A simple man. A man of little formal education, but infinite wisdom and earnestness. Over a quarter of a century has gone by since discovering Maharaj. Maharaj led me back into root intuition and into the sublime qualities of my own faith.

Interestingly, in recent months Nisargadatta Maharaj has come to my dreams. In the first, He appeared in a doorway. He looked at me, and threw a handful of religious icons on the ground, shattering them to pieces. In the second dream, Maharaj, again in a doorway, just stood looking at me. I was moved by his look and placed my hands on his shoulders. As we stood facing each other, the look became pure love, and the understanding was clear. I took my leave of him, and when I awoke, it became clear that I should try to teach, and share that love.

I, like Nisargadatta himself, believed the words of the guru. But it took an *event* of awareness to understand with more than the mind. A moment of facing reality, the big reality alone. No guru can come with you, as they are *already there*! He is not taking you anywhere. He is inviting you to *join* him, in the most real sense anyone can. But you must be present. You must be willing to *join the guru in his freedom*. If you expect the guru to touch *you* into understanding, you need to be ready to let go of ignorance. The guru and the student are not separable from the teaching. Both appear and subside with the teaching. Forget the dream guru. He lives in your mind. He may have powers. They live in the mind as well. Go beyond the mind.

Do not look for a Ramana. Do not look for a second coming of Christ. Do not seek anything inside the mind. The true guru is not in the dream world. *The kingdom of heaven is within you.*

Should Spiritual Teachers Charge for their Teaching: A Spiritual Perspective

I realize that this is a topic that is much discussed and debated, but it came to my attention again this morning, and I wanted to add my two cents!

This morning I was looking at some of the web pages of some of my Friends on Facebook. Many are very nice and interesting, but one thing I kept noticing was the *donation* buttons. Now most of these are spiritual teachers of one kind or another and are requesting donations for the furtherance of their *work*. To me, this is like offering insight with *your hand stretched out*. Now I realize that they are not *charging*, but a donations button lets you know that they *want*, or at least would *like* something from you.

Now, as some of you know, I come from a Christian monastic background that holds poverty as an ideal. I also have to say that I was often in conflict with the Church over this very issue. I was involved with a couple of cathedrals that had very wealthy congregations and clergy that catered to them. One kept hearing that *the church is a business*. This was a large factor in my leaving the established church, as I had no desire to worship in a business.

One of the web pages I visited today was one belonging to a well-known American spiritual teacher. He sells books, DVDs, and other items. I have talked on the internet to this teacher about this very subject, after hearing him defend Eckhart Tolle over the excessive charges for Tolle's meetings. This American teacher told me that he makes very little from his books, which were initially self-published. In an interview in a spiritual magazine, he was asked about this *charging*. Among other things, he stated:

"I'm thankful that people paid my teachers to talk or else I would never have seen their books or benefited from their messages."

"If there is a good teacher out there anywhere who can help the realization of freedom, I certainly wouldn't want him working in a

factory. If I were suffering, I would pay for him not to work so he could give me guidance."

Before I go on, let me point out that this particular teacher is also a professional in a very lucrative profession, and not someone living in poverty. He is certainly in a position to share without charging.

Now I understand that it costs money to print and distribute books. And as long as some are freely distributed to libraries, so the less advantaged can read them, I have no problem with charging a minimal price. Also, if you are asked to travel for a Satsang or other meeting, having your expenses met is reasonable if you cannot afford to offer this as a sharing. But the excuses above are not at all valid and demonstrate a lack of spiritual understanding.

The first statement *assumes* that they may not have this understanding if they had not read these books or *benefited from their messages.* This is as much as saying that this message is not available without the books being published. This totally rejects the Absolute and its ability to *bestow* grace as it will. If *awakening* is going to *happen*, it will happen regardless of whether there are books or gurus, or if they are paid or not. Understanding comes from within. Another important thing to remember is that, in this age of the internet, this message is available to everyone. The teacher who made these statements has two websites on which he could share the entire of his message, but he chooses to put money between the seeker and the message. This first statement is simply a rationalization.

The second statement shows very little understanding of the functioning of the Absolute. My experience has shown that there are, and have been, many *good teachers* working in factories. Their fellow workers benefit from their presence, and those who are suffering find their way to them by the grace of the Absolute. They are not charged by this *factory worker*, as he gives love without wanting or expecting any reward. Your *teacher* may be the trashman or the one who services your car. The important thing to remember is that *anyone* or *anything* can help you *awaken.* A *real* teacher in spirituality *wants nothing from you but earnestness.* If he asks for something or has his hand out with a donation button, question that.

The most important point however is, a true spiritual teacher has *faith*. If he is worried over his financial situation, he is without the understanding that the Absolute will provide what is necessary. If someone is *called* to donate or contribute, *they will*. If the teacher is to live in and adjust to poverty, *they will*. If we do not let life take its own way, if we do not offer our love *freely*, without reward or compensation, then we do not live the compassion we pretend to *be*. Gurus and seekers are led to each other. The Guru does not need to advertise or put out books. He simply needs to be, and trust that the Absolute will see to the rest. If he cannot see this, or be willing to do this, no matter his education, beautiful words, or charismatic personality, he is a fraud.

Murderer's Funerals and This Little Child

Matthew 18. ¹ At the same time came the disciples unto Jesus, saying, who is the greatest in the kingdom of heaven?

² And Jesus called a little child unto him, and set him in the midst of them,

³ And said, Verily I say unto you, except ye be converted, and become as little children, ye shall not enter into the kingdom of heaven.

⁴ Whosoever therefore shall humble himself as this little child, the same is greatest in the kingdom of heaven.

In response to one of my recent postings, I received a couple of comments that told me that it is important to return again and again to the basics. One of the comments complained about my *one size fits all* philosophy. And the other commenter literally went on for days, both with me and other commenters, explaining long philosophical arguments regarding love and its place in this *cosmic trifle* we find ourselves suspended in.

In regard to my *one size fits all* philosophy. I would have to plead guilty. This commenter went on to say that I would be good at the funeral of a murderer. Again, I would have to agree. While I would *tailor* my approach to a particular *seeker*, I would not stray from earnestness in the pursuit of love itself. At a murderer's funeral, I am sure I could find something worthwhile to talk about. All human beings are created out of the substance of light, as well as dust. A person of light sees light even through the skin of human dust.

Recently, it has been implied that I am a *milk-toast*, naive, or some kind of ex-hippie who lives in some kind of *airy-fairy* world of *pseudo-bliss*. It's true, I was raised in Marin County, California, in San Rafael. Marin was, even then, a bastion of the *new age* and pop-psychological thought. But finding myself to be gay, as soon as I met my partner, it was off to *San Francisco*. My partner and I managed residential hotels in San Francisco's Tenderloin district. We were the first to advertise in the mainstream press that our hotels were *gay-managed*. At that time, in that area of San Francisco, there was a lot of racial strife. The area was predominantly black, but gay people, being excluded from most other areas except for the expensive *Castro district*, were finding a home here.

In my career as a tenderloin hotel manager, in addition to helping hundreds of young gay kids find a new life after having been tossed out of their homes by less-than-understanding parents, I have had guns pointed at my face, my life threatened more times than I can remember and an arsonist burned one of our buildings to the ground at three in the morning. My partner and I were both from the *burbs* and were both plenty scared when we started. But after a short time, we not only brought up our buildings but helped change the face of the Tenderloin. Like the people we rented to, we were poor, but we found love alive and well in that setting. We found, in a world of thieves, junkies, and prostitutes, *heart, love, and compassion*. No, I am not a *milk-toast*. I saw many of our former tenants and friends die of Aids, at a time when a diagnosis meant a death sentence. I have literally sat, talked, and eaten with murderers, rapists, and child molesters. I have also consorted with Cathedral Deans, Lord Bishops, and monks. I have had good friends in both groups and seen good and bad in both. I do not write and speak from education. I speak from my life.

That brings me to the second commenter, the one who wants to define love with words and thoughts. Love as I define it, is *all that is*. Some call this Parabrahman, the Absolute, awareness, Nirguna Brahman, and on and on. Love is the tears in your eyes when you suffer, or when you observe a beautiful forest or sunrise. Love is a child's kiss on the cheek. Love is alive in the promise of a seed. We do not need big words or ideas like Parabrahman. We know what love is. We may have been denied it. We may have a distorted or even perverted idea of it, but we know it. Many of us, particularly the intellectual ones, will try to hide from it in our mind. We will insist on talking, using big or esoteric words. We will design systems that lead intellectually to the *door of truth*, and then stand outside the door trying to open the door with our talk, having forgotten the *key*.

What is this *key*? It is stated in the quotation above: "*Except ye be converted, and become as little children, ye shall not enter into the kingdom of heaven.*" What does it mean to *become as little children*? It means to live in unconditional love. My teaching, if I dare call it that, is simply to return to that simple loving trust that you *knew* in childhood. The difficulty comes about when we understand that this unconditional love comes at the cost of vulnerability. As we grow, we keep putting on layers and layers of masks. Education, social conditioning, unbridled regimentation, all play a part in masking and hiding our *true* nature. Education, rightfully held up as *valuable* often becomes the biggest enemy. For it is here where we *seekers* in non-duality find our shelter. We study our own and other religious systems, *we learn new words to describe the indescribable.* But mostly *we hide.* We hide in the mind because we know that the "*truth*" will not bother us there. Every person who has made even a cursory study of religion, philosophy, spiritual ideas, practices, or rituals finds that at one point there is that step beyond the mind into silence.

This silence is the *classroom of the heart.* This is where the child learns. The child sees the sky in silence. Not yet having words like atmosphere, or possibly even *blue*, the child sees the sky as it is. The view brings wonderment and love without definition, by simply being. *This* is becoming a little child; this *conversion* of the sky back to its original substance: love. This is really what the spiritual *search* is all about, this *converting* maya back into love. As we age, we not only begin to see *blue*, we begin to define the sky as the atmosphere if we are educated, and perhaps "*God's home*" if we desire to live in fantasy. But either way, the clear *seeing*, without *blue, ether, atmosphere, heaven,* or any *quality* or name is the clear *seeing* we strive for. This is the reason for the *classroom of the heart.* Silence is not something to be *cultivated.* It is the *absence* of cultivation. It is completely unsophisticated and uneducated. It is the *silence* of the little child. Not, that little children are silent. They are filled with the exuberance of joy. A joy that comes from this *silent* observation without defining boundaries or verbal *prisons.*

This is the *humbling of oneself* like the child. To give up the web of words, leave the *search* and become *empty.* Not empty in some negative sense, but empty of ideas about yourself. Many are so afraid of the *next step.* They fear that *death,* that leaving behind the image of the *seeker*, the *learner*, and the *enlightened one*. But a child has no image of *enlightenment*. They are free to see the *sky*, initially, even without the *sky*, let alone *blue* and all the other complicated *thought stuff*. I once said that *enlightenment* is giving up all that you hold for all that you are. This requires trust. It requires returning to a time when you lived free from words and conditioning. That means stepping out of all your ideas about yourself. Your spirituality must be simple, wordless, visible only in the fulfillment of love. The Bible speaks of the rich man turning away from Jesus because he was asked to give his riches to the poor and follow. This applies to our *wealth* of knowledge as well. All must be burnt up in the fire required to *become as little children*.

When you become *as a little child*, lost in love, living in the *kingdom of heaven*, you are in a wordless realm. Like the exuberance of joy of the child, you want to jump on the furniture and shout to all about this wonderful joy. But you are in a *wordless* realm. All of us who try to *teach*, can just smile, babble a bit, and point to the moon. Like a child's rattle, not even *color* or *sound* to the child, but *joy itself*, we wave our little words, giggle a bit and share love. This great wisdom of the child, this great bravery and trust of the child are simple and gentle, but not "milk-toast". It takes great courage to live as a child in a world of adults. If you don't remember, ask one. But that is what earnestness is all about. To live on love alone, without concepts, images, or words. To live in the trust of a wordless understanding and joy. That is becoming as little children.

Poems

The Love that Lives Between

If you and I,
and all we see,
are products of the mind.
An open wound,
a broken heart,
are often what we find.

We seek for God,
we seek for peace,
we separate ourselves.
We try to find some
answers in the books
upon the shelves.

But God and we
aren't separate,
when all is said and done.
The more we look,
the more we see
that God and we are One.

When words and thoughts
speak not to us,
and "God" dwells in the mind,
The only truth is
Silence now,
no "I am" can I find.

Without the "me",
without the "God",
the Truth is plainly seen.
The only Real that ever was
The Love
that lives between.

I Sat Alone Today

I sat alone today
and left behind the
"I am".

I sat alone today
and emptied my head
of self/no self.

I sat alone today
and dangled my toes
in life's answers.

I sat alone today
and cried for sorrow
and for Joy!

I sat alone today
without the "I am".
I simply was.

Ripples

Love, like a drop of dew,
falls gently on the quite stream
of Love itself,
and "*life*" begins.

Like the ever-widening ripples'
stirred by the single drop,
life goes on until it returns
into the stillness of the stream.

The Ink Flows Freely

The ink in the pen,
like all perceived,
is Love itself.

With words,
either drawn
upon the brain,
or laid to paper,
I lose the very image
given on a cloud.

Clear in heart
but vague
in consciousness,
tears of recognition
run down the cheek.

Oh, that I could
hand it to you
like a ripened plum.

Perhaps you might
seek the tree
to which I point.
Finding the Fruit
is your affair.
Consuming its essence
is silent, singular.

Perhaps the
tree of life
to which I point,
will expose its fruit
and you will be
consumed in the consuming.

I can give only
the Love that flows
from the pen,
pointing where it may.
Given by Love itself,
the ink flows freely.

Unfolding Love

Unfolding from between the soft hiding places
of Father's coat,
we sally forth,
safe in Love.
Imagining mountains and valleys
in the unfolding of the sheets and blankets
around our toes,
life is unfolding in one
sensuous,
awkward,
bumbling pirouette.

Love's Expression

Does this *story* of Love become *real*
in *my* writing it,
or in *your* reading it?
Or is the reality in the
Love expressing itself as *both*?

The Wonder of the Child

To recapture the
Wonder of the Child,
is to look into
the face of God –
and find him smiling back.

Healing with Wise Love

First, we must open a wound
in the heart,

and then heal it
with Wise Love.

Ramana's Smile

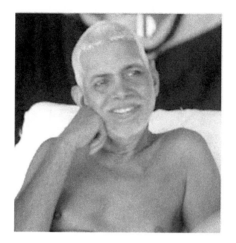

If I allow you to
interpret
Ramana's words
for me,
who will be found
to interpret
Ramana's Smile?

Judge Not

When we judge another's spirituality,
we often say little about theirs
and much about our own.

Ego's Announcement

When enlightenment is declared,
it's the ego that makes the announcement!

The Kiss of Stillness

The kiss of stillness comes from
the wordless understanding of
Love without subject or object,
and unlimited potential,
without the concept of time.

Where only Love Dwells

I take my stand
in that space between
God and myself,
where only Love dwells.

Faces in the Mirror

Through Love's childlike play,
my face, and God's are reflected
in the same mirror.

Gratitude and Trust

Each Dawn, in the Sunrise, I am Gratitude.
Each eve, in the Sunset, I am Trust.

The Empty Vessel

The empty vessel catches the rain.

Complete Understanding

When you completely understand
that there is no complete understanding,
your understanding is complete.

Love in Action and in Silence

The disappointment of finding our image of "God" is illusion,
is quickly overcome by the Realization that we are
"God's" Love in Action and in Silence.

Non-Duality

"God" and "I" are One,
when "God" and "I" are not.

Love in Action

Instead of trying to impress others with our "knowledge"
and clever humor,
why not simply lose the "self" in Love?
There is more Truth in the act of
wiping a sick person's backside,
than in all the Spiritual texts put together.

The Last Duality

After we have discerned the real from the illusory,
the interior from the exterior,
we need to resolve the duality of
both interior vs. exterior and real vs. illusory.

Hang On!

When religion, thought, and mind are seen through,
and the "other" stands naked as illusion,
all that is left is to embrace Life with the
illusory arms of Love, and hang on.

Without Tears

The chill wind blows.
The crimson-yellow leaf
shivers and falls,
without tears.

The falcon and the dove dance.
The falcon, the dance of life,
the dove, the dance of death,
without tears.

Bubbles

Like the Bubbles from a Child's pipe,
thoughts, concepts, and worlds arise in luminous fascination,
only to burst into a sudden shower of nothingness.

An Open Mind

A Truly Open Mind Accepts All
and Clings to None.